A SWAMP THE SIZE OF BELGIUM

PRAISE FOR
A SWAMP THE SIZE OF BELGIUM

Canadian military history has a rich literature of first-rate battlefield memoirs; A Swamp The Size of Belgium is a worthy addition to this canon. Telling the story of an officer deployed to one of the most austere UN missions, it recounts a six month peacekeeping tour in brutal, visceral honesty. Getting to the level of not only sights and sounds, it gives readers the tastes, smells, and day-to-day realities faced by our deployed men and women who support the pursuit of peace. It shatters myths and shows the experiences that rarely make headlines. It needs to be read. I could not put this book down once I started it. Absolutely warrants pride of place on any bookshelf of those who seek to understand what it is to go overseas as a contemporary peacekeeper. - **BGen R.T. Strickland, MSM, CD**

John Vintar is the face of modern Canadian peacekeeping. This is not mythological Kumbaya Canadian UN peacekeeping. This is the hard-core bloody reality of containing conflict in today's complex Africa: A Chinese general, Mongolian logistics, Rwandan force protection and Bangladeshi riverine forces in the hot, brutal sun of dangerous South Sudan. No other soldier has chronicled the Canadian UN experience in Africa like John Vintar. - **Dr. Sean Maloney**

South Sudan was the world's newest nation in 2011. John's writing gives the reader first-person exposure to the personal and professional frustrations of being a United Nations peacekeeper. He focuses on what he did, what he saw, and how he felt rather than lamenting strategic leadership decisions. His writings accurately capture the tedium, frustration, professionalism, dedication, and camaraderie that mark United Nations missions. They also reinforce the strengthening influence adversity has on human relationships, especially those formed through shared experiences.
                                  - **LTCOL (Rtd) R.J, Wallace, RNZE**

A SWAMP THE SIZE OF BELGIUM

by John Vintar

DOUBLE‡DAGGER

United Nations Mission in South Sudan (UNMISS) personnel are regularly attacked, harassed, detained, intimidated and threatened…the Government has committed at least 450 violations of the status-of-forces agreement, including assaults against United Nations personnel and restrictions on the movement of peacekeeping patrols and other UNMISS operations. The opposition and other anti-government groups have committed several dozen more similar acts. As at the time of writing, 43 humanitarian workers had been killed since the war began, in December 2013.

United Nations Security Council Panel of Experts Report,
22 January 2016

Library and Archives Canada Cataloguing in Publication
Vintar, John author
A Swamp the Size of Belgium / John Vintar

Issued in print and electronic formats.

ISBN: 978-1-990644-64-1(soft cover)
ISBN: 978-1-990644-65-8 (e-pub)
ISBN: 978-1-990644-66-5 (Kindle)

Editor: Phil Halton
Cover design: Pablo Javier Herrera
Interior design: Winston A. Prescott

Double Dagger Books Ltd
Toronto, Ontario, Canada
www.doubledagger.ca

TABLE OF CONTENTS

GLOSSARY

AK, AK-47—Russian-designed assault rifle

ALCON—All Concerned

BANFRU—Bangladesh Force Riverine Unit (a unit of the Bangladeshi Navy)

Browning—Canadian-issue 9mm service pistol

CASEVAC—Casualty Evacuation

DAP—Dynamic Air Patrol. Travel by helicopters rather than vehicles

DEET—The active ingredient in insect repellant.

FSA—Flight Safety Assurance

Floppers—Sub-Standard MLOs

Go-Bag—Small pack with survival essentials

HESCO—Pre-fabricated military fortification

IDP—Internally Displaced Persons

IGAD—Inter-Governmental Authority for Development

JAKLI—Jammu & Kashmir Light Infantry (A Regiment of the Indian Army)

Khawaja—Foreigner (Arabic)

Klick—Kilometer

LO—Liaison Officer

MEDEVAC—Medical Evacuation

Malarone—Daily anti-malarial medication

Mefloquine—Weekly anti-malarial medication linked to significant side-effects

Mi-8/Mi-17—"HIP" Russian utility helicopter

MOVCON—Movement Control Office that coordinates movement

of equipment and personnel

Mzungu —Foreigner (singular) (Swahili)

Operation LIFELINE—Regular UN barge resupply missions along the Nile

POC—Protection of Civilians site

PSTC—Peace Support Training Centre, Kingston Canada

Recce—Reconnaissance

SPLA—Sudanese Peoples Liberation Army. The Army of the South Sudanese government

SPLA-iO—Sudanese Peoples Liberation Army in Opposition. The Opposition Army

SRSG—Special Representative of the Secretary General. Chief UN civilian on a mission

UNMAS—United Nations Mine Action Service

UXO—Unexploded Ordnance

Wazungu—Foreigner (plural) (Swahili)

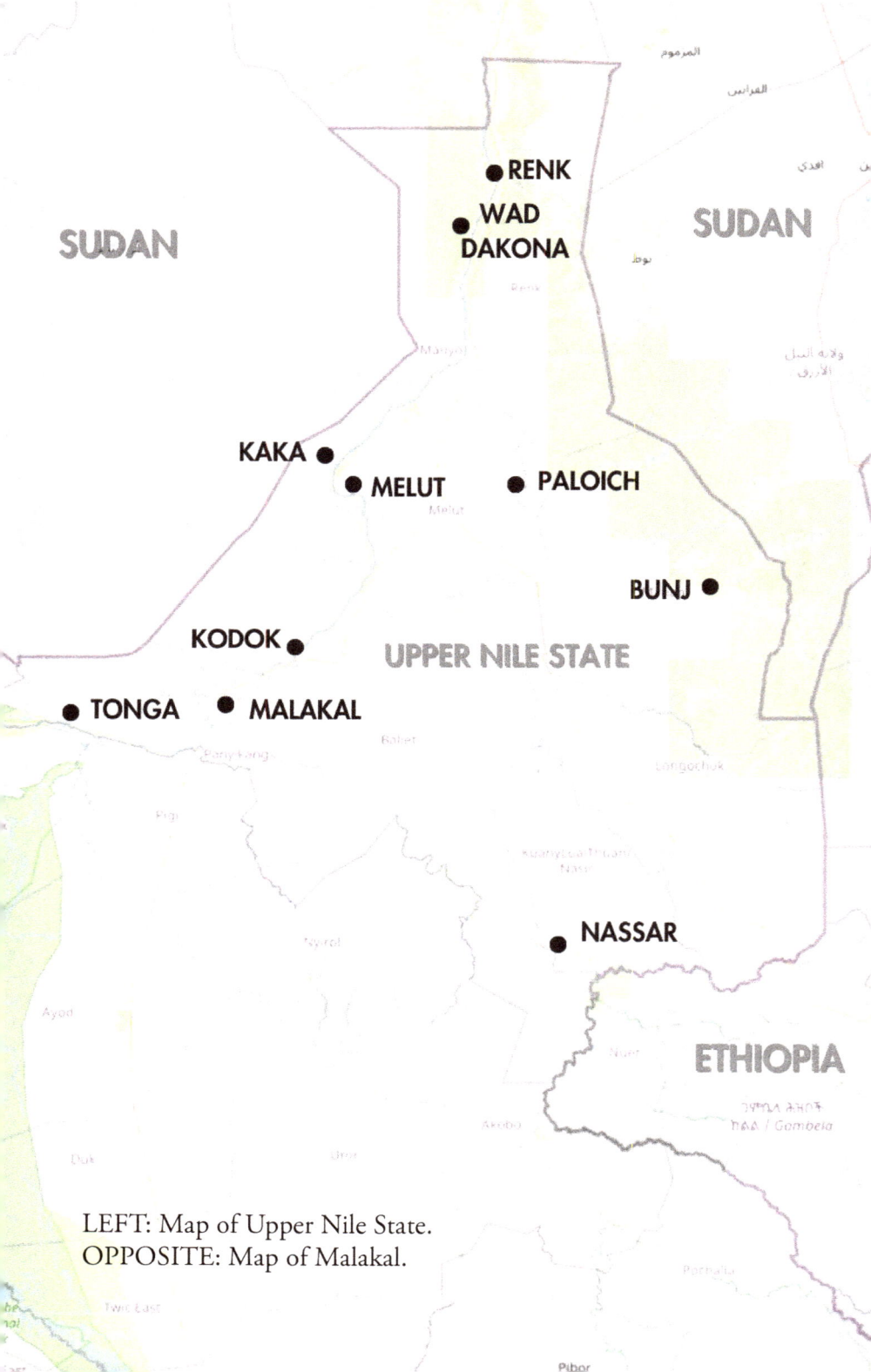

LEFT: Map of Upper Nile State.
OPPOSITE: Map of Malakal.

PREFACE

This book is based on a collection of my emails, sent home during my deployment to South Sudan. To maintain operational security, many critical details were removed from the originals. This includes people's names, some patrol locations, and specific procedures and activities. I assumed all my correspondence was regularly intercepted, and I didn't want to put my colleagues (especially local nationals) at risk. For the most part, these gaps in detail have now been filled in and expanded upon.

Entries are noted as days counted from my initial deployment date, not calendar days written as Day-Month-Year. This was deliberate since on tour, specific dates have less importance, and I placed more focus on the number of days before or after an event. The exceptions to this are the last two chapters when I was back in Canada where dates and days of the week had meaning again.

There are explanatory paragraphs at the end of most entries. These provide additional information that might have been missed in the original submission, or they serve to add thoughts and background information that I remembered after the fact. The last entries written after my return were a continuation of the story for which there are no additional notes.

A few stories in this book were not sent out to a wide audience, or not sent out at all. They were written to record the events that happened but were too sensitive, graphic, or otherwise unsuitable to distribute. When that occurs, it is noted in the explanatory paragraphs.

Conversations are written as best as I can remember them from my patrol notes, recollections written down at the end of each day, or from memory. Embedded emails and news reports are copied verbatim but are occasionally edited to add greater clarity. Most acronyms have been spelled out.

All names have been altered, unless the person is a senior official or otherwise noteworthy figure.

INTRODUCTION

"WHY DO GUYS COME BACK from small missions and not talk about it?" I asked rhetorically, "Because nobody understands, on the one hand…and nobody really wants to hear about it."

"What about the guys in Afghanistan? Do you think they understand?" asked the interviewer.

"No, they don't." South Sudan might have been another planet compared to Afghanistan.

"It's different, isn't it?" she said it more as a statement than a question.

"Totally."

"They had each other. They still have each other."

"I'd be closer talking to a former South Sudanese soldier who emigrated to Calgary, and we could talk about shit, more than I can be talking to my wife."

I paused, reflecting.

"…that's probably not the best thing."

"That's the difficulty coming back from a situation like this, is not being able to relate to anybody back home," she said.

"Yeah."

She spoke gently. "And they can't relate to you…"

That caught me.

"No. They can't."

"So, where does the healing come from?" she asked.

"I don't know," I replied, "…but you've got to tell the story. Part of the healing is telling the story."

———————————

This is the story—stories, really—of my deployment to South Sudan.

This is not a war story, which might seem a bit surprising because the ingredients are all here—a bloody civil and tribal conflict in Africa, a robust United Nations military presence, international aid, and humanitarian efforts, and all the horrible suffering and chaos that war brings—and these factors certainly feature prominently in this book, but it's far from being the main theme. Nor is this a story about UN peacekeeping in general, because the complexities of supporting post-conflict efforts are better explored at a higher academic level. But, like the war, UN bureaucracy and administration play a significant role in this book.

South Sudan became the world's newest country in 2011, splitting away from Sudan in a referendum that ended more than a century of political, economic, and cultural control by the Arab north. The prevailing mood of optimism was short-lived, as a bloody civil war erupted in December 2013. This was political and tribal-motivated combat centred between the forces of the Government of South Sudan and the Opposition. Rapes, abductions, extra-judicial killings, forced recruitment of child soldiers, and other violations were committed regularly and with complete impunity by both sides. International political, military, and humanitarian efforts were completely stretched in the face of this overwhelming level of crisis and chaos.

The United Nations has maintained a presence in South Sudan since 2004. Numerous Non-Governmental Organizations, international agencies, humanitarians, religious organizations, and other enablers have also worked there for decades in the service of peace. It has been, and remains, an ongoing struggle.

With this backdrop, I deployed as a Military Liaison Officer in August 2015—a member of the small Canadian Armed Forces contingent attached to "UNMISS," the United Nations Mission in South Sudan. Unlike large-scale operations like Afghanistan or

Bosnia where entire units from one base or region in Canada would train extensively together before going overseas, we deployed as individuals on these small missions. Each of us was sourced from different units across the country, and we all received our mission-specific training at the Peace Support Training Centre in Kingston, Ontario (but not necessarily at the same time). We arrived in theatre at staggered intervals, and the first time you met someone from the same rotation might be when you actually showed up on the ground. For me, there was no time to develop or be part of a team dynamic. You're very much on your own.

Military Liaison Officers, referred to as "MLOs," are international military personnel seconded to the United Nations, whose job is to interact with all sides in the conflict, conduct patrols, facilitate negotiations, and support the United Nations mission objectives. For the UN Mission in South Sudan, the mandate was to protect civilians, monitor and investigate Human Rights abuses, support the delivery of humanitarian assistance, and help implement the latest peace agreement.

Most people don't know a lot about peacekeeping. On the surface, it seems like a noble idea that has been a hallmark of the United Nations since the 1950s. It evokes a popularized image of a clean, smiling, unarmed Peacekeeper in a blue beret, peering intently through binoculars from an observation post, but that vision doesn't necessarily stand up to the modern realities of conflict. The rise of non-state actors, civil wars, and violent ethnic divisions are factors that have changed both the nature of warfare and the conduct of peace support operations.

UN peacekeeping is a topic that is rarely mentioned in Canadian media. There were occasional reports concerning Canada's promised contributions to the UN, including our 2018 one-year deployment of helicopters to Mali, and our recent failed bid for a non-permanent seat on the UN Security Council. On rare occasions, the press revisits decades-old failures like former Yugoslavia or Rwanda. But these reports are incidental and easily forgotten. For the majority of Canadians, UN missions are invisible.

To reinforce this point, here's a question—Where are Canadian Armed Forces members deployed with the UN right now?

Hold that thought.

Compiled chronologically, this collection of stories recounts my six months in South Sudan: my surroundings, events, reflections, and emotions. For the most part, each chapter is an email sent out regularly to a group of family and friends. I knew that this deployment was a unique experience, and these notes opened a window to events and locations that most had never seen. And, unintentionally, my emails became a reflection of my changing perspective and mood as the tour progressed. I kept writing after I came home because the story didn't feel complete, and I realized that the tour hadn't stopped—the return was a big part of it and needed to be recorded. It was a rough time.

In reading this story, with details and descriptions of my day-to-day life, you have a first-hand insight into my experiences as a Peacekeeper in South Sudan. I make no claim to speak for all those Canadians who have served on these small forgotten deployments. Each tour and each person are different. But I will suggest that there are common threads—of training, cultures, environment, and bureaucracy—that are woven through all African missions.

You might find some of these stories uncomfortable to read, and that's fine. Unpleasant and dangerous things happened on this tour. You might also find some bits funny as hell, and I hope you do because there was a lot of humour and camaraderie, and good times with easy laughter and close mates, and there were many surreal events that we experienced over there.

So, if you want to know what this "Peacekeeping" thing is all about - put on your blue baseball cap, grab your gear, and let's go.

Something's happening outside Alpha Gate.

DAY 10

GREETINGS FROM JUBA

WELL, HERE I AM. It has been quite a trip so far.

Left Calgary on the 21st and did a rapid Calgary-Amsterdam-Entebbe hop with a four-hour layover in Amsterdam, which was enough time to find my gate, grab a bite to eat, and drink a decent coffee or two. I remembered to dig through my backpack to find my anti-malarial pills, popped one out of the blister pack and washed it down with coffee. I started taking the meds a couple of days before travelling. Because malaria sucks.

I had managed to sleep on the flight—left at 1530 Alberta time, arrived 0800 Amsterdam time—so wasn't too messed up. However, the reality of travelling alone, as opposed to being in a big contingent flying into a mission, meant that there was an element of solitude and the fact that, with a lot of time to think, you think. About the deployment, about the conditions, about the humanitarian factors, about all the stuff you don't know and wish you did and really wishing there was more clarity on everything. Except there wasn't any clarity, and maybe I was just jet-lagged enough to worry about things I didn't need to worry about.

It is a common failing of mine.

The Amsterdam to Entebbe hop was another smooth trip, but now I was much more conscious of my body odour. Although I was restless and uncomfortable in my seat, I did manage to get several quick naps of 20-30 minutes downrange throughout the flight. I felt good enough when I got to Entebbe to be moderately coherent and fill out all the forms with no issues. We would have filled out the forms on the plane, but someone at KLM handed the flight crew the customs forms for the US, not Uganda. An honest mistake, like Austria and Australia, I guess. The crew had briefed Entebbe Airport not to be too impatient with a bunch of "Wazungu," a Swahili term for travellers or wanderers, who were slow through customs because they had to fill out forms.

For one of the only times in my military career, the instructions on arrival—how to get through Entebbe Airport, and in fact the entire Check-In process in Uganda—were Bang On. They were detailed, exact, and written in a manner that even Jet-Lagged folks like me could understand. That's kind of a big deal. It speaks volumes to the attention to detail and professionalism of the author. I was impressed! Thus, bearing this amazing Secret Scroll of Knowledge, I sped my way through Customs, jauntily waving my UN "To Whom It May Concern" letter, a happy smile, and my passport, and flew through the terminal and into the baggage area. Where my progress ground to a screeching halt.

Entebbe is a large modern airport, but it seemed smaller that night. I think the big issue is the almost deliberately dim lighting. It was after 2200 hours, and the lighting made everything seem grey and dismal. Like a bad '60s spy film set behind the Iron Curtain. The baggage area was crowded with impatient travellers, and the baggage was slow to get on the conveyor. But eventually, bags started to move, and even more eventually all my bags showed up. Awesome.

Here's a bit of good advice. Five largish barracks boxes will not all fit on a smallish baggage cart. Four almost did. So, navigating an overloaded baggage cart in one hand, and pulling a brown Pelican box with the other, I got to the Exit. Through the doors.

And it felt like all hell broke loose...

There was a sea of black faces holding signs and yelling just outside the doorway, offering cab rides, cheap hotels, carrying baggage, and so on. It was a jumble of sound and voice, and all this added to the discomfort as the humid night air hit me and sweat started in clothes that I had worn since Canada and were already feeling soggy. Then there was Derek from the 7 Seasons Hotel, well-dressed in a collared shirt and tie, who was there to meet me, took two of my boxes to lighten my load, and guided me to the van. I naturally went the right side of the vehicle and stopped short when I saw the steering wheel. Derek said, "You're not allowed to drive this van." I laughed. Ugandans drive on the other side of the road than we do in Canada. Sheepishly, I moved over and hopped in the passenger seat, and we drove from the airport, past the well-lighted UN Regional Support Base, and then took a left turn on a dusty dirt road to the 7 Seasons Hotel. Home for the next week. With an armed guard. Like everything of value in Africa; high walls, razor wire, and 24-hour security.

I checked in. Baggage up to the second floor (third floor in North American terms) which sucked because there was no elevator and the bags were heavy, and in a room that looked positively lurid with dim lights, and bright red shag carpet, and questionable wiring—but excellent air conditioning—I stripped down, showered, hopped into bed, and was asleep in seconds.

The next morning, I woke up to a message on my hotel phone from a buddy that had been on pre-deployment training with me in Kingston a few months back. He was destined for the UN Mission in the Democratic Republic of the Congo, and I had initially thought he had been in-country long before today. As it turned out, he arrived in Entebbe an hour or so after I did, flying in from the UK. Awesome! We had never been particularly close on pre-deployment training, but now he was my best comrade. There is comfort in being in a faraway land with someone you know. You are less concerned about walking around or coming home alone after a beer or two. Safety in numbers. We were to do our in-clearance and initial induction training together. Also awesome.

So, Alain and I explored Entebbe by foot for a few hours. Walked by hotels and government offices on the Kampala and Portal Roads, wandered into a local market area where, as the only two white dudes, we received a few curious stares, made our way to the Victoria Mall and its brilliant coffee shop, then finally to the 4 Points Restaurant for a couple of beers (Oh Tusker, how I've missed you!) and extremely good Indian food. We made it an early Sunday night, since the next day would be the start of our Check-In at the UN base, and we wanted to be completely ready and well-rested.

The next morning started with an adequate but disappointing

breakfast at the hotel consisting of shrivelled, overcooked chicken sausages and lacklustre coffee before we walked over to the UN base. We then spent the next few days waiting in various lines with the Check-In Check-Out team, officers from Mongolia, Romania, and Togo, who were shockingly efficient compared to the days-long agony of manual document entry and bureaucratic lethargy that was my first UN experience in Khartoum in 2006. We brought our baggage to "MOVCON", the Movement Control office for onward transport to Juba, we endured endless lectures on Codes of Conduct, the threat of HIV-AIDS, the UNMISS mandate, security, child protection, gender issues, communications procedures, the role of police in the UN, and so on and so on and it lasted forever.

And we made new friends in this new environment. Most especially with Pierre, a Swiss Army officer, and a couple of officers from Ghana. One Ghanaian was especially noteworthy: airborne infantry, super friendly, professional in his appearance and demeanor. He is my height (6'2"/188cm) and very, very fit. With nine—count 'em, Nine—UN tours, including Liberia, Congo, Sierra Leone, and others. He and I got along immediately—he definitely had his shit together.

We finished the induction training on Thursday afternoon. We were good to go and ready to move on. Cash advance in one hand, "Movement of Personnel" forms (which was basically our airline ticket) in the other hand, and instructions to check in at Entebbe Airport between 0600-0700 hours the next day. So, final prep, then dinner, arrange the hotel shuttle to the airport at the front desk, shower, and crash.

It was early—too damn dark and early—when I got up, washed, put on my uniform, and dragged all my baggage to the main floor. I realized that the coffee in the dining room was fresh. A good omen! But despite the freshness, it wasn't good. It was still crappy drip coffee of questionable quality. Ugh. Bad omen!

Airport check-in and boarding were smooth, made more wonderful by the fact that it was a Canadian aircraft and crew under contract to the UN. The flight was uneventful until we were ready to do our descent into Juba. Where we circled. And circled. And circled.

There were ten aircraft trying to land and another ten or so trying to take off. Juba has one strip and limited taxiways. The pilot announced that he would circle for 20 minutes, and then head back to Entebbe. And in my head, if we went back to Entebbe, I was pondering the options of staying at the Lake Victoria Hotel, which was $110.00 USD per night compared to the 7 Seasons' $60.00 USD—but oh man, the difference in luxuriousness is amazing, and why not treat myself? The Lake Vic is really quite opulent! However, as luck (?) would have it, after fifteen minutes we began our final approach and landed safely in South Sudan.

And waited on the tarmac.

There were three jets in front of us, which blocked a C-130 Hercules transport from taking off, and there was also a Mi-17 helicopter trying to off-load cargo, and a Red Cross aircraft loading bags of food, and just a ton of chaos and it was amazing that nothing collided. I'm not an Airport Controller dude so maybe that was just my impression, and everything was functioning exactly as it was supposed to—but I doubt it. We eventually nestled out of the way near the wing of a monstrous old Russky transport plane—and waited some more.

The chaos got sorted and our plane eventually moved. We cleared through Juba customs quickly, which was easy for me since I already had a South Sudanese visa in my Canadian Special Passport, then took a small minivan to the separate UN terminal for my luggage. Best of all, Mark, our Canadian Operations Officer, was already waiting for me as I left the terminal. We heaved my kit into his Toyota Land Cruiser, and over bumpy and horribly rutted roads (a result of the rains), we shortly arrived at Canada House. My home for the next week.

And with that, it's 2305 hours here, I am wiped out from a long day, and it is definitely time for bed.

Next Installment to follow!

Arriving in theatre is always challenging, especially when you are alone. You don't have a lot of information, you expect most of that information to be wrong, and you brace yourself for friction. This could mean anything from missed flights to lost luggage. You have to stay flexible. To have received detailed and accurate instructions for getting through Entebbe airport was a gift.

One of the realities of a deployment to South Sudan was that I was on a daily anti-Malarial medication called Malarone. Side effects included some gastric upset, but that only lasted a few days and could also have been a result of the new environment and food.

DAY 11

MORE JUBA

THE STORY CONTINUES...

Once the gates opened and we rolled into Canada House, I had a chance to do a quick tour of the razor-wire-topped compound before going inside. I won't go into significant detail about our layout for obvious security reasons, but there is the main house, a small guesthouse, a series of cell-sized rooms for the hired security, and a "water reservoir" that is actually a pool where we can cool off in the Juba heat. Before you get any ideas, the primary role of the reservoir is to fight fires—water pressure is not the strongest here. But to be fair, it's a nice pool too. There is a shed to hold our generators and fuel, as well as a small, covered gazebo to do physical training—it's a rudimentary gym with limited equipment, but it is okay. We also have some chickens to ensure a regular supply of eggs. Yay Protein!

Inside the multi-level main house are a series of apartments with various kitchens and rooms and facilities throughout. It's a great layout, although if a bunch of us are in from the team sites it could be a bit tight. I promptly picked a vacant room and a bed and spread out my kit. I had a free weekend until my training started at Tomping Base located beside the airport, and I spent it doing laundry and getting to know the folks over a Nile Special beer. But first....

The Administration!

Mission pay, allowances, personnel administration, sign for and receive a local cell phone, hand over my shadow file with all my documents including the medical file, secure my extra US Cash in the safe, sign a form for accommodations payment, receive fire

15

briefing, security briefing, alcohol policy, fraternization policy, and so on, and so on.... there were no surprises on anything. Mark was a wealth of info and dealt with all the issues and my questions very succinctly. Meanwhile, the "other" Mark who was our clerk dealt with my paperwork and administration issues. Including pay. Ah, Pay.

I first deployed in 2002. I will say this with certainty—Every deployment. Every contract. Every Single Time—my pay has been screwed up. Coming onto and off active service has always been a shit show. Sorry—I need to explain. I'm an Army Reservist. Reservists have their own pay system in Canada but are paid on a Regular Force pay system when they deploy. Pay is often never sorted out for several weeks, and frankly, it's an embarrassment. God knows how multi-nationals like FedEx and McDonald's can have full-time and part-time staff on a single pay system.... Luckily, thanks to some great people here and in Canada, they managed to get an advance or something into my account—so the mortgage will be paid. Huzzah!

I also met the Task Force Commander—and received my Rules of Engagement brief from him. After which I was issued my pistol and ammo. Surprisingly, to me the Browning was not to the cleanliness standard I expected, so I spent part of the next day on the patio scraping the crap out of it. And the magazines—they were a bit gritty. I was much happier when the pistol's action slid smoothly like butter and the trigger springs didn't make crunchy sounds.

You take care of your kit. Especially weapons. Because you never know.

The weekend flew by. I met some good folks, a few representatives from various NGOs and other international agencies. Got a quick tour around the city and promptly forgot all the details. So easy to get disoriented in Juba. Went to brunch on Saturday at a great place in the city. Traffic here is a challenge. We got pulled over by a traffic cop who wanted us to bribe him. We didn't. Then he wanted to fine the driver for wearing flip-flops. Then our driver pointed out everyone on the road driving motorbikes who were wearing flip-flops or no footwear at all. The cop finally waved us off. I had driven a bit in Khartoum during my last tour, but Juba is a hundred times more nerve-wracking. It's a level of chaos that defies the imagination.

On Monday, I caught a ride with our supply Warrant Officer Jim into Tomping, the UN Base by the Juba International Airport, in one of the aptly named "Bone-Crushers", an ancient Toyota Hilux with completely shit suspension. With the rains and road traffic the ruts had turned into canyons a few feet deep where you must put that truck into the lowest setting for 4-wheel drive and manoeuvre down the pothole at an obscene angle, then rev the truck up and through and finally out of the obstacle. Deep ruts and holes and bumps are the norm here. Or at least they were in our neighbourhood.

Training in Juba duplicated much of what we had learned in Entebbe. In fact, several of the briefings were the same, including the typo errors. The training staff are apparently working on it. It was interesting, though, since there were some very specific briefings about the country and situation. In addition, the "Powers That Be" at Mission Headquarters confirmed I was heading for Malakal in Upper Nile State. And I was happy-ish. All doubt was now removed. I could start shipping my excess baggage. As well, four of my five Care Packages showed up at Canada House. Here's a hint—if you did want to send anything, make sure you pack it extremely well and use a ton of tape, especially around the corners, and pretty much anywhere else. The boxes look like they were hit with mallets or dropped off a tall building. Maybe both. The boxes are going to Movement Control tomorrow with my excess baggage, and with any luck at all will be there when I arrive in Malakal next week.

Read about Malakal. Research it. Check out what has happened and what is happening there. Use BBC news, as it's one of the most objective sources. It certainly appears that I'll be busy up-country.

And in the same way I was thrilled to go to Khartoum in 2006 because Churchill had fought at Omdurman in 1898, I was thrilled to go to Malakal, because there is a place nearby—little known—where Britain and France almost went to war in the late 1890s. Yes. Seriously.

Here's the story.

In the late 1800s, France wanted to link their bits of African Colonies on the West and Eastern parts of the continent along the Sahel. They used the river systems to explore a route from Senegal to Djibouti that runs West-East across Africa—quite a trek, *n'est-ce pas*?

A French officer with gigantic balls named Marchand led an expedition from what is now Gabon in West Africa towards the

East….it took a while, and over the next several months, many of the expedition members died, and about twenty French and over a hundred West African troops and porters wound up at a place called Fashoda on the White Nile River. They set up a fort—told the locals that more white guys were on the way, raised the French Tricolor, and waited for reinforcements…

Meanwhile, the Brits were intent on linking their southern Colonies with Egypt—which although nominally sovereign was really under control of the British Crown. Most of this route followed the Nile south through Sudan and the Al-Sudd, an enormous bloody swamp which lies west of Malakal and south of Bentiu in South Sudan, to territories that later became Zambia, Zimbabwe, and so on. This followed a north-south line from Egypt to South Africa.

Where did that British North-South line intersect with the French East-West line? Fashoda.

Meanwhile, far to the north…

Days after the British defeated the Mahdi at Khartoum in 1898, reports came to the Anglo-Egyptian Commander General Kitchener about white men who had a fort south along the Nile. Dispatching a gunboat and troops, the Brits eventually found Major Marchand and his troops at Fashoda, and immediately disputed his claim to the region. They set up their own fort, and while the relationship on–site was amicable (as anyone in sub-Saharan Africa can attest to—you can't afford to be impolite), in Europe the war-drums were beating and France very narrowly backed down, ordering Marchand to withdraw, leaving a lingering scar upon the colonial psyche of France for decades.

Finally, the Shilluk, the predominant tribe in that region of South Sudan, kept a city for their king. A holy site where the spirits of previous kings would gather and advise the current Shilluk king. It lies North of Malakal.

Fashoda.

To my mind, there's something amazingly significant about this. I need to visit this place.

Moving forward a century or so….

Here, in Juba, the peace agreements are signed. There are flare-ups in the out-lying regions, but I am optimistic that the process will hold, and the country can move forward, if even a little. But this week, I endure power-point slide after endless power-point slide, delivered in a boring monotone by even more boring presenters. I wish I was somewhere else, doing something else.

Soon enough, John.

Oh—and there's no food available in Malakal. At least I'll lose some weight.

I knew before I got to Malakal that there would be issues with food. The dude I was replacing sent me several very detailed and helpful emails to get me as prepared as possible. I spent a lot of cash in Canada buying freeze-dried meals, noodles, canned tuna, canned veg, fruit-cups, things like that. There was a cafeteria in Malakal, open only at mealtime (so it wasn't as though you could go grab a coffee whenever you wanted) which my mates recommended that I stay away from. They had looked in the kitchen, named the place Café Dysentery, and refused to eat there.

Don't get upset at the fact that I purchased supplies in Canada and shipped it overseas at personal cost. As a Military Liaison Officer, I was paid a lot of extra cash by the UN to purchase food. It is a normal procedure for individuals given a daily rate of pay. I just thought I would be buying the food locally, or at least in South Sudan.

DAY 17

JUBA PART III

EVERYONE IN JUBA, from the Mission Operations staff to the Deputy Force Commander, a Chinese three-star General, has expressed their sympathy—the Deputy Force Commander used the word "pity", but I'd like to think he meant "sympathy"—that I'm going to Malakal. Sure, I have to ship my own food up there, and it's kind of the Front Line right now and the "hottest" place in the country, and the Internally Displaced Persons camp, which is more accurately called a Protection of Civilians, or "POC" site, has somewhere around 45,000 people in it, but can it really be that bad? Yes.

Oh well. Everyone has to be somewhere.

The induction training here was painfully boring with a couple of exceptions, but very valuable if you did no pre-training in your own country, as is the case for most of the international military folks here. I am sure they got a lot out of it. But honestly, I'm tired of PowerPoint and I'm tired of the repetition. The number of times I have been shown the same political, ethnic, and geographical maps of South Sudan and re-informed about the major ethnic groups is not value-added. Seriously, six or seven times? The training staff is in the process of revision to align the Entebbe and Juba training, and I wish them luck.

The only interesting map I saw illustrated the major cattle migration routes of the northern nomadic tribes. That was fascinating since, generally speaking, these are routes that have existed for millennia, with variations for climatic changes to river and stream

21

flow. And with that are the tribal conflicts associated with moving your cows onto someone else's turf—trouble starts, women are abducted, scarce grazing land is depleted, blood feuds start, and the cycle happens again year after year.

The direct link back to antiquity astounds me. We in the West have dominated our physical and intellectual environment and have been able to change our routines and rhythms, largely because—to my mind—we got out of subsistence farming or pastoralism. Extra resources brought initially by improved farming methods and irrigation, grain storage, and subsequent trade allowed us to develop institutions that require a static presence to evolve and prosper. The Romans would never have had an Empire had they been forced to migrate annually to feed their cattle.

It bears thinking about. It is important to remember that the people here—of whatever tribe—do not see the world in the same manner we do. North American society is based on a collective Western European-centric history that includes agrarian, industrial, and technological revolutions. The tribes here do not share our history or culture, except to have elements of it imposed upon them, and while many of our root values might be similar, the specific perspectives might not be.

Issues of Law and Order and Governance are good examples. I read up on Dinka and Nuer Customary Tribal Law before coming here, and the central issue and desired outcome appears to be a swift restoration of tribal equilibrium, rather than a ponderous and bureaucratic process that punishes the guilty individual. Therefore, if a man is killed, revenge killings can be actioned against a member of the perpetrator's clan, not just the perpetrator. Cows, which are a vital currency in South Sudan, can also be paid in restitution.

Bottom line—these people were never simple or savage or unlearned—the tribes are incredibly complex mechanisms developed over centuries. Western colonial legal or governance overshadowed but did not fully replace these ancient and proven traditions. My feeling is that our European concepts of jurisprudence, parliamentary systems, religion, military/security structure and technology were packed around traditional culture and practice in a similar manner to sticking small snowballs onto a larger central ball. It's not a clean line.

I digressed from my digression. Sorry.

The final packing and weight distribution and questions such as "What civvies will I leave in Juba for a quick change out of here?" and "Can I bring food and maybe bottles of wine?" occupy me today, since my flight is tentatively scheduled to depart tomorrow morning. I have to call MOVCON (remember the acronym?) this evening to confirm. It may change. In fact, it may change tomorrow too. Flexibility is important.

If you zoomed in on my comment about a bottle of vino, Yes—we are not a dry tour. Yes—we are under reasonable restrictions, as we have been on different missions. Some of the other national contingents have been stupid when it comes to alcohol use (misuse) to the point where, in addition to punishing the offender, all their personnel are now breathalyzed when they come home before curfew. Yes. It is that stupid.

But for me—it would be nice to have a glass of wine with a freeze-dried meal, to add a level of culture to my otherwise austere sea container-esque existence, more of which I will describe once I actually get there.

As agonizing as the induction training was, the week here was a good chance to get to know the people in Canada House. It's a solid group—almost everyone has at least one tour, most have several. That's good. And necessary. I am increasingly convinced that an austere UN tour should not be anyone's first deployment. Otherwise, I don't think the benchmarks are in place mentally, or that the resilience has really developed. Without a base of experience, it is that much tougher to cope.

In the house is a feeling of solidarity and courtesy—everyone pitches in—everyone contributes—everyone is considerate of others. Thankfully, the Task Force Commander treats us like adults.

Although it's early, I am also starting to think about my leave plans, in the hope of aligning my travels with the rest of the folks in Malakal as soon as possible. We need to always have sufficient coverage at the team site, and I don't want to wait until the last minute to submit my leave request only to have it rejected. I realized that there are a couple of rules to follow—if you take a commercial carrier out, the Juba airport terminal is small, noisy, confusing, and not designed to handle the massive inflow of aircraft and personnel that are now here. So, if I don't bring checked luggage, it makes everything easier.

I also learned that the UN has free flights to Entebbe and Nairobi from Juba, and that I could hypothetically get on one of those to go out on leave. However, depending on circumstances, I could:

- Get bumped for a higher priority traveler,
- The flight could get cancelled, and/or,
- Any number of things can change at any time—flight timings for example.

Therefore, there is some risk. But if I don't bring checked baggage and build in some flexibility (maybe an overnight in Entebbe or Nairobi) I could save a bit of cash. The issue will be getting out of Malakal to Juba. The UN must get an "FSA", a Flight Safety Assurance from the local factional commanders that the aircraft coming in won't be shot down.

No FSA? No flights.

The planes are often contracted from civilian companies and aren't expected to run the same risks that military personnel or aircraft would. The other reality is that there are not an endless supply of aircraft or crew in the mission, so you've got to take care of what you have.

So, the Plan is—home for Remembrance Day, travel with Jacqueline to maybe Spain and Morocco end-December or in January, and a weeklong trip to Somewhere in early February. Where is Somewhere you ask expectantly? I have no idea. The thought of hopping a flight somewhere purely on speculation interests me. I'm pondering Denmark to see some old friends, but other options include Addis Ababa, or Entebbe for a gorilla tour, or take the plunge and fly to Mumbai to do bit parts in Bollywood films—which I love, by the way. Who wouldn't want to be in a Bollywood film? Except for the fact that my Hindi is limited to about four phrases (two of which involve ordering drinks), I dance like an uncoordinated white guy, and I'm too old to be the leading man, I am perfect for any role!

That's it for today. Next post will be from Malakal! I somehow doubt that there's Wi-Fi there.

Oh—the Deployment Beard is coming along nicely. A couple more weeks and it should be presentable. There's an awful lot of grey, though, which I attribute to the Mefloquine from the last tour. Or old age.

Whatever.

I liked Canada House. I didn't like Juba. There was a curfew and you had to be off the roads and in your compounds by 8:30 or something every evening. The police/military had checkpoints out, and so did criminals who may or may not have been police/military, who would sometimes shake down, extort, or beat travellers who were running late.

There were also compound invasions, where residents—often UN civilian or Non-Governmental Organizations or Charities and therefore seen as rich, easy targets—would have everything of value stolen, and sometimes receive a beating for good measure. Or worse. I had heard stories of rapes.

Not Canada House. We were a hard target.

The compound had high walls with concertina wire, security cameras, bars on the ground and first floor windows and access points. There were also internal heavy doors to seal off the third floor from the rest of the house if need be. There were also enough pistols, C7 rifles, and ammunition to ensure that anyone breaching our compound would have wound up dead. There were drills for securing the houses and clearing the compound if needed.

During the day, at least one person would be armed (or more if individuals felt like it—I carried a pistol much of the time) and if there were contractors in the building, at least one person carried a rifle.

As I said, we were a hard target, and everyone knew it.

DAY 22

MALAKAL

I THINK WE ALL GO THROUGH IT. When an experience is so new and foreign and once we have started living it—reaching a point beyond its novelty—we feel disconnected. Unbalanced.

It is the point where your connection to your previous world is starting to stretch a bit thin and the memories, faces, and routines get a bit blurry in the remembrance, but where you haven't established a baseline of routine or friendship or familiarity to carry you forward in the place you are now. I feel it pretty strongly at the moment, and it's as if I'm being squeezed—feeling cranky, short-tempered, with limited appetite, and un-restful sleep.

It happens every tour. Lasts for about a week or two. At the end of the process, it is like waking up to a different world—faces and names are familiar, you get the drills down, food has taste and my sleeps are fairly sound and life is now patterned on an unsure routine. But familiar and crappy is better than unfamiliar and crappy. As I said—Everyone has to be Somewhere.

Malakal is different from Juba, as Juba was from Entebbe, and as Entebbe was from Calgary. Three weeks, three new places, all very different, each more austere. No surprise that I just want to unpack my gear completely, set up a sea-can like it's my own, and have the same rack for a few months. It will happen eventually.

I was supposed to fly from Juba to Malakal on Tuesday, but the flight was delayed because we didn't get a Flight Safety Assurance. So, I remained in Juba. Which was grand, mainly because I had started that day off with a nasty bout of food poisoning (no, it was not local

27

food) and it hadn't quite finished wreaking havoc with my system.

I am not going to go into too much detail—no matter how much I swore that this would be an accurate description of the tour—But I am going to go into some, so if you don't want to read about me being sick just skip the next paragraph or two and move on...

Once the flight was cancelled, I had to wander with rumbling intestines and barfy-feelings to several offices in the UN camp at Tomping to get my security clearance and Movement Ticket revised and re-stamped. And in the midst of hours and hours, with waves of increasing nausea and clenched, cramping guts—I managed to tough it out in an office with faulty air conditioning to get my flights revised and when I left without throwing up on the nice lady's desk, I grabbed my barracks box and arranged for a ride back to Canada House. It was so stinking humid and stifling hot. Radiant heat reflected off the dirt road into my face and I was feeling like hell. The sweat was literally pouring off me and soaking through my clothes and my whole body felt wrung out. Waiting by the side of the road in the sun, it was finally too much, and I peeled off my combat shirt, hoping for a breeze or something just to cool me down a bit.

I sat on my baggage wanting to die and praying to hold on just five more minutes. Then Jim drove up in the Bone Crusher to take me back to Canada House. I stood up wobbly and leaned weakly against the truck. He looked at me with worry and asked, "Jesus Christ, are you okay?" but I couldn't hold back anymore and without answering him I doubled over and puked my guts out by the side of the road. Then wondered if maybe I had malaria. But I didn't really care—the purge made me feel slightly better.

I got back to Canada House, left my baggage on the main floor, and stumbled weakly upstairs to sleep—with a few exceptions for sips of Gatorade—for the next 18 hours. By the next morning, I felt slightly more human, and certainly more in control of my world. And my bowels. Thanks Imodium!

I left Canada House at 0630 to check in at the UN Passenger terminal. This is a misnomer, as it's not big enough to deserve that term, really. "Small Barn" might be more apt. I finally boarded the plane after a two-hour wait (with only sips of water, I wasn't ready for coffee) to leave Juba and after a smooth flight, arrive over an hour later in Upper Nile State.

Malakal. My tiny little war-home.

My first surprise upon deplaning was when I realized that a couple of sections of Rwandan Force Protection had surrounded the plane and, facing outward, were holding their weapons at the low ready. Which isn't surprising given that the Front Line is the West Bank of the Nile, where Johnson Olony's Opposition troops are located. Then seeing the UN Armoured Personnel Carrier with a "Dushka" Heavy Machine Gun mounted menacingly on top, the Rwandan soldier manning it scanning left and right.

Yes. This is interesting. I like guns.

With the other passengers, I got onto a mud-spattered UN bus and enjoyed the driver's navigation around the deep ruts and potholes between the airplane and the passenger pen—about 300 meters? Over five minutes of driving. I still wasn't 100% recovered so wasn't loving the rut and pot-hole experience.

I had befriended a Mongolian Officer on the flight—he was from our Sector and belonged to one of the smaller County Support Bases farther north in Upper Nile State. When we arrived at the passenger waiting area, he found an MLO team to take the two of us to the camp. An Aussie bloke from a UN de-mining team hopped in, and finally a small convoy of UN vehicles with Force Protection, some fuel vehicles, and several SUVs (none of them up-armoured, by the way) drove—slowly, winding back and forth across the packed dirt road, avoiding the many potholes as best they could—to the camp's Main Gate. Alpha Gate.

It had rained for several hours the day before, and the ground was sodden and muddy and my overshoes were somewhere in my kit that I had sent as cargo the week before but had absolutely no idea if it had made it here yet. If not, my feet would be in for a miserable time.

The clay-like mud here is tenacious and evil, it clogs on your boots, and then more mud sticks to itself repeatedly until your feet are so heavy that walking becomes a chore of ever-increasing misery. It was exactly the same dismal soul-sucking crap I remembered from my last tour. At least it's getting close to the end of the rainy season.

Once through the gate, we parked at the MOVCON offices and waited and waited and waited for our luggage. The UN teaches you patience. At this point, I was starting to get worried. I had handed over my pistol to UN Security in Juba, and while I had a receipt for it and my mags and ammo were with my carry-on, maybe I should have waited by the plane for the flight crew to have it handed over to me? On the other hand, maybe I should ask some questions. Or maybe if one of the crowd around here looked remotely in charge I could ask them?

Ah screw it—at least I had a receipt.

In the meantime, someone took me to the MLO Team office and I met Tor, who was the acting Senior MLO and the guy responsible for personnel administration, but, more importantly, he had the key to my temporary accommodation. I grabbed that and went back to the waiting area for my kit to arrive. Eventually a van showed up with our stuff and a UN Security dude got out of the passenger seat holding my pistol case and I knew all was well with the world. I verified the contents, signed off on the form, and put the pistol, that I have nick-named Mr. Browning, into my backpack. I hitched a ride to Jim's container (he is the guy I'm replacing and was away on leave at the time), got my carry-on stuff put away, and walked back to the MLO office to meet the rest of the team.

When you first meet a group of people, they are amorphous—the individuals don't really have identities at that point and coming from so many countries with many unfamiliar names it was a challenge to remember who-is-who. We had officers from places such as Papua New Guinea, South Korea, Nepal, Ghana, Mongolia, Ethiopia, Zambia, and Fiji. And now, one Canadian to add to the mix. However, over the coming weeks, each of them will become distinct personalities. I will write about them in a later post.

But the camp—It's large and confusing and a rabbit warren of containers and walkways and razor wire and all the assorted flotsam of the UN. Muddy roads and wild dogs everywhere. Literally everywhere. No pest control policy here obviously. The dogs lie in the dirt or walk calmly along the pathways, mostly a dun-brown or tan colour and the typical Middle Eastern long-snouted shorthair breed. The size of a smaller German Shepherd. Many are scarred and mangy. Some very unhealthy looking. But one dog in particular, who seems to live close to my container, is a cute black and white pup that wags her tail and loves to play. Regardless, I keep my distance from them. They are filthy. They spread disease and should be culled.

After some in-processing paperwork, the big win was that all my kit had arrived at MOVCON. Additionally, four of my care packages were here too. I got someone to help me out with a truck and we grabbed all my pre-shipped baggage and got it stuffed into my container. It's a tight fit. It's also a tight fit because Jim still has a bunch of his stuff here. And a ton of food—including Pop-Tarts! And a bread maker! Also, a toaster, kettle, and microwave.

But Pop-Tarts…think about it. Sugary refined floury awesomeness!

The container is maybe fifteen or eighteen feet long and just over six feet wide, with a bed, wardrobe, and fridge. And a working air-conditioner. Thank God. All other shelving and storage were "liberated" from the camp. Bug net over the bed, and buttercup yellow walls. That colour isn't standard UN issue—someone was tired of the normal white-grey I guess—but whoever painted it also painted the ceiling yellow. Complete lack of fashion sense.

Every corner and seam of the room was covered with layers of tape or glue or caulking to stop the bugs from getting in. It's cozy. If I get to take over this container from Jim—and I sure hope that will be the case—I will seal up all the holes again. I brought four tubes of silicone sealant and rolls of duct tape just for that purpose.

At the end of the day, I managed to get a pack of instant noodles down—my first meal that stayed down in 48 hours—and lay down under the netting starting to second-guess myself and wondering why the hell I volunteered for this shit? And with that thought circling my brain, I tried to sleep. I dozed fitfully—woken up randomly from the incessant sound of millions of frogs croaking and the intermittent baying and fighting of the dog packs throughout the night.

I woke up early the next day feeling hungry. And much, much better. And it was sunny outside, and I realized that I had seen the first day through a filter of nausea that made everything miserable and dismal and grey, and now it was a sunny day and I felt pretty good and this was Home Sweet Home, Baby so make the best of it! After a good breakfast of coffee and a granola bar, I shouldered my backpack, and walked up the drying mud road to the MLO Office to start my day.

The Force Protection were troops from various countries who contributed formed units to the UN. Experience, enthusiasm, and efficiency varied widely depending on the country and the specific units. Our Force Protection troops were from India, Rwanda, and Ethiopia. The Indian Battalion Commander (12th Battalion, Jammu & Kashmir Light Infantry, the "JAKLI") was a very close friend from my 2006 deployment to Bentiu. A good omen, indeed!

He told me later he pulled some strings in Juba to get me sent to be with him in Malakal…I guess in hindsight it was better to be with friends! At least we got to hang out on occasion, eat proper Indian food, and watch Bollywood films together. And his troops looked out for me.

As for my accommodations—I knew I was going to live in a sea container long before I arrived in theatre. As austere an existence as that was, at least I had a fridge and microwave. I also had water containers, a hotplate, and kettle courtesy of earlier Canadians, who left utensils, cookware, and cans of food.

Think of it as spending six months of your life in a really decrepit trailer park.

DAY 24

CARE PACKAGES

NOTHING BEATS GETTING MAIL.

Email is great, and thanks for letting me know how you are all doing! It sure feels like I've dropped off the face of the planet. Care packages are always welcome, and so many of you have made kind offers of resupply that I feel a bit guilty not letting you know the sorts of things I think I need or will need.

I am going to throw a list out. Overall, I think I am doing okay for several months of main meals—seriously. I find that the heat saps the appetite; I will have maybe a granola bar for breakfast, noodles and fish for lunch, and a larger meal and dessert/fruit for dinner. This tour is Bring Your Own Food.

The cafeteria serves rice and beans mainly, but often runs out before the line does. In short, we have food insecurity. Not as bad as the "IDPs" or Internally Displaced Persons, of course. It's a lot less than what I ate in Canada—your average fast-food hamburger combination would be a good two or three meals here.

A caveat on sending food. Small, individual portions are better for me. I don't want to let things sit open, even in the fridge, if I can avoid it. Don't want to encourage the bugs.

Anyway, I noticed there are some things that I do need/want/crave, and this might be a result of the heat, or in some cases a desire to share some Canadiana with my mates.

THINGS

- Brigade Patches—need 10 as hand-outs to the team
- Paper towels
- Toilet paper
- Small bottle of bleach
- Washing-up liquid
- Febreze spray
- Scented dryer sheets
- Plastic or acrylic non-breakable wine glasses—yes. Seriously.
- Baby wipes
- Cheap ear buds (I expect mine will get destroyed in short order)
- Bootlaces for 9" tan boots
- Trouser blousing bands
- Lysol wipes—they come in that plastic container and you can pull one wipe out at a time.
- Canada flags
- Roll of clear map-tac
- Books—cheap paperbacks that you will never ever see again because the humidity will disintegrate them, and bugs will nest in the pages and lay eggs in the spine. I'm not kidding. Something with a fair amount of a War Theme would be a great choice— anyone have the Casca Series?
- T-Shirts—If you send me a T-shirt or any other product with your logo, I will shamelessly model it and send you pics. For sizing—Large.

FOOD

- Small containers of maple syrup
- Protein bars—I've really been liking Vector lately, but anything that doesn't look like it will go all "melty" will be great
- Packs of dry-roast peanuts or cashews
- Go-Go Squeeze snacks—those things are addictive!
- Mott's Applesauce Cups (or similar)—less addictive but awesome. Unsweetened please.
- Small pudding cups—nom nom nom
- Nibs or Twizzlers
- Gatorade powder
- Noodle Cups (Superstore has a 12- pack box of cups—it saves

on dishes, increases landfill. Just kidding. The local employees here burn our garbage once they have sifted through it for anything of value)
- Cheez Whiz (If it comes in a plastic bottle, awesome)
- Dried salami (pepperoni sticks are ok too)
- Plastic bottles of hot sauce, BBQ sauce....

WRAPPING

If you already know how to wrap packages securely, sorry for stating the obvious. However, I had a bad experience last tour where contents broke and rotted and contaminated other packages. I want to avoid that, obviously.

As I've said, I received my five care packages. They were in rough shape. Some of my boxes only held together because of the vast amount of tape used. Literally, there were no corners left to speak of. Or edges. However—most importantly, contents secure! Huzzah!

Small boxes are better than large ones. A smaller box also helps keep the weight to manageable levels. I think 20 kilograms is the limit…Home Depot has a small moving box (16" x 12" x 12") that is ideal.

It is safe to assume that whatever you send will be dropped-kicked off the edge of a building and then run over by a forklift. Use lots of packing material, especially around any glass. I also lined the box with a big garbage bag to prevent any leakage if something broke.

A ton of tape is needed along all the corners, edges, and make a good "+" shape with tape on each side, top and bottom of the box. Have a page with the detailed list of contents and approximate value taped to the outside of the box.

I recommend a web search for any extra pointers. Maybe there's a website on "Packing for the Apocalypse" …

Finally, the mailing address:

MAJ JK VINTAR
OP SOPRANO
TASK FORCE SOUTH SUDAN
PO BOX 5225 STN FORCES
BELLEVILLE, ON
K8B 5W6

Today…A day of Reptilian Wonder. Walking to my place for lunch I heard, then saw, a medium-sized monitor lizard stomp across the path. He was about four feet long, including the tail, and disappeared quickly into the swampy undergrowth.

Then, as I was eating lunch, I saw a small gecko in my container. No idea how he got in, but he eats things that I hate—like bugs—so I'm letting him live. For now.

Malakal town was abandoned except for soldiers, so you couldn't buy any food there. You could buy bread and sometime other items such as crackers in the POC camp, but I refused to buy anything from there, mainly because of how the food was prepared. I also didn't think we should be supporting a false economy inside the camp when the goal was to encourage the IDPs to move out of the camp and back into town.

The cafeteria was completely inadequate for me and most of the Western military. Although I had been warned off the place, I ate one meal there and for 15 South Sudanese Pounds (about $1.00 Canadian) received a single piece of stale bread and one tiny and overcooked chicken sausage. Oh, and a couple of tablespoons of beans scraped from the bottom of the pan. To be fair I did show up late for breakfast, but the portions were not anywhere near enough to live on.

Care packages were my lifeline and the only sure means of getting food. And coffee. I needed good coffee.

DAY 28

FIRST WEEK IN MALAKAL

I SPENT LAST THURSDAY AND FRIDAY trying to figure things out around here. Where things were—moderate success; how things worked—it's the UN, so marginal success; and what we do as an MLO Team—limited success. There are overlapping layers of bureaucracy and redundancy, so sometimes it's important just to breathe deeply, recite a calming mantra, and move on…I really did forget about this glacial level of momentum from the last time here. Silly, silly me.

I was made the G2 within minutes of hitting the ground—that's the "Intelligence" guy for the Team Site (stop laughing). It's good to realize that information (or rumour) is very open in the UN, so it's not like a conventional intelligence-led, operations-driven military campaign. Basically, my job is gathering information, collating it, sending it off to Juba with my analysis and comment, and see if my predictions are accurate. But, at first glance, it appears that terrain analysis and examining friendly and enemy courses of action are foreign concepts to the majority of military folks here (as they might be for non-military readers).

I am looking at conducting reviews of terrain, command and control structures, military organizations, military leadership profiles, Points of Contact, and so on. I need to build a picture of what unit is where, led by whom, with what intentions…and apart from that, I need to understand the Internally Displaced Persons situation—the flow of IDPs from X to Y, their condition, where the Humanitarian agencies can and cannot go. I also look at open-source local media to see what they think is going on.

If it sounds easy—it isn't. The situation is so fluid that information before December 2013—when the current crisis started—is almost useless. The other issues involve freedom of movement in accordance with the UN mandate. Simply put, for several reasons, we cannot get out and be the eyes and ears of the mission to the extent desired. So, I've been trying to rebuild from scratch. It's fun-ish. Especially since no one really seems to know what's going on. I take that back. No one person knows what's going on. You have to do a freakin' scavenger hunt to numerous agencies to piece together aspects of the truth (or truths) and even then, it might be sketchy.

But it's been an interesting week…

Monday morning, I was brewing up a cup of coffee after Morning Prayers (daily coordination meeting) and going through old patrol reports to figure out what was going on. My research was interrupted by a percussive sound, like a couple of car doors slamming in the distance. Everyone in the office stopped and listened, trying not to breathe, straining to hear more clearly… waiting… There it was again!

A couple of booms, some short bursts of heavy machine gun fire … crump… CRUMP… CRUMP. North-West. Across the Nile. Lasted for about ten minutes or so.

Shortly after the shelling and machine-gunning stuff stopped, the Radio Room came on the net and let us know that there was shelling going on and to continue monitoring these means. That was funny. Seriously funny.

If you can't be timely, at least be accurate.

Depending on media reports, there are about three different versions of events you could believe. I will tell you with certainty that Malakal was not "Rocked by Gun-Fire" as some outlets would have you believe.

On Tuesday and Wednesday, I went out on a couple of "patrols." I put that little nuance on the word because it is nothing like what we in the Canadian (or most militaries) would consider patrolling. It was "hop in the truck and drive." Our first mission was to visit the Bangladesh Navy Maritime Unit on the banks of the White Nile, a couple of klicks down the road, Northwest of our camp. A pusher boat and barge loaded with UN sea cans is docked there. They cannot unload the containers because the crane in Malakal Port is broken.

Some spare parts were ordered a while ago and were flown up to Malakal from Juba. They sent the wrong parts. Back to square one.

So, this Patrol-thingy…

No planning. No preparation. No inspection of the vehicle. No one brought a Go Bag (an essential piece of kit—a backpack with vital goodies—first aid, water, food, radios, etc.). No flak jacket or helmet. No patrol orders at all—not even a "Hey if something happens, do X," and I was not pleased. Even if only a couple of kilometers down the road, you need to go through the drills, because laziness is really, really stupid and dangerous. Need to change that mindset ASAP.

I insisted on grabbing my flak vest and helmet at the very least, so that if the situation did change suddenly—and that tends to be how situations change around here—at least we could hunker down with the Bangladeshis and the Rwandan Force Protection until things stabilized.

It was an interesting visit, though. Stood on one of the barges overlooking the White Nile and peered across to the West Bank of the river, where there are still skirmishes between the "SPLA," the Sudanese People's Liberation Army, who are the Army of the South Sudanese Government and their opponents, the "SPLA in Opposition." Johnson Olony commands the latter in this Shilluk area. Read about him, there's a lot of info out there.

For me, it was good to chat with the Naval Unit leadership and enjoy a couple of biscuits and a good cup of chai and listen to stories about Operation LIFELINE, the barge convoy resupply that periodically comes up from Juba. LIFELINE is the movement by barge of UN supplies—relief supplies, humanitarian aid, contingent-owned equipment, UN provisions for the various national militaries, and so on. It's a journey from Juba to Malakal and takes a couple of weeks from start to finish. And along this route are checkpoints, and blockades, and troops and gangs, aged and underpowered watercraft, and unexpected sandbars and groundings.

Look at the route between Bor and Tonga—on the edge of the Al-Sudd, which is a swampland system that is over 30,000 square kilometers in size, that can extend to over 100,000 during the rainy season.

For reference, 30,000 square kilometers is the size of Belgium.

The barge patrols carry Bangladeshi naval personnel and force protection, although piloted and crewed by Sudanese civilians contracted by the United Nations. They also carry MLOs so that negotiations can take place at the checkpoints. Although the barges fly the UN flag prominently, there have been instances where the barge has been shot at with everything from the ubiquitous AK-47 to Rocket Propelled Grenades, mortars, and on one occasion…. a tank. Some of the rounds hit. One of the RPG rounds failed to detonate. The barges and pusher are a big, slow-moving target. It is dangerous duty.

If you are on the barge patrol, you must bring all your own food and water because there is no resupply. You sleep (generally) on the deck. You are looking at the same scenery and doing the same thing for weeks at a time. At night, any light attracts all the bugs along the river so it's a complete blackout. You're unable to eat after sundown because your plate of food is too insect-covered. No internet. No mobile coverage.

Not an easy time.

After this visit we learned that there was no change to the situation—we cannot unload the sea-cans, the crane doesn't work in Malakal, and so on—we shook hands all around, and with smiles and waves, we drove back to the camp. I didn't have a good sense of the camp layout except for my own small areas, so we did a diversion to go through part of the POC camp.

If you recall, POC stands for "Protection of Civilians." These initially unplanned and ad hoc camps sprung up after the incidents of December 2013, when really bad things started happening (again) and it was along tribal lines and civilians fled their villages and towns to the UN camps for some sort of safety and security and the UN opened the gates. In addition, as the fighting kept going and instability rose in the outlying areas, more and more people fled into the camps.

In the POC camp within our compound in Malakal, there are over 45,000 people living in an area measuring 800 meters by 800 meters. In tents.

The communities are split up and housed on tribal grounds. They have created schools and community associations in the camp. And alcohol stills and weapons makers. And internal protection groups to stop women and children from being assaulted. And bored youth who can't wait to kill someone from another tribe. Or maybe their own.

We drove slowly down one of the wide paths, fighting for space with a pressing mass of people and other UN and Aid vehicles. People trying to sell things along the side of the path in the crush of humanity.

Some of the SPLA soldiers in Malakal have family in the camps. The soldiers will dress in civilian clothes, sneak in, and visit their folks. A couple of times, the SPLA were discovered by another ethnic group and lynched. Some killed. Some wounded.

The Force Protection troops on the gates have been attacked numerous times. The youth have turned into angry mobs on occasion, and it's a disturbing sign where in cultures that once revered their elders, decades of war have eroded that respect. The youth often act in defiance to the wishes of their tribal leadership—causing trouble, rioting, killing. Once, as they attacked the gate, some of the mob tried to grab the Force Protection troops' weapons. The Rwandans shot the main instigator in the foot and arrested him. That stopped the riot for that day.

Every now and then the UN Police will go in to clear out contraband items. There are plenty of those around…

It's dangerous and the humanitarians that go in there every single day to deal with disease, rape, violence, and sheer human misery are the bravest people I know.

Impressions of the POC site…

Endless vehicles—Water trucks and aid trucks and UN trucks and Force Protection trucks. Kids wandering around looking fed but far from well and mothers with tired eyes moving slowly and hunched down the muddy pathways. Broken old man on crutches missing a leg trying to negotiate the uneven ground. Shelters that barely pass for shelters leaning crazily in the shin-deep mud. Bodies washing and bathing in the ground water flowing through the ditches. Ever-present mangy dogs dodge both people and traffic and one squatted in front of a truck and hurriedly defecated before nearly being run over. Smells of rot and mud and garbage.

And relief when we were through it and back in our part of the camp.

Wednesday's patrol involved a couple of trips into Malakal for some meetings. One in the morning and a follow-up later in the afternoon. It was a chance for me to see the town itself and interact more with our SPLA Liaison Officers and meet the local SPLA leadership. Once again, the roads were full of ruts and potholes and we never really got above crawling speed, even past the airport and down Charlie Road.

I remember Malakal briefly from 2006. It was a bustling place, really. A small international airport, a university, decent downtown, shops, guest houses, and so on. Different tribes and different religions co-existed relatively peacefully (surprising, given the decades of war). Malakal has been an important junction of trade for over a century.

Now it's a ghost town. The area we saw wasn't devastated like a post-WWII town with rubble and the obvious effect of bombs, artillery, and fire. This was instead an abandoned city, with broken windows and looted compounds and missing bits of dwellings when someone needed sheets of corrugated metal or bricks or metalwork for their own simple hovel. Broken and dented and shredded cars and trucks litter open fields and the sense of rust and decay is palpable.

Yet within this was movement. SPLA soldiers—most in varying patterns of camouflage, some few in civilian clothes, but all with AKs—were the principal occupants. At checkpoints, or under tall trees to escape the oppressive heat, or wandering down the road. Soldiers everywhere. And for the most part quick to return our waves and to smile at us. Unthreatening. Non-aggressive. But as you should know by now, all that can change in a moment. Always be polite. Always smile. Always give way to SPLA vehicles on the road.

Amidst all the Soldiers in town were a few women from the POC site—we saw them in groups of five to ten throughout our drive through town. Traditionally dressed, carrying goods on their backs or on top of their heads. Bunches of sticks were the typical load. They appeared relaxed as they sauntered down the road, and according to our SPLA Liaison Officer, they came from the POC camp to find or buy items to bring back.

There are no civilians in Malakal, because it was so recently the front line (and technically still is, I guess). Until the security situation improves, civilians won't move back. When they move back, aid agencies and NGOs will re-establish themselves in the town. The Governor of Upper Nile State and the mechanisms of governance can move back to Malakal from their temporary location in Renk and become fully engaged in the re-building process. And with stability comes predictability. Schooling, harvests, commerce, governance.

All this hinges on an improved security situation—on the ceasefire holding.

The morning meeting, and especially the afternoon meeting (with a couple of dudes from the US Embassy) were valuable and everyone smiled and was welcoming and said the right things. There was another related meeting today in a different location with an opposition leader, and that also went well apparently (I wasn't in on it). I'm not saying a lot for good reason—sorry.

Let's just say that a lot of people from the international community are watching Malakal and there's a lot of pressure for a lasting peace agreement—one view (and I think it's valid) is that if the ceasefire can be maintained here in Malakal, then the rest of the country will likely follow. So, some countries are sending a strong message to all the players on both sides.

But if things go badly in Upper Nile State and especially Malakal—if it all destabilizes and explodes and Malakal changes hands over and over again and the humanitarians can't do their work—well…there's already been twenty months of that.

Being slotted into the G2 position wasn't surprising. Western-trained MLOs (we include the Aussies and Kiwis in this grouping as well as many of our NATO partners), are generally assigned staff positions within the MLO cell in addition to other routine duties, such as patrolling. These staff jobs can include anything from personnel, intelligence, operations, and logistics.

It is definitely not a stab at the MLOs from other countries, but in many cases, they did not have depth or breadth of experience with the continental staff system. Most countries recognized it, and the term used was that the military personnel from "skiing countries" tended to do a lot of the heavy lifting. And that was fine for several reasons, since it made the days go by more quickly when you had something to do, and we tried to stay busy.

DAY 36

THE KIWI AND THE HEAT

SECOND WEEK DOWN.

Jim—the Canadian I'm replacing—got into Malakal on Tuesday. A day late because of torrential rains here on Monday. He leaves here 72 hours later (Friday morning), returning to Juba and then Entebbe and home. He was here during the hard action last spring when Malakal changed hands several times amidst vicious fighting.

I owe him big time because he set me up for success with his analysis of the situation and what needed to be done to get us out patrolling, and the camp personalities, and who the Floppers were and weren't. For the uninitiated, a Flopper is a person whose capability, competence, professionalism, and ambition is lower than low. A Non-Performer. A Bag of Hammers. A Shit-Pump.

Jim's pretty angry after this mission because he actually gives a shit, and his frustration was largely because he simply couldn't defeat the collective institutional malaise. He'll be fine as soon as he gets home—his sense of humour will see to that, I think.

On the flight with Jim came The Kiwi. A very experienced New Zealand Army officer with a wicked sense of humour and a broad smile who sees the world much like I do. Young (well, younger than me isn't hard to achieve on this tour) and a sport enthusiast and quite fit and likes a pint or two. And a bit mad—his physical training yesterday consisted of running the perimeter wearing body armour. He and I are going to be working together for the duration of our tours and I know we'll get along just fine. Except for the crazy physical training shit…he only has a plate carrier and if I wore my

49

full rig with flak jacket and plates I'd look like a Mutant Ninja Turtle. A dead one. Lying in the road. Because the heat and sweat would have killed me.

Kiwis and Canadians share several traits, one of which is that we live in the shadow of a bigger nation. It affects the national psyche somewhat, I think. That'll manifest itself later.

Returning to the story at hand…

Because of various realities—like if you try to do all your entry administration yourself it will take you forever because there is no order or reason to the process, and you will get lost and confused—Jim and I took The Kiwi around to all the various offices around the camp to get the in-processing bullshit done as quickly as possible. Get a handheld Tetra radio. Sign here. Get an email account. Come back later. Fill in this form. And this one. And that one. Come back much later…

We then discovered that there was a waiting list for single accommodations (anywhere between six and eleven people—we think the dude working in the Accommodations Office wasn't interested in being helpful and just made up a number)—and that the Kiwi would have to temporarily stay in a large transient room that is allocated to the MLO team. Our office has the only access, so we grabbed the key and went to check out the room. And we were disgusted.

Apart from the sparseness, and the four beds haphazardly set in either corner of the room, the peeling linoleum flooring, and the dampness and sense of general disuse, there was an overpowering odour of rot and decay. It smelled as though a dog had crawled under the container to perish. Which is quite possible. The last attempt to cull the wild dogs involved a poison that dehydrated them….so they snuck under containers to whimper for a couple of days before they died.

Before you get sensitive about this—these dogs aren't Lassie. These are wild dogs that spread disease, run in packs at night, spread rabies, and need to die. I object to the process the UN uses here because a bullet—although louder—is more humane and quicker than poison.

As for this stinking abattoir of a room—there was no freakin' way The Kiwi was staying in there. We drove back to the MLO office, handed the key back and told our G4 (Logistics) guy to contact camp services to get someone to clean up whatever was making that horrid smell.

I bet you he hasn't contacted them—it would interfere with his intense Facebook strategy.

So, where to stay? The three of us, led by Jim, who after six months here definitely knew his way around, went back to camp services to work out a deal somehow. Long story short, we managed to wrangle that The Kiwi would get Jim's container on Friday (about ten seconds after he vacates the place). Until then, mainly because I had a ton less stuff in my accommodations, and I managed to do a decent Feng Shui (in my opinion), The Kiwi stayed with me.

We scored a spare cot from the Norwegians—it is wider and far more comfy than the Canadian or NZ variant, grabbed The Kiwi's kit, which had arrived on an earlier cargo flight and was waiting in a sea can (Huzzah!), and got him settled into my container. With a bed and a cot and kit, it's cozy and a bit cramped, but you help out when and how you can. And it's only for a few days.

In his kit, most importantly, he brought a large supply of "Back Country Cuisine" meals—freeze-dried from New Zealand. Brilliant selection. Great flavour. Good nutrition. He's been willing to share. I'm letting him try my "Mountain House" meals in exchange. As I said, he's going to be a good mate.

And he gets the bread maker. Bastard. To be fair, it was the previous Kiwi's—who didn't like to make his own bread, so Jim took possession of it.

Patrolling was slow this week. I didn't go on any—because of the shitty weather, there weren't that many tasks, and I'm trying to line up something that's a bit complicated but that will help achieve an effect if I can make it work. Fingers crossed. Sorry—none of that makes sense, does it? Essentially, I'm trying to plan some complicated patrols, and I helped set up other patrols for success.

Just as importantly, I took advantage of the time that Jim had left in Malakal to meet many of his humanitarian contacts, and other agency friends that are here…a representative from Human Rights, a Catholic priest who was in the area for years, Civil Affairs, OCHA (Organization for the Coordination of Humanitarian Affairs—a UN organization), and World Food Program. They often have an extremely accurate and pragmatic perspective since they've been here for much longer than the military. One of the folks I met—a quiet gent, very pleasant, and always helpful—had been kidnapped and held hostage for a few months in another conflict zone. And later came back to work in South Sudan. A fascinating person, and we're planning to have a pint this weekend and chat. Especially over the Wales—England Rugby game.

Also—next efforts—trying to get myself and The Kiwi and whatever new MLOs we receive for the Team on some flights to our outlying sites. Apart from Malakal, we have teams in several other strategic towns and villages where they are doing pretty good work patrolling, liaising, and coordinating and showing the UN presence. We're a little more restricted here in Malakal for several reasons, mainly the absolute distrust of the UN by the local military authorities. The advantage of going to the out-stations is that we can get a true picture on the ground, talk with our guys out there for more information, look at force protection issues, and so on.

The platform of choice for these local hops is the venerable Mi-8 helicopter, a Russian-designed beast that is big, bulky, ugly, and damn near indestructible, when they work. They handle both passengers and cargo and are an absolute workhorse. They are also extremely loud and you can't even hear yourself think in them. Good times. Bring ear protection!

The Kiwi is going to be assigned as one of the G3 (Operations) staff. As I'd mentioned in the last email, I'm the G2 but doing a lot of Ops stuff. We both have ideas and ways to improve what we're doing with a process, structure, and so on, so he and I are already seeing it as a collaborative effort. Small victories are critical. Most important is to make the list of priorities and pick your battles—you can't do it all in six months. Or a year. That would be like stuffing a marshmallow into a parking meter.

What you do is just pick a few performance yardsticks and try to move them forward. There are a couple of the MLOs that are very good and efficient officers—our South Korean, Ghanaian, Nepalese, and Zambians are good examples of hard-working Officers who "get it". But many don't get it—and as I saw last time I deployed; some are very content to let others do the work. That's an understatement—they are lazy as shit and make the same money as the hard-working MLOs.

Whatever. The world isn't fair.

I know I haven't described anyone in real detail, and I'm sure that the team seems amorphous to you. That's intentional since they haven't taken on any personality or uniqueness. You aren't seeing the Team dynamics or our interaction because I'm not seeing it either. Be patient—right now to me they are just starting to become distinct personalities with their own actions and voices. It's maybe too early to talk about them.

To put it all into context is more important—to experience the sights and feelings and environment. I think it's important to write down these factors first, while the feelings are fresh and the discomfort new, because it's going to be a routine soon and I'll forget all the extremely good and bad bits.

Like Heat.

Oh, the Heat.

I know that—as far as heat and humidity are concerned—different places make you feel heat differently. Saigon heat felt and burned intensely, but differently than Khartoum's dry searing waves. Toronto's summer swelter can't compare to Mombasa's deep humid slow bake, where in seconds your shirt was soaked through with your own sweat.

But heat here is different. It's always different.

Different from all those other places and it's worth talking about because it's part of your day and a topic of conversation and something that always lurks in your head. When the conditions are right, the temperature drops but the humidity stays high and the towering cumulus form darkly on the horizon. And that will bring torrenting sheets of rain that pour and pour and leave deep muddy pools of water and that horrible clinging clay on your boots. The clay. Tenacious stuff.

It's not enough to say, "It's hot."

All this heat can ruin your day if you aren't careful—sun stroke and heat stroke and prickly rashes and dehydration. You factor it into everything you do—in the liters of water you drink or take on patrol, and in your supply of Gatorade and Oral Hydration Powder…

The combination of heat and sun and humidity defies

description—walking out into the afternoon sun the heat slams itself into you and drains your energy. Walking to my container for lunch along the main road is quicker than a web of side paths but completely exposed to the sun. As I trudge along, my steps get shorter, my pace slows and the sweat dampens my shirt and pants. My feet are hot and everything feels soggy. The sun beats on the road and reflects back into your face and it feels like you're fully clothed inside a sauna. The humidity compounds the misery.

Nights like tonight bring no relief. The slight drop in temperature at sunset brings a greater feeling of humid dampness in the air. Not as sharp, but more enveloping. You're wrapped in a hot blanket that hasn't stayed in the dryer long enough and you feel smothered and suffocated.

I suppose you get used to it. Maybe it's more accurate to say that you get used to enduring it.

In hindsight, meeting The Kiwi was the best part of the tour. He and I got along famously, worked together, ate together, spent our free time together, and genuinely enjoyed each other's company. We had both received similar, high-quality pre-deployment training, we both had kick-ass first aid kits, and we were both armed with pistols (he had a SIG-Sauer as opposed to my antiquated Browning High Power).

We also distrusted the same people, and I find that is a good foundation for a strong friendship.

Throughout the tour, The Kiwi was my support base, and I was his. This support was critical as the tour progressed and the daily stressors and frustrations built up every day. You need a good mate like him to keep sane.

DAY 42

GENERAL OLONY

THERE ARE TWO PARTS TO THIS WEEK'S EMAIL. There could be three, I suppose, but I'd prefer to focus on the immediately more interesting stories and put some away as half-formed ideas until they solidify enough to make a good long account, or several short ones…I'm learning that some subjects take longer to write about than others.

It was a busy week. The Kiwi and I were basically running the Ops shop while the other two G3 folks were away for several days. Both being new we made shit up as we went along and, with the luck of beginners, it seemed to work out.

I spent the first hours of my Birthday having a relaxing Sunday morning. Coffee (Ethiopian). Light breakfast (oatmeal). Did a load of laundry. Propped the door open to air out the container and had some tunes playing. Then around 0830 or so, I got a call. Something's up. Get to the office.

Since my uniforms were hanging on the line and still damp, I threw on some civvies, grabbed my bag, walked to The Kiwi's cabin and knocked on the door. After a minute, I heard the key turn and the door open. Bleary-eyed and half-asleep, he poked his head out…

He started the conversation, "Hey Mate. Good morning."

"Something's up. Reports of IDPs—lots of IDPs—coming from the Bangladeshi Camp. I'm heading up to the Office."

No hesitation. "Right. Meet you there." (Damn good people, these New Zealanders.)

When I got into the office, the Duty Officer and his assistant were already manning the place, and I recorded what we knew, and what we needed to know. After some hasty coordination, we kicked them out the door to investigate the situation. We spent the whole day coordinating, assessing, directing, and tracking the Team. Those guys on patrol were awesome. It was a long day, and a good day.

Here's the story from Radio Tamazuj…more or less accurate…

SPLA prevents displaced people from entering UN base in Malakal

Soldiers from South Sudan's national army SPLA prevented dozens of displaced people from reaching the UN's 'Protection of Civilians' site in Malakal town of Upper Nile state over the weekend, multiple sources told Radio Tamazuj.

According to the sources, UN peacekeepers were escorting around 270 displaced Shilluk people, mostly men, from Wau Shilluk on the Nile's west bank to the Malakal base when they were stopped by SPLA soldiers.

The soldiers demanded that the men be handed over to them for detention but allowed the women and children to proceed to the base. The UNMISS peacekeepers did not hand the men over but escorted them back to the west bank, the sources said.

The current status of the men is not known. Malakal is controlled by government troops while the west bank is held by rebels.

Separately, the UN's state coordinator in Upper Nile State reportedly issued a directive that peacekeepers will no longer admit newly arrived civilians to the Malakal base because the compound is full, according to a source.

UNMISS spokesperson Ariane Quentier did not respond to questions emailed yesterday from Radio Tamazuj regarding this matter and the SPLA incident.

Update: 9:41 AM, 1/10/2015

The report of the directive is not true, according to Quentier. The UNMISS spokesperson further confirmed the incident with the SPLA, putting the number of men turned back at around 130.

As of 24 September, there were 45,462 people sheltering in the UN base in Malakal, according to UNMISS figures. Thousands of civilians have arrived at the base recently following a month-long blockade of food deliveries to the Nile's west bank by the SPLA.

As I said—the patrol was awesome out there. Damn good work and helped prevent any escalation. To their credit, the SPLA troops acted with a lot of restraint, too.

I was looking forward to the week because of a planned helicopter patrol out near the border on Monday. I wanted to be on it. It was cancelled and moved to Tuesday. Then the Tuesday patrol was cancelled. That was starting to look like the World was conspiring against me and I was getting a frowny face because I like helicopter rides…but then another opportunity opened up and I was on the manifest for a Dynamic Air Patrol. We called them "DAPs."

We met General Johnson Olony. A leading figure of the SPLA Opposition. It was memorable.

Our helicopter landed in the midst of the sprawling settlement in Tonga, throwing up clouds of acrid dust as it hovered and then finally settled down on the plateau. Even the presence of our armed Force Protection who were first to exit the aircraft and take up positions— didn't reduce the smiles, or handshakes, or halting conversations in a combination of English and Sudanese Arabic. Everyone was very friendly and pleasant. I shook hands with one gentleman and commented on his beard, noting that he must be a very young man, since his beard was so black and mine was so grey. He laughed, shook my hand again and introduced himself as Peter. No visible rank but he clearly carried authority among the soldiers judging by how they behaved around him. He sat beside me in the meeting.

My job was to observe and take notes. My boss sat in front of me, facing the General's empty chair. With Peter beside me, and since I wanted to be prepared for the chance of having my notes seized at the end of the meeting, I scrawled my most horrible chicken-scratch. Illegible notes serve no value, or will take so long to decipher that any value is lost…

There was a stir. The General was approaching.

Olony strode up to the group of us, who were sitting in curved rows of iron benches and plastic chairs under the tallest shade tree in the camp. UN and Force Protection and former Rebels together with the Inter-Governmental Authority for Development representative. Known by their acronym of "IGAD", this East African agency has a mission to promote regional cooperation and integration to support efforts in achieving peace, security, and prosperity. They had brokered the latest cease-fire and were trying to make in-roads with the Opposition to put the plan into place.

The General's stride was powerful, and we all stood to greet him. Black, as the Shilluk are black, with a sheen of sweat on his close-cropped head, he dominated the group with his presence. Dark, piercing eyes. An aggressive stance that was not—could not—be contrived. And standing almost seven feet tall, muscular, thick through the arms and chest. More than physical, he exuded power in a raw, visceral form that I'd never seen before. Like a bull ready to charge.

"I have a PhD in fighting," he said once in an interview, speaking with derision of the other rebel leaders who had earned Doctorates from Western institutions. This was not a man to underestimate. He was General Olony.

The meeting did not start well.

Olony sat down, and after the first introductions, he began to speak. In his tribal language and in Arabic, loud enough to be heard not only by the circle around the tree, but by the increasing number of soldiers who gathered to hear his words. Through an interpreter, he launched against the UN, IGAD, and especially the President of South Sudan, Salva Kiir.

Vehement and increasingly loud. Sharp sentences punctuated by gestures. Others chimed in to show agreement or reinforce his point. And sometimes to correct the interpreter. Our Commander tried to interject but was stopped short. This was a one-way conversation, and it was going to stay that way until Olony decided otherwise.

"The UN can solve the problems but works not for the interest of the people of South Sudan. Not helping Our People. They are only helping the Government."

Between statements, he would lean back until the interpreter was finished, and then shift his bulk forward to emphasize his next point…

"There was shooting after the agreement was signed. The Government did it. The UN withdrew the sanctions against me. That was good." (Well, that was because one country vetoed the sanctions…but whatever).

"What about Warjok? Malakal is occupied by Those People. Why did they occupy it? The fighting is tribalism fighting, not government and rebels. They must leave the occupied areas—Lelo, Warjok. From tomorrow I will decide if I will push them out of the areas."

This last point was made with him stabbing the small table in front of him with his massive hands. He then focused his attention on the peace-brokers from IGAD.

"IGAD. You representatives are from Africa? You don't want peace. You are businesspeople and want the war to continue. You know with others helping us we can chase Kiir out of Juba. We are granite. You cannot break us. We will get another country to help us."

"Malakal is Shilluk, Wau is Shilluk, as are Lelo, Detang, Warjok. If they do not move. We will move them."

I was frantically scribbling the conversation and names in real time, so as not to miss anything, and asked Peter if I had the places correct. I did. They were all villages across the White Nile from Malakal, that the Government Forces had occupied several weeks ago…

"Kiir and Musaveni (the President of Uganda) are together. Kenya and Uganda want to rule South Sudan. We will call Kony to give us reinforcements." (Kony is the Head of the Lord's Resistance Army. A violent armed extremist group that operates in Uganda, South Sudan, and the Congo. Hmmm…)

"Civilians are being killed. But all UN in Juba are from one tribe supporting Kiir. Good governance is needed. If the UN governs South Sudan for six years, there will be peace." (That's awfully optimistic, Johnson.)

"If you hear bullets there across the river. It is not us. It is the government killing people."

It went on and on, and I will tell you that all this was a little nervous-making.

Then the IGAD representatives spoke. And our commander spoke. And my boss spoke. And bit by bit countered many of Olony's arguments…

"You don't support us"—"But we have many Shilluk in our Protection of Civilian site in Malakal."

"You don't investigate them when they shoot people"—"Yes we do, and we report it to the UN in Juba and New York"

"We have no voice"—"But the next Governor appointed to this area is from the Opposition. It was announced today."

"You promised to call and did not"—"Give us several numbers and we will call you every day"

And IGAD spoke with factual calm and talked about the process and next steps and they brought copies of the agreement for Olony and his staff to review. And I suddenly noticed that the dynamic had changed. More than that. The language had changed.

Most people were now speaking English.

I flashed into the reality that the initial harangue was more for his listeners than for us. And that's why he spoke in his language. So his troops would understand and be impressed by the Big Man giving the UN a massive blast. When the issues came down more to tactical fact and negotiation, English became the common language. And while the mood lightened slowly, the central issues still remained— we were in no position to force the SPLA away from the West Bank of the White Nile, for example—but the dialogue had started and the ice had broken. That was a start.

While the talking went on, I watched. And took copious notes. There was a lot going on and a lot to observe:

- An old man was brought forward to talk. He came from a contested village to describe how his family had been killed and that there was no incentive for him to return to Malakal. He listed numbers of people killed, and cattle taken. Whether you believe the stories or not, you need the right people to come and investigate and interview.
- I noticed one female soldier.
- There was a bodyguard with an odd-looking submachine gun in addition to his AK-47. Heckler & Koch maybe? A Beretta model from the 1950s? And there was another dude trying to look totally bad-ass with tough-guy scowl and aviator shades who was holding an AK tricked out with a top rail and red dot sight. Odd weapons or configurations you usually don't see, and since I'm a firearms enthusiast, I notice them.
- No, I didn't see any child soldiers. Didn't mean they weren't there…Olony was being sanctioned for forcibly recruiting hundreds of them.

Time passed quickly, and it was soon time to go. But first, we met some captured SPLA soldiers who appeared well-treated, not abused, who spoke freely about their conditions, and how they were getting tired of Red Cross biscuits and really missed sorghum. That's a very positive sign, actually. That they weren't mistreated, not that they hated Red Cross biscuits.

We need to go back there. Bring some humanitarians for an assessment, Human Rights to interview the allegations of civilian killings by the military, IGAD to talk about the next steps in the peace process. And I hope I am on the next patrol.

As the group walked back to the helicopter, my boss and I strolled ahead of the others…a lone soldier walked parallel to us a few feet to the right. The boss talked to him in English…nope. He spoke Shilluk and Arabic and some Swahili. Suddenly a bunch of stuff came back to me, and with a few phrases of Arabic that I dredged up from my last tour he and I had a short conversation. And our smiles got wider and the gestures more animated and if we couldn't understand every word, we got the gist of it and laughed together as we walked. And it was simple stuff—How are you? What's your name? My name is John. I am from Canada. Everything is good?

It made a difference.

We boarded the helo and while it was a very hot day, the interior of the aircraft was a big oven and the heat was even more stifling inside. I sat in the back near the closed ramp and sweat ran from my face and slowly dripped from my beard onto the metal floor and yet it wasn't so bad because you knew there would be an end to the misery when we would take off…just a few minutes more.

The JAKLI Force Protection commander sat across from me, magazine off his rifle, mopping sweat from his face with a handkerchief. Everyone else looked miserable until the rotors turned, we lifted in a hover, and as the helicopter moved forward, the breeze came through the open windows and cooled us. I dug through my pack and pulled out my earphones and connected them to my phone and cranked some tunes from Die Aerzte. Listening to German pop-punk in an old Russian helo piloted by Rwandans over South Sudan's White Nile. Completely Surreal.

My sweat felt cold on my clothing and skin, but it was such a relief after the past sweaty hours. As we followed the path of the river, I was suddenly hungry.

———

Wasn't much of a Birthday for me, really. But it really wasn't as though I had anything planned and I probably would have been self-pitying and pouty and wandering around with a long face. So instead, at least we did some cool stuff.

For a period of about three weeks, it seemed that all the crap happened on weekends, which was incredibly inconvenient for us. No civilians worked weekends. Our Sector Headquarters staff didn't work weekends. And most importantly, the SPLA (and Opposition) didn't work weekends either, so driving down to Malakal to rouse one of our SPLA Liaison Officers was never well-received. I know this because they told us.

Meeting General Olony was very interesting indeed, because it was good to meet a man who lived up to the hype. He was memorable in a lot of ways. The UN considered imposing sanctions on him which did not occur because of a dissenting vote in the Security Council.

At the end of our meeting in Tonga, I felt compelled to speak with him. I strode up to Olony, standing small in his shadow (I'm 6 foot 2 inches/188 cm tall), and thanked him for taking the time to see us. He gazed down at me, scanned my uniform, and asked, "American? Or Britain-ian?"

"Neither Sir," I responded, "I. Am. Canadian!"

He laughed and held out a massive hand to shake. It was like putting your hand into a goalie's glove.

DAY 48

ONE MONTH MALAKAL

IT WAS A FRUSTRATING WEEK IN MANY WAYS.

I am starting to have a backlog of things to write about and they are crowding one after another in my head like a highway in rush hour. Some stories sneak their way to the front along the shoulder while other, bigger stories sit. Stalled. Waiting to crawl ahead.

Stupid bottleneck of a brain.

I have officially reached Groundhog Day. After a month here—Happy Anniversary to me—the days have finally glued themselves together and I have trouble recalling what happened on one specific day versus another. Everything is the same, and I want to share my usual daily routine because it is a Routine…but it's also an insight into what life is like here.

0530-0600—FAR TOO AWAKE.

I wake up. Lie in bed. Get out of bed. Ponder life's deeper meaning as I put the kettle on. Put on t-shirt, combat pants, socks, and boots.

Grab my soap, towel, roll of toilet paper, and go to the ablutions. The ablutions are all screwed up because ours are located near the Humanitarians and NGOs who were brought in during the fighting—so they use our facilities. And leave it in a completely shit state. So, the camp management locked the containers. Good luck finding a key when you really, REALLY have to go to the bathroom. Maybe the fact that Camp Management never actually told anyone about their cunning "Hide the Key" plan frustrated me most, because a bunch of us spent two days playing "twenty questions" to get some answers on who actually holds the keys.

So, back to the routine.

I do ablution things. Head back to my container. Take my sleeping bag off the bed and air it out.

0630–FIRST ALARM

Alarm goes off. I'm already awake so it's irrelevant. I prepare my coffee—I have a Bodum French Press that also doubles as the cup itself. Brilliant. Even more brilliant is some Ethiopian coffee one of my mates from the United Kingdom left for me when he finished his mission. That coffee is dark, fragrant, heavy, and delicious. For something solid (apart from coffee grounds), I eat a granola bar, or maybe a piece of bread and peanut butter (of which I have three jars).

0700-0730–STUFF

Email or check the news online or call home. It's a Malakal morning but a Canada evening and vice versa, and it gives time to catch up.

0730–SECOND ALARM

My other alarm goes off. Programmed to say, "Good Morning John. Take your Malarone pill right now! It is seven-thirty" The "Daily" anti-malarial. Same time every day. Much better on my system than Mefloquine, which was the weekly pill I took last tour, and which caused me some issues. Like paranoia and near-homicidal rages.

Around this time, The Kiwi pops round and I shut down the laptop and grab my day bag. For those interested, it is a BDS Tactical Bug-Out bag, with added pouches on either side for a water bottle and small First Aid kit. It's my short patrol pack, which is enough to keep me going for up to a day. It also has a convenient pocket for a pistol and two magazines. Some days Mr. Browning (my pistol) comes along.

Lock up the container and trudge the 400 meters or so to the office.

0740-0830–PREP FOR THE DAILY BRIEFING.

I call it Morning Prayers and the term seems to be catching on.

As the G2 I prepare the meteorological report, check open source media for news (Radio Tamazuj and Sudan Tribune mainly), look at the Juba and Upper Nile State Situation Reports for any pertinent points, update the Patrol Risk Matrix (a basic matrix where we assess critical factors which will determine whether we conduct a patrol or cancel it), continue to enjoy the smooth delicious coffee…and greet my fellow Team-Mates as they come in.

0830-0900—MORNING PRAYERS.
A series of Situation Reports, called "SITREPs" from the key staff to ensure everyone knows what has happened in the last 24 hours, what's planned for the next couple of days, if there are any personnel or logistical issues, and so on. The Senior MLO, a Norwegian Colonel, also presents his points at the end. Then off we go…

0900-1200—MORNING ROUTINE.
A range of activities. A short patrol either to Malakal Town, or the Bangladesh Navy Camp on the White Nile, or through the POC Site. We might have follow-up questions from the Morning Brief, which can result in info-gathering visits to the Humanitarians, the State Operations Centre, UN Police, or Security. Or updating Operating Procedures, planning upcoming patrols, or chatting with the SPLA Liaison Officers who are assigned to us here at the camp.

1200-1300-ISH (MORE OR LESS)—LUNCHIE MUNCHIE.
Now this is an interesting fact. Most of the folks will take a two-hour lunch. I'm referring to a lot of the civilians, not specifically the military. Well, them too. So, if you are even thinking of interacting in the afternoon with one of the civvies here, or even most of those in uniform, don't even show up at their offices before 1400 hours. They won't be there. It's frustrating.

For my lunch, I will walk back to my container and heave a sigh as I open the door and look at my still unwashed pile of laundry on the floor. I haven't really been able to crack the code on the cleaning ladies—locals from the POC Site, by the way—doing my laundry. The Kiwi left clothes and quite a lot of laundry powder. The clothes were returned. Days later, the empty container that had held the detergent was back in his container.

I'll put the kettle on and usually have a pack of noodles mixed with a can of tuna. I'll read a little bit. Rehydrate. Enjoy the coolness of the air-conditioning. And then go back to the office…

1300-1730—AFTERNOON ROUTINE.

Again, could be a short patrol. Or Team administration—grab a vehicle, load up all the empty water containers, and drive through the POC site (which you have to remember is inside our perimeter) to turn right to the southern gate of the Indian Battalion's area and proceed past the trucks and BMP armoured fighting vehicles and Soldiers over towards the Rwandan Battalion area, where the water purification point is located. The water is collected from the Nile River and put through a two-stage process, as I understand it. It's supposed to be potable. Loading up everyone's water is a regular administrative task, and while it can be extremely muddy and messy at times because of flooded muddy roads (yes, even in the camp), everyone takes turns and pitches in.

1730-1830—PT.

I have a walking/jogging route that is 1.4 km long. It is within the camp but borders another section, including the POC site. As I walk, I look at the holes in the chicken wire fence, and the person-sized gaps in the boundary wire and shake my head at the half-hearted security measures. The perimeter, as I like to say, is "porous."

The ground is—like every other road around here—pot-holed and uneven. It is safer to walk at a brisk pace rather than jog and risk turning an ankle, but many of us jog the less-bad bits and walk the really bad bits, stepping around the deep ruts and holes, and around the many wild dogs that lie in the dust and mud-clay, taking on the road colour so that at times you don't see them until they get up to move out of your way. With temperatures in the high 30s and extreme humidity, it is easy to work up a good sweat and clear the head of the day's frustrations.

1830-1900—CLEAN UP.

Shower. I do this before sunset. The bugs—especially the mosquitoes—haven't made their appearance in any large numbers by that time. But if you wait until 1930 or later, you will be devoured.

Back in the room—apply some bug spray and DEET cream and thrown on some civvy clothes to feel slightly more human. Ponder the many and varied dinner options available (ha!). Have a glass of wine or a beer to help the pondering…

1900-2000—DINNER.

Either a freeze-dried meal, or some pasta, or soup/stew. For soup, I'd mix several cans of veg and meat together in a soup stock (also from a can) to cook something "home-made." There is no food in Malakal. The lack of fresh fruit and veg here is an issue. As is the lack of grains and meats. And dairy.

Those are all the Food Groups.

2000-2230—RELAX.

Visit friends in their containers. Email friends back home. Watch some shows or a movie (I put a bunch of stuff on my hard drive before deploying so I wouldn't be short of entertainment). Listen to music. Do some upgrades to the container—usually involving sealing up holes or taping things to other things. At some point the pistol is out and loaded and stays that way until morning.

2230—PREPARE FOR BED.

Straighten out the bug net, replace the sleeping bag after shaking it to make sure no bugs are hiding there. Make sure the pistol and flashlight and Tetra radio are in easy reach. The pistol is usually under the pillow. Crawl into bed and re-adjust the bug net to make sure it's well tucked-in. Flip the light-switch.

2230-0630—SLEEP. OR AT LEAST TRY TO.

And throughout the night, I wake up to the sounds of howling packs of wild dogs, or strange scratching around my container, or imagined noises. And when I turn on my headlamp while inside the bug net, the first thing I see is the white netting and it takes seconds to adjust to this and see beyond the net into the container. It's quite claustrophobic, actually.

Wash. Rinse. Repeat.

The only difference in the week is on Sunday, which is a maintenance day. We check into Ops in the morning, but can do laundry, wash-up and do some basic maintenance on our vehicles—check fluids and belts and equipment—and we can do it in civvies.

The main activities for me, which include eating and PT, really don't change. Except that around 1930 on Sunday nights, it's poker-time in the Senior MLO's office. For 10 South Sudanese Pounds (less than $1.00 Canadian) we spend a few hours playing Texas Hold-Em. It's enjoyable in a way I didn't think was possible, but when you have a Norwegian, Canadian, New Zealander, Fijian, South Korean, Nepali, and Papua New Guinean (as an example—the line-up can change weekly) sitting around a table, playing together, laughing, and learning when to check or hold, it builds camaraderie and spirit. It's a simple, silly game—played for next to no money—but it is heart-warming and time-passing and it becomes the first topic of conversation on Monday morning with good-natured joking and comments about how the winner would spend all their vast fortune.

That's my routine.

The reality is that most of what happened on the deployment followed this predictable model. The day-to-day activities didn't really change very much. There was a lot of repetition, and sometimes (often) you wouldn't know what day of the week it was. Except Sunday. We always knew when it was Sunday because we could sleep in. Even the unpredictable things became predictable—checkpoints, roadblocks, friction, ineptitude, laziness.

I eventually cracked the code on the cleaning ladies and laundry ladies, who weren't the same person. The cleaning was included in the container cost (USD $22.00 per day). So, I would put 200 South Sudanese Pounds on a bag of laundry with a portion of soap, and Hey Presto! that evening, I would have laundry folded and mostly dry and ironed on my chair. The only laundry-related problem was with my gym gear and Under Armour material, which did not respond well to a hot ironing. In fact, a lot of my gym clothing got a little melted over the tour. But at least they were clean…

DAY 50

THE SEARCH

ON SATURDAY MORNING, Samirah's first words to me were, "Wanna go find a dead body?"

It all started out innocently enough when a bunch of us were having a Friday evening drink at a friend's Farewell Party and Samirah described going out to see a corpse earlier that afternoon. The victim had been shot along one of the main IDP routes that they travel to get from the West Bank of the Nile to the camp here in Malakal. It's not a long distance, but fraught with danger.

Almost always at night, sneaking from Wau Shilluk to the riverbank. Then, in flimsy canoe-like boats, they paddle along against the current, steering amidst the fast-flowing green-brown water until they land near or at "BANFRU", the Bangladesh Force Riverine Unit camp on the banks of the river. From there, paralleling the road between BANFRU and the UN camp, they make their way through low scrub and small stunted trees to the POC site.

Apart from those who are fleeing those areas because of security concerns—especially with threats made by both sides to either expand the West Bank holdings or drive the SPLA away from it—there are also many who come to Malakal because of food insecurity. Malakal has regular food distribution, and there is a trade of goods between our site and another one across the river. It's maybe 20 kilometers in a straight line, but much more to get here.

Sometimes the SPLA stops them. Sometimes there's in-fighting, robbery, theft, and assault. And sometimes boats overturn and passengers flail against the current only to exhaust themselves and drown.

The UN agency people who file witness statements and reports aren't always trained investigators. They are lawyers and advocates and back home they might have an army of police, forensics teams, subject matter experts, laboratories and testing equipment and detailed analysis to try and pin down what happened. That doesn't exist here. No one is a trained investigator except the UN Police and even then, the skill and knowledge varies from country to country and person to person. I've only had some of the basics—and I mean basics—taught to me on pre-deployment training back in Canada. But if there's a spent casing, most MLOs could tell the difference between a 7.62 x 39mm (AK-47 ammunition) and a 12.7 caliber heavy machine gun casing. Or to cordon off an area and not disturb the ground, and take notes, collect evidence, snap pictures, etc. The small amount of training we had is significantly better than no training at all.

One of the four pillars of the UN mandate in South Sudan is the investigation and reporting of human rights abuses. Or at least to support it.

On this Friday night, the initial discussion concerned the pictures they had taken of the body and what the bullet wound was and whether the body had been moved and all that other stuff. So, I asked to see the photos. They were graphic and they were of a dead male and because he hadn't been dead very long when the team found him, he hadn't bloated or been eaten yet but the flies had swarmed on his eyes and mouth and on the dried crusted blood from the wound and they sat clustered green-blue on the dark black skin that was somehow pallid in death.

I told Samirah what I saw, and what the pictures suggested.

Single gunshot wound to the upper right chest, two inches to the left and up from his right nipple. They hadn't flipped him over to check the exit wound. Lots of blood by the side of the road, two big pools then a drag trail off the road, all of it mostly covered with a patina of dust from the many trucks that drove the road to BANFRU and back from our base every day. His body was found about 25 meters off the road—he had been dragged there by his feet. Probably by his pants first, since they had pulled off as someone dragged him away. The pants—tan and bloody-dark—lay bundled off to the side. There were scrapes and scuffs from the dragging over hard clay and gravel and thick low scrub. He was almost naked, his genitals covered by his shorts, his arms stretched over his head. I figured he had bled out quickly rather than died immediately and that's what I told Samirah and some other Human Rights dude who was looking over our shoulders, taking it all in.

Yes, maybe I wanted to be helping some of these folks accurately record info on the off chance that one day, in the future, maybe a Truth and Reconciliation type of committee might get a bit closer to the truth of the event. Doubtful. Ha!—more than doubtful. Probably not ever going to happen.

I guess I became their go-to guy if any other victims were found. And that's why Samirah walked into the office the next Saturday.

The initial story was that a number of folks had been trying to cross at night from Wau Shilluk to get to Malakal Camp and somewhere along the way a single gunshot had been fired. One guy died. The victim's family and an eyewitness were in the camp being interviewed by Human Rights, who were taking the info down and trying to pinpoint the exact location.

I grabbed my Go Bag, walked over to their office, and waited. My initial thought was that another patrol of guys could drive me out there to the murder site, and then bring me back to base since they had to do a town patrol anyway. But things were taking a long while so I got Emin—another MLO—to hop into another truck with me, but then we couldn't sort out the Force Protection and when we were about to start some of the civilian witnesses and family members tried to get in the car and I stopped that cold. No Non-UN civilians in my vehicle—Shit, we have enough issues with the SPLA thinking we're spying for the Opposition and cozy-cozy with the Shilluk without them seeing an MLO being a taxi service for IDPs.

We stopped before we had even started. Someone found another car and driver and let the civilians pile into that SUV and lead the way through Alpha Gate. And Hey! The Indian Force Protection troops were actually where they were supposed to be, and they followed us as we drove the pot-holed road the couple of kilometers to BANFRU. As we neared that gate of the small compound, we suddenly turned left onto a smaller grey-coloured clay trail that, while mostly dry, had some deep mud sections. I put the Toyota into low gear and easily got through the ruts, although the smaller SUV housing the Force

Protection behind me had more difficulty, and with whining engine and spinning tires lurched its way through the worst of the muck.

About 100 meters past this morass the vehicles stopped and the Shilluk family members and witnesses had already dismounted and were already moving, spread-out, towards where the body had been last seen. It was hot and the sun was as relentless as the humidity, with the heat reflecting off the baked clay and back into my face. We started walking as a group towards the location and then Samirah told me some new information—the shooting had apparently happened on Thursday. 48 hours earlier. Oh Dear God—this was not going to be at all pleasant. It would be decomposed and eaten by dogs and birds and maybe crocodiles.

And I didn't want to be there.

We approached an area, surrounded by open-spaced shade trees, scrub, open patches, then further along, high reeds and water that looked to be about twelve to eighteen inches deep. The water was the Nile, but you'd have to go through high reeds for several meters before you got to the open water and swift-running current.

I walked slowly and scanned the ground back and forth looking for anything...just anything that would seem out of place. And the Shilluk girl pointed towards the overgrown riverbank near a tall tree, surrounded by water, about ten feet beyond the dry ground where we all stood. Samirah asked, "Did you bring your gumboots?" and I shook my head. This was getting worse. A body that's been dead for a couple of days and immersed in shallow water and I didn't want to get my feet wet and now I especially didn't want to be there...

And as I was being reluctant to step into the water, and as I stood debating whether to go in or not, a male relative had already rolled up his trousers, and slipping off his flip-flops stepped into the muddy water and moved towards the tree where the body was last seen. We all watched and waited, and I took a few notes and marked the location on my Garmin.

The man moved branches aside with his hands and peered under the tree, then shook his head and yelled something to the interpreter before moving deeper into the reeds. He disappeared from sight, but you could hear the crackle of vegetation and see the waving of the reed-tops to mark his progress. He walked a wide semi-circle before reappearing, and his face clearly told us that there was nothing there.

All of us walked a bit further along the banks but the body wasn't anywhere we could see or smell, and we collectively made a decision to head back to our base. We figured the crocs ate him.

Although we didn't encounter anybody apart from ourselves when we first arrived at this place, over time a number of civilians from the POC site appeared one by one, looking for firewood, or a place to fish, or a ride to Wau Shilluk. Two small boys, maybe around five years of age, walked in front of me holding a couple of small Nile Perch, strung on a stick, in their tiny hands.

It brought me back to being a kid fishing up in Northern Ontario, or along the Maitland River, other random streams and rivers, and the excitement of the catch and the friendship of sitting with a pal, both your lines in the water. Gazing as the water slid past and the cloud reflection and the sudden tug as the fish took your bait and the exhilaration that followed.

These kids were catching fish, surrounded by people looking for a corpse.

I never sent this out as an email, as I felt it was too intense an experience, and I didn't feel that this was proper to share. I found this search emotionally draining, and while this was an occasional patrol for me, the Human Rights folks dealt with issues and events such as this all the time. What was most interesting about this was that I had wound myself up, steeled myself to the fact that we were going to see a corpse, that it wasn't going to be a pleasant experience, and that I was afraid of my reaction. I didn't know what I was going to do—laugh, vomit, or cry. Maybe all three.

Not finding the body was a combination of relief and disappointment. That's pretty messed up. Relieved that you didn't find a corpse, then disappointed you didn't find a corpse, then the reality hits that this was a human being. Relatives were looking for him. Mourning him. Grieving. I realized it wasn't all about me and my experience or squeamishness.

After that, most of my work with the Human Rights folks involved looking at pictures and providing my observations based on my limited investigative training. That was No Problem. Easy. Like it wasn't even human.

DAY 57

THE MALAKAL GENERAL

MEETING THE SPLA GENERAL took less effort, but in some ways, more work.

While his headquarters was more easily accessible than Olony, who I had written about before, it involved driving. And while that might not seem a chore, and while the distance might not be great, there were challenges—especially the first bit where I crawled along in first or sometimes second gear, leading the small convoy of MLOs, Force Protection, and Big Guys along the single straight red dirt-mud road. Imported dirt, I believe. "Murum" I think it's called, it makes a better road material, even in the rainy season. It is brought in from around Bunj. The local soil is black and very slippery and clings when wet. But it didn't stop the massive potholes and ruts that made me cringe in my seat afraid that we'd bottom out the SUV.

Even along the straight road, there were twists and turns and choices—to either follow the tire tracks of the more travelled route or dodge around deeper holes in favour of slightly shallower crevices. It didn't matter. The driver and passenger in front lurched back and forth like drunkards, while in the back seats, I felt for them. Buffeted and worse—unable to see or control the path and anticipate the pitch and yaw of the Nissan.

The Rwandan Force Protection had it worse. They drove in pickup trucks with a metal frame attached to the back with a forward machinegun mount overlooking the cab, and seats facing outward for the troops. On each side of the pickup, three or four soldiers sit on a bench with their feet off the sides of the truck resting on a pipe-rail-thin support. It cannot be all that stable and I cringe at the thought that if a truck rolls, these guys could be seriously hurt. But a more likely scenario is that in a moment of forgetfulness, a soldier will lose balance and get launched off the side.

But once you got onto Charlie Route, it was a straight run through the town and past the checkpoints and the soldiers who, in civvies or uniforms, all had AK-47s and sometimes didn't wave back, but usually did. I remain amazed that waving at the most bad-ass looking dude in South Sudan would result in a happy grin, a softening of the features, and a friendly wave in return…sometimes with both hands waving and a grin and Hallo or Salaam Aleikum in return. But sometimes not. Sometimes a frown. A snarl or sneer. A slight lift of the weapon in your direction.

I had driven to the SPLA HQ previously and was pretty sure where I was going, but Adam, one of our SPLA Liaison Officers, confirmed my route. It was an easy left at the checkpoint then through two gigantic morasses of mud. I stopped, put the car into "4 Low" and turned on the Diff Locks before trying to get a good run into the sludge—straining and lurching and bumping, afraid to slow and terrified to stop—we navigated the first and then second seas of mud and slime. Do you remember the Force Protection vehicles, and how they are configured to carry troops in the open? Picture that vehicle going through mud almost the height of the tires. Those dudes must have been soaked and reeking.

After that mud bath, the Nissan briefly came to rest just outside the lonely gate of the Headquarters. Lonely because there was only the gate. No fence or wall or barrier. Just the gate. You could—if you weren't afraid of being shot repeatedly by an over-zealous soldier—drive around it on either side. But that isn't the way it works here.

Once the Force Protection and others had caught up to me, I approached a dirt roundabout in front of could have been a British style garrison headquarters—the buildings of the same era were scattered throughout the town—and drove in a semi-circle until I was pointed back towards the gate. For a quick exit. Ha! We would never even make it to the vehicle if things went bad. The Force Protection vehicles pulled in ahead and behind us, and the Big Guys did whatever they did—dismount, pleasantries, handshakes, and so on. I honestly wasn't paying attention because I was scanning the area.

Unlike Olony, the SPLA General was only slightly taller than I am, with a bit of a belly. His upper front teeth had been forced out into something of a chipmunk-ish overbite as a tribal ritual. He had small but expressively dark eyes and a pleasant but professional demeanor. He was very well-turned out, often wearing a pressed short-sleeve shirt with General rank on his shoulders, gorgets on the collars, darker green trousers, and socks, with well-shone oxford dress shoes. This General was no guerilla bush-fighter—he was professional, intelligent, eloquent, and engaging.

To underestimate him would be dangerous, as it's dangerous to underestimate anything in this country. He was a broad Thinker. And while this General was not projecting the visceral force I had seen in General Olony, in this one I felt a greater depth and common understanding. One who would act—but with reason, for a reason. Logically.

I liked his words.

I first met him when a delegation from a Western Embassy came to call and pass on their message, and he listened because the delegates had a good message and there was a force and power behind it. But the General wasn't taking any shit from us either. He admitted that he had taken the offensive and captured ground across the White Nile River after the cease-fire had been signed. This action was taken in order to secure Malakal Airport, because this was his line of supply. Otherwise, the Opposition could shell, mortar, and rocket the airstrip and cut off the flights. Frankly—as much as everyone wrung their hands at his actions, we all benefitted from his "violation" because it ensured regular Humanitarian flights. Regular UN flights. And regular SPLA resupply flights. Contracted with big Russian heavy transport aircraft, or a Boeing 727.

However, the Opposition reacted strongly to this offensive. They were enraged. The assault across the White Nile was operationally sound from the SPLA perspective, but it was a serious ceasefire violation, it encroached on tribal lands, and there are claims of human rights violations. The news reports talked about Mi-24 helicopter gunships being used…

Sometimes the meetings were held inside a large central room with a high ceiling where enormous geckos crawled along the paint-peeled walls, and I was once lucky enough to have been positioned near a window where a faint breeze would occasionally cool me down. The room was sweltering.

But at other times, in keeping with a tradition through the continent, chairs would be formed in a semi-circle around a tall shade tree that stood just outside the headquarters building and his desk—enormous and heavy wood—would already be set up with his chair positioned and files already placed for the meeting. And we would sit under the tree while lower-ranked personnel sat off to our right. On the other side, in the shade of another tree, sat the personal security detachment of ten or more soldiers, machine guns resting blackly on their bipods with the belt of ammunition coiled on top, their AK-47s carried with extraordinary nonchalance.

The General stood up as we approached, and I waited my turn to greet him. I stood to attention and gave him a good salute and I like to think he appreciated it. I shook his hand and got a good handshake back and maybe he likes my beard, or my smile, or the fact that I don't talk much at these things. I watch and listen and take notes. And think a lot about it afterwards. I am always interested in the motivations—why does someone do X when Y would make more sense? What are the factors? The Motivations? The Benefits? Or is it just an order from his boss? Interesting questions get asked. And sometimes the unasked questions tell you more than the spoken ones.

The meetings are always good with him. You must be on your game because he's sharp—often referring back to his notes and challenging us on what was said, and what was actually meant. His English is excellent. But the greatest success, to my mind, is that after every meeting, even if we don't agree on some issues, the door is left open for the next meeting. That's critical in negotiation.

And once we say our cheery and smiling goodbyes, it's the same route back. Lurching along from pothole to rut, looking in the rear-view mirror to make sure we aren't outpacing the Force Protection too badly. Looking ahead for individuals or small groups of soldiers moving through the ghost town. Women from the POC site heading back to the camp with firewood or a bag of random goods on their head, scavenged from the ruins of a house and either sold or traded at the market inside the camp. And then the empty stretch of road with the never-ending bump bump—dotted with small groups of soldiers walking up the road—until we reach the Hesco barriers and enter Alpha Gate.

The General in this story is Major General Kezekia Puot. He was either the Acting Commander 2nd Division, Deputy Commander of the Division, or the Deputy Sector II Commander, or all three depending on who you spoke with. He was later replaced in Malakal by Major General Boutros Bol Bol, the Commander of SPLA 2nd (Rhino) Division.

I always enjoyed the interaction with Puot, and felt we had a good working relationship. He was, as I said, intellectually sharp. He exuded a degree of professionalism I hadn't previously seen. 2nd Division were relatively disciplined compared to some of the other SPLA units that had been in the area. While there was a lot of shit that happened around Malakal—shootings, abductions, detentions—it wasn't necessarily institutionalized, or necessarily done with chain of command authorization. It appeared to usually be bored, lonely, and drunk (or stoned) soldiers. Or members of SPLA-aligned militias just being assholes.

The roads and the mud, even from the base to Malakal, a distance of only a few kilometers, was terrible. The average driving time was 45 minutes to SPLA Division HQ in the rainy season, which dropped to 20 minutes in the dusty dry season. Wherever you're going, you aren't getting there fast.

I never did see the point of bringing Force Protection to the SPLA HQ. They had enough troops and firepower there to completely demolish us if they wanted to. I suppose it got the Rwandans and occasionally the Indian Force Protection troops out of the camp. Maybe it made everybody feel like they were helping…

DAY 58

THE PATROLS THAT SUCK

NOT JUST BECAUSE THEY ARE IN BAD LOCATIONS, or the road conditions are brutal, or it's pissing down rain, or you get stopped and turned around by the local military—although those are all really good reasons why patrols can linger in bad memory. Sometimes they just suck because of stupidity.

Sometimes they're funny.

We were doing one of the framework patrols—head to a specific location every couple of days, check it out, see what's going on—and part of our route back is a drive through the POC site. A lot has been going on in there over the last few weeks, with IDPs being moved from the old site within our camp boundaries to a new setup with better tent spacing and facilities that is still within the wider perimeter, but not within our camp proper. Make sense?

We can still protect them, and in their new tents they won't literally be living along the main road from Alpha Gate in the middle of the camp. Those first sites were ad hoc communities, set up when the bad things happened, and the UN opened the gates to let people in to stop the killings. The cars and vehicles that they used to flee Malakal to come into the camp sit empty, rusted, and gutted, outside our northern and southern gates.

After 20 months, the POC site—especially the original part— is the embodiment of every single Charity Organization visual in a television commercial that is designed to tug at your heartstrings and open your wallet. On second thought, that's not true. The real images are far worse than anything they would dare show you on television.

I remember being home after the last tour and seeing those charity heart-string-pulling pictures of a little girl who just wants to have food and go to school. Won't you please help? I recall thinking, "That kid looks fine. Not malnourished at all."

Perspectives change with experience, I guess.

It's bad here. And the single narrow mud-clay road is bumpy like every road and the locals share the space with water trucks, and other trucks, and force protection, and endless UN SUVs, some with a blue UN on the side which identified UN humanitarians, or a black UN which identified everyone else. And kids are playing or bathing in ditch water where dogs wade in to drink and clothes are washed.

Realistically, it's safe for us. But you should still follow the usual drills—doors locked. Windows open a little bit to hear what's going on. Eyes on swivels. You run over one kid, or a goat, or nudge a little kiosk-shop with your bumper and things might not go too well after that. There have been riots in the past. It doesn't take much, in my view, to bring a group of stressed, crowded, hungry, thirsty, traumatized, bored people together in outraged mob-think. Even if you don't cause it, if someone else does something that ignites the collective anger and you're in the way…then you have just walked into a big problem.

One day, a few of us go out on a regular patrol. The Kiwi, Yves, and yours truly. Yves drove. Kiwi was shotgun, and I was in the back of a Toyota Land cruiser that has a bit of an oddball seating configuration, because there are only front doors and rear clamshell doors. So, if you are planning to sit in the back, the front passenger seat folds forward, and then pivots to give enough space to squeeze into the back seat. Getting out in case of an emergency is slightly problematic and I figure my best bet is to push myself into the rear compartment and kick out the back door. Because if someone's in front…I'm not getting out.

Yves has been to South Sudan before. Twice. Not Malakal, but that doesn't matter, because he possesses a deep wisdom and knowledge. Not only does he have the answer to every question, but he also has the answers to questions you haven't thought to ask. And anything he does will be backed up with a reason (or five) why his method is better than yours.

We all know That Guy…

We're crawling through the POC site, down the main road to the gate by the Indian Battalion's section of the camp, through that with a wave to the guards and a couple of UN Police and again, along the main route. Yves was driving…did I mention that already?

Dark clouds surrounded us that day and the gloom and threat of rain had reduced the usual foot traffic of IDPs, so it wasn't surprising that fewer "shops" were open. These little businesses were rickety and small structures of old tentage, tarpaulins and bamboo lashed together and in front were the wares—from light bulbs, light switches or wiring looted from Malakal homes, a couple of stools and a steaming old kettle on a charcoal brazier showing that it was a little tea or coffee shop, sellers of woven reed curtains or bunches of firewood. All sorts of things to buy or trade for, laid out by the road. In this collection of sellers, there were some surprises that stood out—at a largish plastic patio table was a dude with a laptop and a printer. Ha! A little mini-copy shop. Next time we want to ask if he can send a fax or email….

Of course, there are always places that sell bread. It's a staple. Usually made from corn but also from sorghum. Small round loaves—like a pita but different, heavier in both texture and taste—for about one South Sudanese Pound each. Or deep-fried little sweet rolls about the size of a thumb but twice as long.

If you want to buy food there, fill your boots. Just don't expect me to carry your slack when you get ill. I will never eat anything out of the POC market area, mainly because I'd rather not have dysentery or an intestinal parasite. I'm funny that way.

Just as we passed a cramped intersection of tiny uneven dirt paths, wide enough for a truck (almost), Yves stops the SUV. "One moment," he says, then unbuckles and gets out of the vehicle. Closing the door, he walks over to a bread-seller. Within a second, he's surrounded by people. This is not awesome.

Let's recap—We're in an SUV. The Driver bailed out. In the middle of the POC Site. On patrol. Because he felt like having a snack.

The Kiwi and I sat, stunned, for a second…then both burst out with some choice expletives. We were aghast and as the seconds ticked by, increasingly enraged. This was stupid, reckless, ignorant, and…did I say Stupid? What the hell? You're on patrol, not a goddam shopping trip.

In a minute or two—it felt a lot longer—Yves, blissfully ignorant, opened the door (we unlocked it for him), hopped into the truck, and holding deep-fried treats in a plastic bag, smiled, and asked, "Do you want one? They're good."

There was a noticeable pause.

I started by very calmly explaining to Yves that he would never, ever do that again, especially with me in the car, or I would hop in the driver's seat and abandon him. The Kiwi also explained the security situation, and that putting one's comrades at risk was inappropriate and could lead to bad feelings on all sides. Well, the conversation went something like that anyway. It might not have been that polite.

We continued the drive. Mostly in silence. As I had said, the risk of rain was high, so the amount of foot traffic was reduced. But it's always valuable to see the amount of movement from the old site, the goods for sale, and the pattern of life. I know that a whole bunch of UN and Non-Governmental Organizations track all that sort of data, but sometimes seeing things for yourself is more valuable.

Just past the southwest gate, there is a buffer zone area between the gate and the actual camp perimeter with a high berm and towers. It is maybe 100 meters in width, and grassy. The pile of abandoned cars I spoke of earlier were there, as were around 60 young men of fighting age. Just hanging out. And probably checking the folks coming into the camp. We drove through this buffer, past the gate, with another wave to the guards, and up the road to yet another gate, which would bring us to the new site. Outside this gate and along the road were some SPLA troops, including a pair of their Military Police. Just hanging out. And probably checking who is leaving the camp. But no trouble this day. Waves and smiles all around.

The new camp was filling more and more every day. A couple of thousand IDPs had already brought their belongings to their new homes. More room per person in terms of square feet, more space between tents, higher ground and good drainage, better and cleaner ablutions, even some space for a soccer pitch. And some good planning for allocations—for example, those who are infirm or vulnerable are given tents closer to the ablutions. There are community patrols to ensure women and girls are protected when they go to the washrooms—especially at night. Really, the POC site is a decent-sized town with a high population density. Some kids were kicking a soccer ball around on the pitch, and I thought that was positive. Something—some beneficial physical and social activity—can only help, because being stuck in that camp every day with no real activities isn't healthy.

Rather than go up to the northern perimeter gate, which would have lengthened our journey, we took a side road into our part of the camp, wound around the Helipad where the Mi-8s sat white against the grey clouds drifting along the horizon until we reached our parking area near the double-stacked sea cans that MOVCON uses for storage. This parking area was—of course—muddy and rutted. Yves picked a bare spot to park the vehicle and shut it down.

The Kiwi and I let him walk on ahead as we grabbed our Go-Bags and body armour from the back of the Land Cruiser. Hauling the kit back to the MLO offices, we talked about the unexpected bread stop, shook our heads in despair, and shared bitter laughs at the stupidity of it all.

And for me—yet another name added to the list of folks I will not patrol with. Or if I am patrolling with them, I'm driving.

They'd better not ask to buy bread.

———————————

If I had one major complaint throughout the tour, it was the sense from so many people, including the MLOs, that the POC site was a benign environment. That you could shop and wander and smile and everything was just wonderfully peaceful. Most of the time it was, but the reality was that this place was a powder keg waiting to explode.

Among the MLOs, there was no general sense of situational awareness; no healthy paranoia and distrust of everyone; no degree of suspicion. Relaxing like that can get you killed. The sheer ignorance astounded me daily. Being suspicious and a bit on edge are healthy survival skills. I always thought about the possibilities…what if someone has a gun, what if there is a riot, what if someone is killed in front of us…?

We weren't even supposed to patrol the POC site, but we made it part of our normal framework to get a sense of what was going on, because the reports we did receive were scanty and often inaccurate, and when something did happen that required MLO presence, it was often at Hotel and Juliet Gates, which were located at the southern end of the camp. It made sense to patrol it.

The camp, certainly the old part, and even the new part, was extremely depressing. I could never look at kids playing without thinking what their life was going to be like. And I realized how lucky we are in Canada, and how ignorant we are of the fragility of our own fortune. We just assume that it's the natural order of things.

DAY 64

THE LONGEST DRIVE

IT WAS A GOOD WEEK.

Did cool stuff. Well, not really "cool", but non-Malakal stuff and right now, it's the best we've got.

I planned a patrol to get to a place called Baliet, about 60 klicks away from here. We hadn't been out that way in some months, and it was worth a shot. If we could get out there to confirm the route, meet local leadership, get contact information, a village profile maybe, we could set a positive foundation for future patrols.

We were, in fact, trying to shape our bosses to build a patrol and engagement framework that started with the MLOs going into a location, followed by humanitarians a couple of weeks later, and then maybe multi-day long distance patrols. The way the patrol program was currently structured—if you could use that term—appeared as if there was no rhyme or reason. It was as though someone randomly looked at a map and said, "We'll go…. Here" before jabbing a pushpin at an obscure village.

There were other issues, too. Some dudes had planned Long Duration Patrols on weekends to locations when there had been no UNMISS presence for months—weekends, where you could maybe (maybe) get a casualty evacuation "CASEVAC" flight into Juba, but they were working on the airport runway on weekends and even then you'd have to get a Flight Safety Assurance from the SPLA and probably from the Opposition depending on your route—and that was problematic. And if the weather socked in and the birds weren't flying, you're screwed. Don't get sick or hurt on weekends, basically.

So, the end result was that—working with Sector Headquarters—we organized our own patrol programme, and our own patrols.

The real reason I needed to plan and execute this reconnaissance was to get rid of the bad, bad feelings from that patrol a few weeks back where my gut instinct was right, and where we got stopped and turned around after a pretty intense couple of minutes. That experience had rattled me, had been eating away at me, and I had to shake it.

This patrol was going to be different—better planning, better coordination, and better execution. Because I was going to plan and lead it and I had every intention of making it a good one. But all the positive indicators weren't there at first and I agonized a bit, but by early in the week things started falling into place. UN Security had contacted the local authorities, they were aware of our intent to visit, and they said the security situation was good and we were welcome. The SPLA Liaison Officer was coming along—a former schoolteacher fluent in several tribal languages, and Arabic, and of course English. It hadn't rained for a few days so the chance of the roads not totally sucking was pretty good. And best of all, the local General had a copy of my Operations Order and Route Map (yes, I believe in informing everyone) and he was very pleased that we were going out to towns in that direction.

Even though no one appears to have read my orders, every agency was more or less where they were supposed to be at around the time and place I'd noted as a rendezvous point. There were some surprises…instead of 10 or so troops of Force Protection, I had 30 or more Indian troops in a couple of 2 ½ ton trucks, and they had even brought a wrecker in case one of our other vehicles bogged down and needed to be recovered.

I grabbed the lead guys from UN Security, Force Protection, and UNMAS de-miners and did the final patrol coordination just outside the gate. I just wanted to confirm "Actions On" (what you do when X happens. Or Y. Or Z), order of march, signals, blah blah blah. All the stuff that you'd usually do well in advance…but you take what you've got and try to improve it for next time.

We got rolling through Alpha Gate and down Airport Road until the southern turn through town. It didn't take long to realize that the Force Protection vehicles, although big and heavy enough to get through a lot of mud, were extremely slow, and especially cumbersome around the potholes that littered the roads. This was going to take a while....

When we arrived to pick up the SPLA Liaison Officer—the LO—from his house, he was nowhere to be found. The local guy sitting in front of his home didn't understand me, but there was a steady stream of soldiers walking up the road, so I stopped one and he spoke English so he confirmed that Adam wasn't home at the moment. I went on the radio and got hold of Ops and we found him after about 20 minutes or so, sent a vehicle to get him at his location and—slightly delayed—started down Bravo Route to areas south of the town I'd never seen before.

I had done a decent map reconnaissance and knew—or thought I knew—where the checkpoints were, and I put a series of report points on the route map and included it all in packages that every vehicle received—Orders, Route, Call Signs, Casualty Evacuation processes, and so on…

I mentioned it before—Malakal was a ghost town, except for soldiers. Houses were abandoned, but not burned out. The road was pretty good except for a couple of spots where it passed over a culvert or waterway and had sunk in, so the track was either deeply rutted and muddy or just sunk in, and Abi (my driver) tried to navigate them without causing us too much distress.

What I didn't expect to see was the rusted hulk of a Russian T-55 tank facing north…tracks thrown, rusted, and looted of anything valuable, including the lightbulbs removed from the searchlight. I really need to get my picture taken on that bad boy.

And down the road a couple of klicks…the First Checkpoint. This was at the first T-junction and there were a lot of soldiers, mostly sitting around under trees, smoking, drinking tea, idling away the time just as any bored soldier would. But the approach of several vehicles, whitely painted and flying UN flags, diesel engines rumbling, made them sit up and look at us with curiosity. A Sergeant, recognizable by his three chevrons and red sash worn proudly over his camouflage, walked up to our vehicle as we stopped.

I had insisted that Adam sit in the front passenger seat. The Sergeant saw him—saluted, we rolled the windows down and explained where we were going. Another salute and we were waved on. Excellent. Had we not had Adam with us, it would have been a very different and unpleasant story.

Moving East now and a bit South, we came upon the next SPLA bivouac position, and it was austere, set on higher ground, and newer because the rows of individual cabins fabricated from corrugated iron still shone silvery in the sun. It was well laid out, all things considered. Adam recognized a cousin of his among the soldiers, so they let us pass. There was a steady flow of individuals and small groups of soldiers heading into town. Most in uniform, in flip-flops, holding their AK-47s by the barrel resting on their shoulder. Most waving at us as we drove past.

At the road's next southern curve, the ground sloped almost imperceptibly downward. As we turned the bend, we stopped.

We had to stop.

Ahead of us, as far as we could see, was the road…barely even a road anymore. A morass of mud and water that almost covered the ruts from earlier road traffic. 19.4 kilometers from Base…and we were done.

Shit.

A couple of guys went forward to do a recce, on foot. The rest of us waited. SPLA soldiers walked from the morass past us, and most of us made sure to smile and wave. They were carrying an AK in one hand, their sandals in another, and trousers rolled up beyond their knees. Many of them looked at us, shook their heads, and laughed. "Very Bad!" they'd say, nodding with their head down the track they had come from.

Our guys came back after some time and gave me the report. The mud and sludge went on for over two kilometers. There wasn't any dry soil on the roadsides, either. The water level was high and if you went off the road, you probably wouldn't be able to recover, even with the wrecker.

Had a quick discussion with the Team. Screw it. Turn around.

It's tough to turn a big truck, let alone a wrecker, on a narrow road. But everyone managed it after a number of seven and nine-point turns. With us in the lead again, Adam in the front seat, we drove back to the base. Not successful in our mission, but overall, the coordination was pretty good, the things we needed to work on and improve became obvious, and the interaction with the local military was excellent. Take the good with the bad.

For me, I slept more soundly. I felt better. The worrying stopped. I had shaken off the bad patrol and replaced it with a good one.

And the best part was that Abi and I are the leaders in "The Malakal Golf & Country Club—Longest Drive" competition. Obviously, we don't have a golf course here because it's all rough and water hazards and you probably could not get a golf cart sent here if your life depended on it. Oh, and no golf clubs either. But we had vehicles.

The farthest road patrol counted as "The Longest Drive". Not distance counted on a helo or a barge. Road-based mileage. You had to endure bumpy crappy roads and get as far out of town as you could while on patrol and track the odometer reading. At the end of the month—there's a prize—it may involve a beer or two.

The Kiwi figures he'll win it before month-end.

I'm praying for more rain.

Although the patrol wasn't a success, since we never made it to our objective, it proved a couple of things to Sector, the MLO Team, and me. With proper planning and coordination (including information), a lot of the friction went away with the SPLA, and within our own organizations.

That's a valuable lesson.

After a string of poorly planned patrols, I was hit with waves of self-doubt and my dreams at night were all about being out on the road, and they never ended well. In many of them I was captured and held hostage (prophetic), so I needed to be in control—to plan and execute patrols properly. Sector "planned" the patrols, but never went out on them. They didn't live their mistakes. Once I started planning and leading patrols, the bad dreams stopped.

I had introduced a one-page operations order that we use in Canada. It's actually a lot easier than the ponderous, multi-page, content-free drivel that Sector issued as an "order." We eventually had relative success with the format after about four months.

Bringing an SPLA Liaison Officer was always a good idea if you were in SPLA territory, of course. If you brought them into Opposition territory they might have been killed (yes, despite the Peace Agreement) but they were key to getting us through checkpoints. We'd already experienced what it was like when we didn't bring an LO—once or twice we were turned back, and it wasn't very much fun at all.

Getting to the south side of Malakal was very interesting indeed. Not that there was anything particularly different in terms of ruined houses and desolation, but it was different. When you fly into Malakal from the east, you see the main roads and some of the obvious SPLA positions, and it was good to see them from the ground as well. Hell, it was just good to get out of the usual framework patrolling and push the envelope a little bit.

DAY 73

A NEWS REPORT

SORRY THAT THERE'S BEEN NO EMAIL THIS WEEK. Lots on the go and frankly haven't been able to get my head into the writing. I was preoccupied. All resolved yesterday. This pretty much tells you what's been happening…from the UNMISS website…

UNMISS secures the safe release of all personnel held by SPLA-IO in Upper Nile State

The United Nations Mission in South Sudan (UNMISS) successfully carried out an extraction operation on Sunday, 1 November, safely securing the release of 13 UNMISS contractors, who had been crew on board a barge convoy transporting fuel to UNMISS' base in Renk, Upper Nile State, and who were detained by SPLA in Opposition soldiers at Kaka, on 26 October. A group of 18 international peacekeepers and Military Liaison Officers, who had also been a part of the barge convoy, were released earlier on 29 October. The convoy equipment, a total of three vessels including the barge, have also been returned and are on their way to Melut, Upper Nile State.

On 26 October, the 31 personnel, comprised of 18 UNMISS uniformed personnel and 13 South Sudanese UNMISS contractors, were taken hostage by heavily armed SPLA in Opposition soldiers, and the barge convoy, its equipment and cargo, including 55,000 liters of fuel, were confiscated. While the barge was returned today, the fuel cargo, communications equipment, an inflatable boat, and seven of the 16 UNMISS weapons taken on 26 October were not returned.

UNMISS reiterates its call to the SPLA in Opposition for the immediate release of all its equipment and cargo.

UNMISS would also like to clarify media reports over the weekend stating its questionable involvement in the transportation of weapons. The Special Representative of the Secretary General, Ellen Loej, strongly refutes these accusations "the barge was not transporting weapons cargo of any kind, in fact, all fuel cargo was bound for the UNMISS base in Renk, as a resupply," said SRSG Loej.

She added "while we, today, are relieved by the safe release of all UN personnel, the need for all parties to the conflict in South Sudan to fully respect unfettered free access and movement of UN personnel and assets cannot be underlined strongly enough. A similar incident should not and hopefully will not happen again."

Oh Yes. There's a story here.

One of the realities of sending emails and other correspondence back to Canada is that you must employ a high level of operational security. In short, I am not going to send out detailed emails about a future or ongoing operation. When I went on interesting patrols or did anything out of the ordinary, I might talk about it in general terms via email or on social media, but only well after the fact. The trick is only having as few people as possible aware of your future plans. Once I've already been somewhere on patrol, who really cares? Patrol reports or other documents within the UN system would confirm that I had travelled. And since our reports were unclassified, pretty much anyone could access them… Here's another bit of zany paranoia. I automatically assumed that my email traffic and general communications were monitored.

DAY 74

THE HOSTAGES

HERE'S THE BACK STORY.

It's about the detention—hostage taking, really—of a UN barge convoy that was moving from Malakal down the Nile to Renk for repairs and resupply. It is the filler to the UN press release I sent out earlier.

UN barge convoys go up and down the Nile between Juba and Malakal regularly but infrequently. It's the most efficient and secure means to transport large quantities of goods north—humanitarian supplies, spare parts, vehicles, foodstuffs, and so on. On each of these barge convoys, a couple of MLOs will be tasked to go along to negotiate any SPLA and Opposition checkpoints along the route. The only other way to get things into Malakal was by aircraft, and that was not efficient as this mode of transportation was prone to weight restrictions, weather, flight safety assurances, and technical breakdowns.

Naturally, before UNMISS would launch any of these barge convoys, there is a significant communication process to let both the SPLA and Opposition know that the barges were coming, to document what was on the barge by providing a detailed manifest, and basically answering the who, what, when, where, and why.

Our convoy was a bit different in that we weren't cruising south to Juba via Bor. We were going downstream, north, to Renk. All our travel would be within Upper Nile State, and therefore it should have been within our ability to influence and inform.

The manifest included the specifics of the Bangladeshi Force

Protection, including number and types of weapons, names of personnel, and so on. There were Sharing of Information letters. Details and personal information of the barge crews. We had a letter from Juba signed by Paul Malong, the Chief of Staff of the South Sudanese Armed Forces and we provided copies to the SPLA Division Headquarters in Malakal, Paloich, and Renk. The SPLA, therefore, was reasonably well informed that a barge convoy was coming.

But the Opposition, based largely on the West Bank of the Nile, with Headquarters in Tonga and Pagak, was a lot more complicated. We didn't have the same direct contact with them as we did with the SPLA on the eastern side of the river. Why was that? Because the Opposition, and especially Johnson Olony's forces, occupied the west bank of the White Nile between Tonga up towards El Gelhak. The Opposition under former vice-president Riek Machar's leadership tries to portray itself as a unified whole, but the reality is that Johnson Olony is more of a Shilluk War-Leader than a loyal member of the Opposition. And the chain of command appeared to be fragmented at the best of times.

So, for our communication with the Opposition—apparently one of our MLOs had been on the Thuraya satellite phone with a dude in Tonga on a daily basis. This contact——Brigadier Joseph Aban—said he had passed along the message about our barge convoy to all the Opposition commanders along the Nile. We hadn't been to the West side of the Nile or met with the Opposition often enough to have developed a high degree of mutual trust. This sat phone communication was pretty much all we had. That was a major miscalculation.

Ultimately, UNMISS needed a level of assurance from both sides that we would not be harassed or looted or shot at or sunk.

Funny—we were always shot at.

During the last barge movement in July, when the convoy rounded the final bend of the Nile and came into sight of Malakal from the south, they came under fire from AK, RPGs, mortars, machine guns, and a tank. With the SPLA on the east bank in Malakal, the Opposition forces held the west side of the river and once the SPLA opened fire on the barge, the Opposition opened fire on the SPLA. And then the convoy sailed right in the middle of the crossfire. The firefight lasted for about 90 minutes.

Results? A few holes in the barge. An unexploded RPG warhead in the wheelhouse. But no injuries. Draw whatever conclusions you want on their marksmanship, but I will mention that the Nile at that point is only a couple of hundred meters wide.

We hoped that no one would get shot. Or shot at. Or anything....

The preparations had started reasonably well, but by the time the barge and Bangladeshi Navy Force Protection and crew and cargo were ready to go we MLOs had to scramble a bit. We were under pressure from UNMISS HQ in Juba to get moving and moving fast. Like tomorrow.

We had to put two of our folks on the barge. The MLOs had been selected earlier, but there were constant delays in sailing and preparation, and each day of delay led to conflict regarding which MLOs could be available because of travel, leave, or other tasks. There was a last-minute change to one of the slots, and with the scrambling to sail the MLOs had a bit less than a day to get all their stuff together, including food, water, lifejackets, and the essential paperwork that the UN insists upon before there is any movement of personnel.

The convoy eventually left the landing at BANFRU and chugged its way north along the White Nile, with a barge, a pusher, and two old Landing Craft Tanks that looked like D-Day invasion boats loaded with bladders of diesel fuel. They followed the current towards Melut, and from there they would travel on to Renk. We wished them all safe travels.

We had regular communication with the convoy through the Bangladeshis, who had long-range radio communications between the Force Protection and BANFRU. The MLOs also received a daily call from the MLOs on the Thuraya sat phone. We knew that the barges sailed up to Melut without any significant issues. The next day, they pushed off downstream, hearing gunshots on two occasions, which were strongly suspected to be from SPLA positions. They approached Kaka on the west bank, about 30 klicks north of Melut.

It looked like a normal checkpoint. A fast boat with some troops heading towards the pusher, waving, and saying Hi. But farther downstream, a barge with a T-55 tank on top slipped its moorings and started moving towards the centre of the river, effectively blocking any forward passage of the barge, pusher, and remaining vessels.

The MLOs went with the boat crew to head ashore, meet the commander, and negotiate the free movement of the barge. It all looked good.

Stories change or shift at this point because depending on where someone was in time and space they saw and interpreted something totally different from another witness. So, I can't speak to the individual accounts because I wasn't there. But here are the facts:

• Within a very short period of time, the UNMISS personnel were accused of having former SPLA or Intelligence officers among the civilian South Sudanese crew
• The Opposition had disarmed the Bangladeshi Force Protection
• The barge was grounded along the bank
• The 18 Force Protection and MLOs were separated from the 13 barge crew members
• All communications assets were seized. We received one sat phone message from the Force Protection commander that gave us a tiny bit of information.

Then silence.

News reports—notoriously inaccurate throughout this entire incident—mention 100 or so Opposition troops that stopped the convoy. Bullshit. It was about 1,500 Opposition troops. Heavily armed with tanks, a huge number of Anti-Aircraft guns, including ZSUs, and machine guns.

I looked at satellite imagery of Kaka—the inner perimeter is over 3,000 meters, with about 30 fighting positions every 100 meters. That's just the inner perimeter, not including what's along the banks of the river or actually in town itself. Kaka is also near a road that runs to Sudan, so you're looking at a pretty major logistics hub for the Opposition. None of this is super-secret stuff either—any average Captain could have done a map recce and extrapolated all that info. I had no idea with the Intelligence folks in Juba were thinking.

For the next day or two in Malakal we all ran around like idiots and Juba ran around like bigger idiots trying to figure out what to do, but one very valid criticism is that UNMISS said nothing publicly for a couple of days.

Nothing. No press releases. No news reports.

No "Condemnation" of the fact that one of Riek Machar's subordinates forcibly seized UN assets with UN personnel and was holding them hostage. I'm no lawyer, but I think this qualifies as a war crime or something.

I understand that the silence might have been to protect the detainees, but this strategy completely backfired. The SPLA accused the UN of supplying the Opposition with 55,000 liters of diesel. UNMISS' silence was seen as collusion with the anti-government forces, blah blah blah. From where I sat in Malakal, UNMISS' initial silence was damning, and set up significant barriers in our later relations with the SPLA throughout Upper Nile State.

Now, there was a shitload of high-level negotiation going on between the UN representatives in Juba and the Opposition leadership in Addis Ababa. New York and the Security Council may have been engaged. I don't know. I wasn't really in the loop.

I do know that UNMISS finally got the conditions in place to go to the Opposition headquarters in Tonga on Wednesday, October 28th to meet Olony to release the detainees the next day, on Thursday. When the UNMISS team flew to Tonga to engage with Olony, he wasn't available since he was apparently ill. By all accounts, he was also in a foul mood, which means he wasn't ill and just didn't want to meet our team. Here's Warlord Lesson 101—When there's bad news, discussions are better left to subordinates so that your personal prestige doesn't diminish.

At this meeting, the UNMISS and the Opposition delegates discussed the issue, and its possible resolution. The Opposition kept dropping irrelevant arguments, none of which explained why an Opposition unit detained UN personnel, equipment, and civilians. Eventually, UNMISS received the assurance that the military in Kaka would release everyone on the next day. This was great news.

Meanwhile, back in Malakal, the rest of us entered Operational planning and crisis mode. Juba provided a thousand-mile-long screwdriver to micro-manage us…and we largely ignored them.

From the military side, the real driver of this Operation was The Kiwi. He was tireless—coordinating, planning, influencing, and with extraordinary common sense and skill managed to get the civilian leadership, Security, the State Operations Centre, and Juba onside with a solid plan. That's a freakin' miracle in itself. His efforts shaped the extraction operation and turned it from a complete shit-show to something that actually might work.

Okay, here's the Plan.

Helo #1 would fly from Malakal to Tonga, pick up some Opposition Leadership, then fly to Kaka. There wasn't enough fuel to do a round trip, so once the mission was successful, it would fly directly back to Malakal. Helo #2 would fly from Malakal to Kaka direct, and then fly with the Opposition leadership back to Tonga, then to Malakal. Confusing? It isn't really. Think of it as a triangle from Malakal-Tonga-Kaka. One helo flies the pattern clockwise; the other helo flies it counterclockwise. It was the only way to make it work.

It was a restless night.

For the MLOs, the long and short of it was that The Kiwi and Abi were kicked out the door Thursday to get the guys and I was in the MLO ops centre so that The Kiwi could call me on his sat phone and we could speak clear English and suss out the situation. Because he and I were the only two native English speakers and we couldn't afford a miscommunication issue.

The next morning, the helicopter launched late for a number of stupid and bureaucratic reasons. Here's one blisteringly idiotic example—the Emergency Movement of Personnel forms did not get approved in Juba until after 0830 because no one came into work early to complete the paperwork.

Let's think about this for a second—recovery operation. Hostages. Huge implications for the Mission and peace process. The Special Representative of the Secretary General had her personal attention on this. Lives were potentially at stake. And in spite of this, someone managed to maintain regular office hours. Unreal. That person and their supervisor should both have been fired. Fuckers.

Eventually, the bird was in the air. And we waited.

Here's a hint—in a crisis, when there's nothing to do, do nothing.

Don't make stupid work or decisions based on info you don't have. I get it, it's human nature—Everyone wants to Do Something, and it was funny to watch people look for things to do to occupy their time or give the illusion of helping me when in reality they were just getting in my way. When the bird's in the air, there is absolutely nothing you can do until it reaches the objective. I read the news and kept my mind clear. Contingency plans were already in place....

But when the bird landed—Game On! First SITREP went out.

From: UNMISS-MLO-MALAKAL-OPS
Sent: Thursday, October 29, 2015 11:57 AM
Subject: SITREP – TONGA/KAKA

ALCON,

SITREP

1. Spoke with MLO 1145 hours – Team had landed in TONGA.
2. ETD TONGA to KAKA 1200 hours. ETA KAKA 1400 hours.
3. MLO will call from KAKA once on the ground and will confirm Helicopter Landing Site
4. MLO Recommendation – second helo should be in the air NLT 1330 to optimize time on the ground.

SITREP Ends

Regards,
John

OPS – Military Liaison Office
State Support Base Malakal
Upper Nile State—UNMISS

SITREPs went out every time The Kiwi called. I wanted everyone on the same page. The Kiwi would call, everyone would shut up, and as I was talking to him, I'd write the main points on the big whiteboard with the time of call so that anyone walking into the office would know what was going on at a glance. This saved time and energy for us to work on all the other things.

From: UNMISS-MLO-MALAKAL-OPS

Sent: Thursday, October 29, 2015 1:12 PM
Subject: KAKA SITREP

ALCON

SITREP

1. As of 1308 hours, flight has landed in KAKA.
2. Next SITREP from MLO in 15 minutes after initial assessment.

SITREP Ends

Regards,
John
OPS—Military Liaison Office
State Support Base Malakal
Upper Nile State—UNMISS

I worked in the MLO office, which I turned into the Military Ops Centre to the disgust of the civvies who ran the State Operations Centre. Apparently, I was supposed to report there to work on the operation. Nope. I was in my office hours before they showed up at theirs. I have a massive map occupying an entire wall of the MLO container to track progress. And we never did coordinate these details in advance so it's too late now. Sorry.

There were a couple of options that we had worked through earlier:

1. UNMISS recovers every individual and every piece of equipment including the barges. If so, then the barges, if serviceable, would be crewed by the former detainees and sail South to Melut.
2. UNMISS recovers all personnel and equipment less barges. If then, recovery by helicopter. The Force Commander in Juba would decide whether to release the helicopter or not.
3. UNMISS recovers UN personnel only, not civilian barge crews, or nobody. If then, recovery by helicopter.

From: UNMISS-MLO-MALAKAL-OPS
Sent: Thursday, October 29, 2015 2:11 PM

Subject: SITREP—TONGA/KAKA

ALCON,

My hard copy notes of the conversation at 1350 hours with MLO at KAKA, given verbally to State Operations Centre.

SITREP

1. Meeting ongoing between TONGA iO and KAKA iO leadership
2. Meeting with MLO will occur after that pre-meeting. Expected to meet for approx. 1 hour.
3. MLO has not seen any UNMISS detainees
4. An Anti-Aircraft gun had an accidental discharge—in the event of shooting stories/rumours in KAKA
5. Recommendations for second helo:
a. Pers required to be flown out (UN or civilian) are unknown
b. No force protection recommended for second helicopter
c. Worst case scenario is to fly all personnel out
d. Could use current Force Protection for barge if serviceable
6. MLO requested to advise KAKA SPLA Opposition of arrival of second helo within 90-120 minutes.

SITREP Ends

Regards,
John
OPS—Military Liaison Office
State Support Base Malakal
Upper Nile State—UNMISS

Reference Point #4—The Anti-Aircraft gun shooting. This was funny as hell.

I was on the sat phone with The Kiwi when the 23mm ZSU cannon fired. We were talking through the static and I suddenly heard a loud "WHOOMP clang". Then silence.

Pause.

Me, "Uh…what was that, exactly?"

The Kiwi, "(muffled laughter) Guy fired an Anti-Aircraft gun behind me by accident."

Awesome.

There was a whole bunch of shit happening on the ground. A big sit-down meeting, the usual airing of grievances against UNMISS and made-up fantasy bullshit from the Kaka leadership to somehow justify the capture and detention.

One of the allegations was that an SPLA helicopter gunship was seen flying over the barges north of Melut. So, the Opposition stopped the barges. Bullshit. And it still doesn't explain why the Bangladeshi military personnel and the MLOs were held once their identity had been confirmed.

It appears, then, that if you are a local military Commander and bat-shit crazy and you're working for the Opposition, then you don't have to listen to anyone. Not Johnson Olony far away in Tonga, not the Administrative HQ in Pagak, and certainly not former vice-president Riek Machar, who was sitting in Addis Ababa trying to do some high-level negotiations with IGAD and UNMISS. All indications were that Machar had absolutely no control over the Opposition in Tonga or Kaka, anyway.

My guess was that local Commander decided to keep the barge and the diesel for a potential offensive farther north in Manyo County, west of the Nile from Thor Gwang up to Wad Dakona. He probably didn't realize that he was about to commit a war crime. Sadly, he probably didn't give a shit either way.

The Kiwi was running in and out of the meeting, giving me updates. There was a lot going on, and time—always a precious commodity—was running out. We needed to get things moving fast.

From: UNMISS-MLO-MALAKAL-OPS
Sent: Thursday, October 29, 2015 4:59 PM
Subject: FINAL SITREP—TONGA/KAKA 29 OCT 15

SITREP

Discussion at 1515

1. Meeting complete. iO will release all UNMISS personnel.
2. Personnel condition is unknown, MLOs have not seen them yet.
3. iO will NOT release the barge or crew at this time
4. MLO will advise that 2nd helo will be arriving KAKA within 90-120 min.
5. UNMISS are to liaise with KAKA SPLA Opposition—they will complete their investigation in a couple of days.

Regards,
John
OPS—Military Liaison Office
State Support Base Malakal
Upper Nile State—UNMISS

During the crisis we had some irregular communication with the Force Protection Commander in Kaka, and what we heard wasn't good. Two guys were down with dysentery, one had fever, food was restricted, they were given only Nile River water to drink, they were given no access to meds for the ill people, all personal goods and electronics looted. Even if they were physically able to function, The Kiwi and I had decided that psychologically putting the detainees back on the barge would be stupid and we planned to disobey any ill-conceived order that came down from Juba.

Discussion at 1537

1. 18 UNMISS pers are at the Helo waiting to board
2. Dr is assessing physical/psych condition. MLO assesses pers at a 3-4/10 condition
3. Waiting for launch authorization

Luckily, the Doctor who went with the extraction team and did the initial assessment put a lot of these guys at three or four out of ten for either physical or psych. Good call. They were mentally and physically exhausted. While only the UNMISS folks were being released, not the civvies or the barge, at least they were coming home and not riding on a barge for two days, and that was what we wanted. But the only thing we were getting out were the UNMISS people. Not the civvies, not the equipment, not the barge. Despite Dr. Machar's personal word that all UN personnel and equipment would be unconditionally released. Ha!

Discussion at 1616

1. 1st Helo with 18 pers (all to be medevac'd) departed KAKA 1616 hours for MALAKAL.

2. 2nd Helo ready to depart (waiting for Force Commander release?) within 10 minutes. Missing 2 x passports, weapons, pers equipment, all electronics. iO claims they will return the items within a couple of days.

3. 1626 hours—2nd Helo departed KAKA for TONGA (ETA 1730) and MALAKAL (ETA 1815)

Here's a hint for all you folks—If you ever plan an operation and are sitting back at a big HQ…. don't micro-manage the operation and inject restrictions that could jeopardize everyone…let the Incident Commander make the call and support their decision.

In fact, The Kiwi and I had gone through the courses of action and our decision points the night before. There is a lot of trust and mutual respect between us, and he knew I'd have his back.

The authority to release the helicopters to return to Malakal was retained by the Force Commander, an Ethiopian three-star general sitting in Juba. If this seems like micro-management to you, it is. The Kiwi was on the ground and he made the right decision to leave when they did. There was some insistence from Juba that the Force Protection and MLOs stick around for awhile to press the issue of getting the barge and crew released, but frankly, the bat-shit crazy Brigadier on the ground was getting pissed off with us, and his troops were getting ready to go fight farther north.

As the guys boarded the chopper, bugles were literally sounding and a couple of hundred Opposition soldiers deployed north to fight.

Discussion at 1700

1. Med pers standing by.
2. Reintegration processes ready to initiate.
Regards—thank you all for your hard work today!

John

Our guys flew home, landing at the base helipad to a crowd of well-wishers. Handshakes and hugs and smiles. The evening sun shone brightly, and it reflected our mood. A bus was ready and all the former detainees were shuttled off to the camp medical clinic for a full checkup. There was a mental health counsellor in camp that I had on standby for any psychological issues or briefings.

Some of the detainees from the Bangladeshi Force Protection looked absolutely haunted coming off the chopper. Of our two MLOs, one looked great—smiling, resilient, and happy—while the other looked stretched thin. But day by day he has gotten much better and now he's laughing. We are all keeping our eyes on them both.

There were two other things I needed done. I had a word with one of my humanitarian mates who had spent almost three months in captivity in Darfur—I asked him to take the two MLOs aside for a quiet chat about his own experiences, and to keep an eye on them for me. He would know their reactions far better than we would. Then I talked to Human Rights, asking for them to interview the MLOs when they were ready (but as soon as possible) because I wanted this all on record—the capture, the conditions, the denial of medicine— for any future investigation against the Kaka leadership. I figured that the UN leadership would be less inclined to ignore findings compiled by a civilian component.

So, that was our Thursday. The Kiwi and I had a celebratory scotch that evening after dinner, and he packed it in early to go to sleep. It had been a long, exhausting day for him especially, and none of us had slept well the night before.

On the next night, the MLO Team had a Welcome Back party for our two mates. We laughed, and drank, and listened, and made it very clear that we were a tight-knit family. But constantly in the back of our minds was the fact that there were still 13 hostages in Kaka, and they couldn't be forgotten.

The high-level negotiations kept going because Saturday night we got a short-notice mission that we would run another extraction operation on Sunday. The orders from Juba were so agonizingly nit-picky that the seating configuration of each helicopter was already done for us. Think about this. Juba—the HQ that was 500 kilometers away—told us what the seat allocations would be on our helicopters. Reading that order, I lost my mind. Rather loudly and profanely, in fact. If Juba had wanted to be helpful, they could have provided another helicopter, or more pressure on the Opposition, or something constructive. Basically, we gave whoever over-planned our extraction the collective middle finger and did our own thing. Which was the right thing.

HERE WE GO AGAIN.

Once again, I was the main point of contact for the MLOs on the ground, and this time—to play nice—I placed a borrowed whiteboard and myself in the State Operations Centre by 0830 and set myself up at an empty desk. There was only a 90-minute delay this time and because much of this was a repeat of Thursday's Operation, there were only a couple of factors to consider—if the barge and other vessels were serviceable, and if the crew was in any condition to get it back to Melut that night. In which case we'd need to provide an MLO to overnight with the barge and fly from Melut to Malakal the next day and provide some force protection troops as well.

First bird in the air. Wait.

Once the first bird landed, and the patrol had been on the ground for a while, we realized that they hadn't yet seen the barge or crew. This wasn't good since we were getting close to the point where we needed to send the second bird, either empty to bring the crew back, or with Force Protection to man the barge. We were basing all this on an expected call from the Extraction Team.

The phone finally rang and the MLO Patrol Leader (not The Kiwi, unfortunately) advised me to launch the second helicopter with troops, even though we didn't have all the required info at the time. No one had seen the barge or the crew, but time was being wasted and we needed to give the guys in Kaka the resources to let them be flexible in the solution.

Looking at everyone in the SOC, I said, "Launch the second bird now."

First Response? Paralysis.

Second Response? Second-guessing. Of epic proportions. Maybe we should wait. Maybe we need more information. Let's wait ten minutes. Maybe, maybe, maybe…

I asked what value a delay would bring and further argued that ten minutes or more would not make one bit of difference here, but with an hour of flight time we would have more info from the ground team by the time they arrived. It got stupid for a minute or two, and one of the planners, smirking, asked, "Are you in a hurry?"

My brain exploded. And I lost it. "YES, I AM IN A HURRY!"

I went on to explain my reasoning again rather loudly, and being louder and angrier seemed to help—we need to give the tools to the people on the ground. Delays do not help us and might hinder them. We are sitting on a high value asset that is critical for them to return home, and every hour lost is an hour of daylight lost and our last time out from Kaka is 1630 if we want our guys back before they get shot down. So yes, I was in a fucking hurry.

The bird launched in ten minutes….

And while it was in the air we got the next call—barge was serviceable, crew looked ok. They were going to leave for Melut within the hour. One of our MLOs was going to stay behind and travel on the barge to Melut to make sure nothing bad happened along the way.

Win, Win, Win.

The helos returned with the patrol, and with a few boxes of stuff the Opposition released or could find. But some of the Bangladeshi AK-47s were missing. The Brigadier in Kaka said they were currently being used up North but he'd bring them back when he was finished (ha-ha! Bullshit!) Other missing items included all the electronics—sat phones, mobile phones, laptops, and cameras. Even though we didn't get all the weapons back, as we searched through the Bangladeshi tactical vests, we realized that they contained full AK magazines. So, they took the weapons but didn't think about taking the spare ammo.

Not too smart, fuckers.

Extra uniforms were not returned. These were Bangladeshi Navy uniforms that were a nice blue camouflage and wouldn't hide you from anything. And there were 55,000 liters of fuel missing.

OK. We got all the people out relatively unharmed. That was outstanding. And we got some of the equipment, and all the vessels. All in all, a busy week with a decent result.

But I was completely enraged—angered that some Warlord Asshole figured he could rob us, detain us, and play mental games with my mates. His name, by the way, is Paromi Angoy (or Angui). He held UN personnel hostage and gave them inadequate food and water. He denied medical care to ill UN personnel. I hope he is remembered in the years to come.

I felt and still feel this incident very keenly. As I noted earlier, there was a last-minute change to our manning for the convoy. One MLO was bumped out and replaced at the last minute because of flight schedules and leave.

Me.

I should have been on the barge.

This entry was never sent as an email.

I started writing it within days of the situation and maintained notes and emails for reference. The real writing first started as an angry rant as I was flying home on leave in early November, and it sat there as an unfinished and profanity-laced tale until I returned home at the end of the tour. Every time I looked at the unfinished story, I knew I would have to get to it eventually, but the thought of digging deep to complete the account made me feel physically ill. Once I completed the story, I inserted it in the correct chronological order to make it all fit. This was a pivotal moment for me.

I am not intending to completely slag the UN in this entry (well, maybe a bit), even though it might come out that way. What I am criticizing is laziness, a lack of an all-informed network, micro-management from Higher Headquarters, and the reality of Operations attempted by people who appear to have never actually run an Operation.

In my view, because of a complete lack of action or sanctions or public condemnation of the individual who took UN personnel hostage, the UN appears to have no real power against local warlords. That should be cause for concern.

At the very least people should have been fired.

DAY 77

THE FAUNA & THE RIVER

DOGS

THE DOGS HAVE PICKED A SPOT just outside my cabin to hang out. My place backs onto a road—muddy, crappy, and rutted—and the dogs sleep there during the day and often at night once their carousing and howling and fighting is completed. Half a dozen or more at a time, sleeping in little divots they have carved out for themselves, lazily lifting their heads to look warily as you walk past.

I also noticed that there are a couple of three-legged dogs—one at the north side of the camp near our offices, and another farther south by my container. The amputations—the cut and stump—are clean and precise, as if a vet had worked on them. It isn't impossible, but I am still not sure why someone would save the verminous bloody things. There are literally hundreds of wild dogs in the camp, and nothing is being done to destroy them. But I digress…

Needless to say, I have named both amputee-dogs "Tripod."

Some of the dogs have mange and scabs over much of their bodies, struggling even to toss their heads and necks from side to side, as dogs are wont to do. They trot, head, hips, and tail down from one place to another and in spite of my disgust I feel bad for them. They must be in pain. No matter how scabrous they are, or sleepy, all the dogs will move out of your way—whether you are on foot or in a vehicle—quietly and without protest. At night, rain pouring down during a hurried walk to the ablution container, your flashlight picks up the dog's eyes reflected, and the dog will wait patiently until it knows your route, or will step aside onto a parallel path not wanting

125

to get its feet wet, or will traverse the pathways reluctantly by braving the water and mud to avoid you, daintily dipping one paw at a time into the muck.

There was also "Still the Dog" who was a dead dog that was lying in a rut beside my jogging route along the perimeter. I called him that because for more than two days he was still there. Some dude eventually came to get him with a wheelbarrow. By that time, he was bloated and maggot-infested and the putrid aroma was something you ran quickly through to avoid.

There are also occasional litters of puppies throughout the camp. I know this because once in a while—and twice this week—I saw errant little pups, so adorable in their stumbling gait, wandering around containers giving a high-pitched squealing yip until their mothers came to rescue them and bring them under a series of containers where they den with the rest of the litter. Monitor lizards, of which we have a few, eat small animals…. like puppies.

These canines are the shorthaired long-snout dun-coloured pi-dogs that infest the Middle East and much of Africa. Vermin-ridden and disease-carriers. And they all need to be killed. Because now they move in packs of more than a dozen within the camp. With greater numbers comes a change in Pack Mentality. It's only a matter of time until they decide to start going from Cute to Bitey.

I had once mentioned that there was a black-and-white canine in my end of the camp who was alert, perky, and had a lot of personality, for a filthy verminous dog, of course. She is regularly fed by one of the civilian staff and will trot obediently after her every morning as she goes to work. That is just like a "real" dog, don't you think?

I have nick-named her "Sparky the Wonder-Dog."

If I had more time, patience, and an imagination…I would draw an animated cartoon of "Sparky the Wonder-Dog and her side-kick Tripod" although I don't know exactly what adventures they'd have in Malakal. Based on the late-night battles that go on, I think it would be a canine version of "Fight Club."

ANTS

Early in the tour, I stopped on the dirt road and stared for a few minutes in fascination at a trail of ants that had engineered a route by moving massive amounts of dirt off each side of their highway and were travelling in the tens of thousands at their ant-like business. The trail was a couple of inches wide, and all the movement, which initially looked like nothing but chaos, became clearer after a few minutes. There was an orderliness and discipline that became apparent. Traffic on the left and right, heavier loads in the slow lane, push the dirt off the trail…. They were not significantly bigger ants than the standard North American variety, I thought, but they were reddish although that could have been from the dirt as well. Industrious and able to survive throughout the rainy season—now that it is approaching the dry season I expect to see more and more of them.

BIRDS

Small birds, maybe sparrows or something similar, brown on top with a teal body and a splash of crimson on their cheeks flit and dart among the trees by our office. They are also ground feeders, snapping up bugs with their tiny, pointed beaks. Tiny—about the size of a sardine. I know it is absolutely bizarre that I would somehow equate the two in a sentence, but it's the first thing I thought of when I saw it. A streamlined little bird-body in tiny fish proportions…

By comparison, the storks or marabou or whatever the hell they are called are monstrous with a wingspan that must be greater than the length of an SUV. I was visiting our Nile outpost and as I walked around to look at a guard tower in an obscure corner of the perimeter, I startled a marabou that was intently poking through a pile of garbage. It slowly flapped its enormous wings and flew up to the top of a lamppost. When it landed the whole post swayed back and forth alarmingly. This reflects either on the weight of the bird, or the shoddy grounding of the post. Or both.

Somewhere in the lower end of the avian size scale was a white-plumed water bird that looked like a swan—sort of—because it was blindingly white, yet was the size of a mallard with a longer neck. I think it was lost from its buddies as it settled in the middle of our quadrangle of containers. Wandering tentatively through the grass and muck, it seemed in search of something, but had an interesting back-and-forth wobble with its head and lanky neck that was so strangely comical I had to laugh.

BUGS

Then there are the bugs. Big, small, annoying, deadly…. they all live in open combat. With us, and each other. Too many to describe, but some examples are noteworthy. There's the thing we laughingly called the Kamikaze Cockroach—a beetle the size of a small smartphone that, with hundreds of its colleagues, thunders into walls and doors at night, only to leave a morning scene of carnage that reminds me of the first few minutes of Saving Private Ryan. Harmless, maybe, but one of those impacting into your neck feels like a small aircraft making contact. It isn't funny unless it happens to someone else.

Geckos get a pass. I like them. When they are relatively small. Because they eat things. Like bugs. Which I hate. A lot. I have some living in the walls of my container. Geckos, not bugs. Although probably some bugs, too…

BIG AND NASTY

And, as I've mentioned before—there are also the denizens of the Nile. Including either crocs or alligators. I don't know which is which, or which one is in North America and which isn't. Because I do not care. Seriously. Both Alligators and Crocodiles both embody a prehistoric form of freaking unstoppable Evil with a Capital E and caring about the difference is a little like caring whether you are shot by a pistol or rifle. It's still going to hurt.

The Kiwi was on patrol a week or so ago with one of our SPLA Liaison Officers. Some of the roads have deep drainage ditches on either side where the run-off is supposed to go and where people wash, or clean their clothes, or drink. The patrol was negotiating the potholes along the Airport Road when the Liaison Officer suddenly pointed out an Alligator (or maybe Crocodile). In the runoff ditch. It was quite some distance from the river. So, it had emerged from the Nile, went south a couple of klicks along BANFRU road, turned right, and decided to wander along looking for food. Maybe dogs. Or birds. Or people.

Awesome.

At the end of the day, the creatures, in all their configurations, are just a part of essential life here. Especially the bugs. You can't escape them; you can only endure them. And you can kill as many as you can, showing no mercy, especially to those little bastard mosquitos, whose bite brings malaria. Or to the common little blackfly, travelling from piles of excrement deposited by the camp dogs to your plate of food. Or the beetles that seem to emerge from gaps between cabin wall panels and give a pleasing "crunch" when underfoot. It's satisfying to see the collection of them stuck on the fly strips, which decorate my container like festive Christmas ribbons.

Bugs affect the things you do and essential timings of the day. Physical fitness for me should ideally finish before 1830 hours so I can shower and be in my cabin before the sun goes too far down. Otherwise, the light on the lamppost beside my cabin goes on, and every freaking flying biting insect decides to congregate there at the light and devour me as I walk past, bare flesh post-shower towel-clad.

But there are also scenes of sheer magnificence.

A flock of white ducks, that in their numbers and brightness are like an exhaled breath, rise on the wing from a swampy marsh. The scene overwhelms and catches you with the contrasts of reed of deepest green, robin-egg blue sky and white, oh so white, of the birds' plumage as they move in union like a cloud ever higher and farther away over the Nile towards Wau Shilluk.

There is the Nile. Always the Nile. Border. Barrier. Highway. Fast-flowing and timeless.

Coming from Lake Victoria in Uganda and through the Al-Sudd past the Bahr-el Ghazal and Sobat Rivers and beside Malakal to wend north, joining with its Ethiopian Blue Nile cousin in Khartoum, and then to Egypt to be absorbed into the Mediterranean. Civilizations have been built along its banks—trade in materials, knowledge, slaves, power. Empires have risen and fallen along its banks.

When I patrol out to BANFRU, I often come here to stand along the banks, or clamber up a guard post for a wider view towards Lelo in the south, to a bend in the river to the north. A few quiet moments alone to think.

Marchand saw this view. So did Vere Ferguson. So did von Slatin. So did millions of souls throughout history…

I stand there, awed and humbled.

———————————————

Like everything else in life, if you look at something long enough, you eventually start to see it.

The animals were part of our world, and I thought they were interesting and worth observing. Looking at the local creatures broke up my headspace and gave me cause to reflect on nature. I loved it—the contrasts of human chaos and natural beauty. It was a form of escape, I guess.

But it wasn't all idyllic of course—there were dangerous snakes in Malakal (I never saw one, thank God!) and as far as I know, no anti-venom. So—if you get bitten, you will die. No CASEVAC in time. You're well and truly screwed.

As for the end of the story, short as it was… The Nile. Breathtaking. Such history and importance throughout the millennia. It was such a peaceful and calming thing to go to the riverbank and just ponder the world around you, let the mind wander, and think back to what others might have seen throughout the years. I always felt good going there because it wasn't the camp and there were usually birds singing. It was easy to think of how things in the outside world had changed, and how Malakal had regressed…

DAY 79

MEMORIES OF BENTIU

YEARS AGO, WHEN I WAS IN BENTIU, when it was just "Sudan" and people thought they loved the UN, we had a couple of language assistants. One—a Dinka—was named James. A friendly dude with a ready smile, he was without the traditional tribal scarring because his family had been refugees in Khartoum and he became part of a generation of a diaspora that grew up culturally and linguistically more Sudanese Arabic than Dinka. But still very much Dinka.

He was also shorter than most Dinka, being maybe 5'10" or so. Much shorter than I was, anyway. When we used to patrol up in Panriang, a Dinka-dominated area in the northern part of Unity State, James would come with us, an essential part of the team as far as I was concerned. Because his family lived in the town, he was a known quantity, and he was invaluable in noticing details we would have missed—new people in town, a different pattern of life, greater or lesser quantities of goods in the market, and so on.

He was a couple of cows short of the bride-price for his girlfriend, and at times he would disappear to visit relatives far and wide to plead for a loan of cows, and once or twice he danced around the issue of me giving him a couple of hundred US Dollars to help with purchases. I refused of course. The dowry, paid to the bride's family, was—from what I was told—a complicated series of negotiations across a wide range of family members.

Whenever the topic arose of me providing some investment into the James Marriage Project, which was never a direct request you know, I used to ask him, "James, why not use the cows you have now and get a different wife?"

"But John," he'd reply, eyes laughing as he smiled, "I love this one. She is very, very beautiful!"

…and then we'd change topics.

The other language assistant was named Juma. Stoop-shouldered, with a larger head and slightly bulbous eyes, he always seemed a bit embarrassed, reticent to give opinion for fear of giving offence, perhaps. Juma was also shorter than I was.

Whenever we patrolled in the areas around Rubkona and Bentiu, Juma would come with us. He lived in a tukul in Rubkona with his family. A wife and an unspecified number of children. And maybe that's why he was careful with his opinions, because he had mouths to feed and language assistants weren't real UN employees and there wasn't a whole lot of employment, let alone job security, in those days in that town.

But there was one time we had to road-move it up to Kadugli—it took the whole day—so that a bunch of us—me and a couple of Central or South American dudes—could actually fly up-country to Khartoum. He gave us his opinion. And the pragmatism of it shocked us.

We were sitting around the airport bored senseless until the flights showed up. I had gone for a smoke and wandered around to use the outdoor facilities, and when I returned, the Latins were asking Juma a lot of questions. They revolved around why the men in southern Sudan just sat back and did nothing, even when bad things were happening to their women. And I remember with shocking clarity that there was a huge Latino Machismo factor at play where they could not at all comprehend why a man wouldn't fight or die bravely defending his woman's honour.

And I think, in their constant questioning, that they pushed a button. And Juma spoke quietly but with vehemence.

"What are my choices? If a group comes through the village and wants my wife, they will take her. How can I stop them? How? With what?"

"If I fight them, they will kill me and still rape my wife. And she will have nothing left after that. If I don't fight, they will still rape my wife. But at least I will be alive to help her afterwards."

After that was a long period of silence. He was speaking from a view we had never seen and a place we had never been.

Having worked with them a lot during that deployment, I liked both James and Juma. They were good dudes, but I lost track of them when I returned to Canada in 2006. From time to time, I'd think about them, or go through old pictures and wonder how they were doing.

Shortly after I arrived in Malakal, I tossed a question out to our Canadian MLO in Bentiu, asking if they had any language assistants, and if he had ever heard of James and Juma. Nope. Nothing. It was one of those million-to-one questions, but I wanted to ask—I figured they were dead anyway, long long dead—and already half-knew the answer. This confirmed it in my mind. Sad.

There are a large number of local nationals who are UN employees, working everywhere from MOVCON to Camp Services. I don't know many of them, but they are around, sometimes trying to do some camp improvements, sometimes working in administration or supply, sometimes hauling away dead dogs in a wheelbarrow, and sometimes holding onto a manifest that indicates there is a care package for me.

I was going home on leave last week and went through the typical routine of checking-in at MOVCON, handing over my pistol to UN Security guys to do up the paperwork, telling the local security guard "No. you're not inspecting my baggage. I'll open it for a real UN employee, but not for you. Piss off." And so on. Then the waiting, waiting, waiting under the trees where the bus finally came to get us, and we drove through Alpha Gate and down Airport Road. The road had been smoothed and de-pot-holed by the Indian Engineering Company and we rejoiced in the relative comfort of the ride. I sat beside a window and despite the air conditioning blasting, the sun streaming through the window burned and glared. I crooked my arm to rest on the window edge and shaded my face with my hand to give some relief.

The Force Protection had set up a cordon on the airport apron as the bus pulled up beside the turboprop aircraft that was going to get us out of Malakal and into Juba. From an overnight in Juba at Canada House, with the promise of a Nile Special beer or two, I would go to Entebbe, then home to Canada. I expected delays and bottlenecks, but as the bus door opened and the MOVCON guys were waiting at the bus door and the ladder to board the plane, it looked as though the first step in the multi-day journey was going to go smoothly.

As we got off the bus, there was a UN MOVCON guy at the exit doors wishing each of us a pleasant flight. He looked vaguely familiar, and I saw his UN identification around his neck and read his name. And stopped cold.

It was Juma.

I had to be sure, so shook his hand and asked, "Were you in Bentiu in 2006?"

He smiled, and the years dropped away, and I was suddenly back there, and he said, "Yes. I was a language assistant."

I smiled back at him, "Juma, you and I worked together."

Then his eyes saw past my beard and recognized me and the broad smile and joy of expression grew. We shook hands heartily and vigorously and laughed and held up the line of passengers leaving the bus but didn't care.

Despite Malakal being one of the worst places in the country, there were a couple of events that somehow made me feel as though I was meant to be there. Seeing Juma again was one of those moments. He had managed to get his family out to Uganda when the civil war started, and I was very thankful for that.

Another factor in this Karma of being assigned to Malakal was because of the Indian Battalion's Commanding Officer—we had served together in Bentiu in 2006, we had stayed in touch over the years, and I always considered him to be a true friend. His troops treated me well throughout the tour, they took damn good care of me on patrol, and they had my complete faith and trust. Jai Hind!

So, to me this was no coincidence. I was meant to be in Malakal.

That's pretty messed up.

DAY 88

HOME LEAVE

BACK IN ENTEBBE. This is the end of a short leave back home. Took me three days (more or less) to get home…

DAY 1—MALAKAL TO JUBA.

Overnighted in Juba at Canada House. Crammed back a couple of Heinekens and did laundry and re-connected with my mates. The boss seemed interested in the barge incident.

DAY 2—JUBA TO ENTEBBE.

As I waited in the UN passenger area in Juba, my phone buzzed and the Ops O in Canada House asked if I had heard about a cargo plane crashing into the Nile. I looked around—no hectic pace of activity that would usually follow a disaster—and listened to the large aircraft like Antonovs and Illyushins taking off. Must not have been a UN flight that crashed, then. It wasn't.

It was a contracted cargo aircraft that according to the manufacturer hadn't done its maintenance and safety checks and wasn't even airworthy. Oh, the plane apparently had a lot more passengers on board (based on the number of bodies found) than were listed on the manifest. Hell, it might have been dangerously overloaded for all I know. It didn't stop or even slow down our flight.

Welcome to another Juba morning.

As we finally took off from Juba, I felt relieved. A weight lifted off my soul. I was more relaxed, and things looked brighter, especially as we punched through the cloud layer and into the bright light blue of sky and sun-shadowed cumulus.

Landed in Entebbe with no issues and grabbed the shuttle to the hotel. I felt like a new man after a shower and strolled around for an hour or so to work up an appetite and thirst, and I enjoyed the fact that I was the only white dude out for a walk. And while I was certainly an object of interest, in Entebbe I have never been harassed or bothered…sure, guys on motorbikes would always pull up beside me and ask if I want a boda-boda (motorcycle taxi) but were always cool when I told them I'm just out for a wander.

Entebbe is an African city that disproves the fallacy that all African cities are crime-ridden shitholes. It is clean, and organized, and structured, and I enjoy it immensely. I could live there.

The day was sunny but cool compared to Malakal, and I enjoyed the freedom to walk around without threat or the need to be armed. Which doesn't take away from the need to keep eyes open and situational awareness, which paid off when I felt was starting to walk off the well-worn paths into a sketchy residential area and retraced my steps. I wonder about much of the older architecture, which looks a lot like what I'd imagine British barracks or accommodations circa 1930 to be. I also explored the Commonwealth Graveyard and you can't help but look at the graves from 1916 or 1917 and imagine Entebbe in those days, or what these young men died of…wounds? Maybe. Disease? Much more likely.

There were only four military graves here. Well-maintained among the other deteriorated headstones. Poor fellows. Dead and buried far from home. It was less than a week to Remembrance Day and I felt it was important to see them and give them the respect and a moment of silence that they deserved. I'm glad I went there.

As I strolled along, I was already feeling peckish and felt the need to have a snack. A good one. Something I'd heard about from The Kiwi. A mystical unicorn-like appetizer at the Lake Victoria Hotel that deserved closer examination. Since I was already walking in the direction of the Lake Vic it seemed like a logical choice, and it wasn't as though I was going anywhere in particular.

I got through the security at the hotel gate with a wave and a smile—I am sure they thought I was a guest—and made my way past reception to the back patio and took a seat at an outside table. And waited for some service. It took a while…

But I wasn't in a huge rush. I soaked in the scenery. Inhaled the fragrances. Smiled widely like some sort of idiot at the happiness I felt. And I tried to get Malakal out of my head.

I did some mental calculations to pass the time, and as near as I could figure, I had gone over two months without fresh fruit or vegetables, or meat that hadn't come from a can. Time to change that trend…I finally flagged down a waiter and asked for an Avocado Vinaigrette, which was the appie that The Kiwi had mentioned. As I said—it was like a unicorn, since I had heard a lot about it, but just had never seen one. I also asked for a bottled water.

I sat alone with my thoughts, watching guests stroll back and forth, until the snack arrived. And it looked…interestingly green. Large pieces of perfectly sliced avocado resting on a bed of lettuce, sparingly garnished with some slivers of tomato. The vinaigrette was unique—made with what I think was some Dijon mustard and vinegar. While it was nicely presented, it didn't look quite as awesome as I was led to believe…I really was expecting a rainbow or brass band or something. No matter. I cut effortlessly through the avocado with my fork and dipped it in the dressing…Here we go, fresh veg!

And it was one of those first bites where you close your eyes and inhale first because the flavours and the taste are so perfect. The texture and taste of the avocado cut by the tang of vinegar and the slight Dijon flavour giving a unique twist. My God. I fought the urge to wolf it down, and I took my time despite myself, making sure I enjoyed this fully.

After a couple of months of a barely adequate diet, this was Heaven.

Now you might be surprised that there was no mention of a beer with my appetizer. That was deliberate. I was saving that for a point where I didn't have to walk very far, and in my head, I knew where that beer would be best enjoyed!

Leaving the Lake Vic, I walked back along the main drag towards the hotel, but rather than return to the room, I walked across the dirt road to the Four Points Restaurant. Strolling past the small open courtyard, I took a seat at a high bistro table in the thatch-roof-covered section, where the TVs usually show a variety of sports, and ordered a Tusker. As the waitress brought the tray, I could see that the beer was deliciously cold, with condensation beading on the bottle. She opened the bottle, but I insisted on doing the pour myself… watching intently as the beer streamed carefully into the glass, tilting as the beer filled the glass in order to achieve the picture-perfect foamy head.

I put the glass down for a second beside the bottle to enjoy the sight and prolong the agony for just a bit. Then lifted the glass, inhaled the crisp aroma, and drank deeply. Ah, tremendous!

The wait staff must have thought I was insane.

Entebbe. Good food, good drink, good people. Let's leave you for now….

DAY 3—ONWARDS TO CALGARY.

The next night, I flew back home. Entebbe-Amsterdam-Calgary. About 20 hours in a plane. But I was able to do a very affordable upgrade to Business Class for the last leg of the trip. This made all the difference in the world in terms of comfort and food. It meant I would be arriving home much better rested, and that was important. It also meant a selection of port with my cheese plate.

Landing. Customs. Routine. Jackie standing there beautiful as I walked through the doors. And her surprise that I had shaved my beard. And the smiles and laughs and happiness of being back in my house—amazed at the vastness of it—and the scampering frantic energy of Brandy as she remembered me and went crazy with her tail wagging with so much energy.

The subsequent days were a haze. But what fun! Accomplished a lot in a short time….

Shopping at Mountain Equipment Coop, and Home Depot, and Camper's Village, and a whole bunch of places, buying noodles and snacks and 30 or so freeze-dried meals and other supplies like duct tape and God knows what. Packing them tightly in boxes and bringing them to the Base Military Family Resource Centre so they can get shipped to Juba and maybe make it to Malakal a week or two after I get back there.

Being there for the Brigade Sergeant-Major handover and pleased that the timing worked for me to attend. Important to give a good send-off. Then the mess for a pint (only one—jet-lagged rather badly!) and a chance to say Hi to some folks I hadn't seen in months, including the Brigade Commander.

A military fundraiser, where new friends were made and it could have been a fairly early night if someone hadn't opened that second bottle of 15-year-old elixir and I really have no idea how I got home or in bed, but according to my bank statement I was coherent enough to pay the cab with my debit card. Clearly, this is a result of jet lag, and maybe Malarone.

I spent Remembrance Day commemorating the fallen and pleased that 41 Service Battalion was so well represented, and happy beyond words that my niece and her fiancé took the time to attend. Then, of course, The Officers' Mess in Mewata Armoury, where it was another reunion with good friends and a pint or two together.

And then, days later, the Garrison Pub. A refuge of Pubishness. Jackie and I split a Garrison Burger (no bun) and fries. It was excellent. But the half-burger filled me completely and this was another realization that my stomach had shrunk. The subsequent intestinal rumblings were an unpleasant reminder that I hadn't had much grease in my diet for quite a while.

Sleep. A disaster. So jet-lagged. Terrible sleep for the first days. Up at 0400 hours. Struggle to stay awake beyond 1900 hours. Walls hit—where you go from energetic to exhausted and in need of a nap within seconds, which is great when you can just climb the stairs and crawl into bed. It's less great when you're driving down Crowchild Trail at 90 kilometers per hour.

Blur, blur, blur.

With that week came the nagging feeling and increasing knowledge that I wasn't really home. I was physically there and tried to get myself mentally there, but knowing I was only in Calgary for just over a week made any transition more difficult. Being really jet-lagged didn't help. I just couldn't really jump that vast chasm to be fully in Calgary, and had I tried to do so, I think it would have made the return to South Sudan even tougher. I had never really left Malakal.

But home leave, short as it was, gave me the opportunity to relax, be with loved ones, enjoy family, and sleep in my own bed! It was wonderful. But obviously, I needed to go back. So—much like my initial deployment in August, I am easing myself back into theatre. It also buys me time in case there are delays or other issues…lessons learned from last tour, where there were delays every single trip.

First step—from Calgary to Entebbe.

Spending a full day here so that I can relax, de-jet-lag, and (most importantly) figure out if I'm on tomorrow's manifest for Juba. This is where I am now, at the Lake Victoria hotel, sitting beside the bar, drinking Americanos as I type.

Second step—Juba.

More austere but safe in Canada House with a day to hang out and shop if I need to. Most importantly, I need to get my pistol back, give it a good cleaning, and repack.

Then, finally, home to Malakal.

Ha. "Home" …that's funny.

———————————

Going home to Calgary was important. I wanted to attend the Change of Brigade Sergeant-Major and I really wanted to spend Remembrance Day with Soldiers. I craved that physical grounding that being Home would provide.

The transition from Malakal to Juba was quite shocking, as was the move from Juba to Entebbe. Not just the physical or environmental differences affected me. The feeling of being back in Entebbe was more about a pervasive and extraordinary sense of comfort and happiness. Let me jump back a bit—when we were on the plane taking off from Juba to fly to Entebbe, a very heavy weight lifted from my shoulders. I described it briefly above, but it was extraordinary. It was palpable. I think everyone on the flight felt that way to a greater or lesser extent, because we were going somewhere peaceful and predictable.

Looking back, part of Entebbe's allure—apart from fresh food—was the feeling of safety and security. The feeling of not being apprehensive all the time. The feeling of "Nothing bad is going to happen to me here and I can sleep in a really nice bed and walk around if I want." After having spent a week there for Induction Training, it was familiar, and I knew where to eat and drink.

But I'm not naïve—I followed the basic safety rules—I didn't go out after dark to wander around, if an area felt sketchy, I stayed away from it, I didn't flash large sums of cash around, and so on. These are rules, by the way, that you can apply to every major city in North America or Europe…

Upgrading the flights to Business Class was very affordable (around $600.00 Canadian) and very, very timely. I am a tall guy and there is never enough leg room and the meals are always lacklustre in Economy class. The flights were very long and not very comfortable and suddenly here was an opportunity I could not refuse!

And yes—there actually was a selection of ports to accompany my cheese plate.

DAY 95

BACK TO MALAKAL

DESPITE MY BEST ATTEMPTS to ease into the return to Malakal, the reality of coming back was a plunge in very cold water.

The time in Entebbe was terrific, the day and a bit in Juba was good as well, but although I was reticent to return to Malakal, I couldn't wait to get back there. Confused? Me too. Love-Hate relationship, perhaps, because at least when I'm in my crappy little container with my not so comfy bed and rumbling clunking erratic air conditioner, it's MINE. And it's routine and I know what my freeze-dried meals taste like, and all the other crap is at least familiar. Better the devil you know…

More than anything else, I missed my mates. Who in some cases didn't recognize me without my beard, which I had shaved off to go on leave because Jacqueline didn't think she'd like it. To be fair, it did make me look a wee bit older. Coming back to the Team Site, I looked like an average tall white guy in a baseball cap and Oakley sunglasses. One of those who didn't recognize me was my mate Paul from World Food Program. He apologized after the fact, as did several of my other friends.

Current situation-ish around here—We have a lot of folks in the outstations or on leave, so it's pretty thin on the ground for staffing. We must manage expectations this week and are prepared to drop lower priority tasks for the fastballs that come screaming across your path without warning. Don't get me wrong, it isn't as though we are ever really that busy…but everything is situation-dependent and sometimes we are sitting around with almost nothing to do,

147

but seconds later, it's All Hands to the Pumps as we try to defuse a situation and every single person needs to step up.

My thoughts are a bit of a jumble today. Lots on the go over the past few days and I don't have the sense that I've really settled down yet. So, apologies. Just think of this as a peek into my brain after a couple of mugs of coffee. I'm going to jump from the confusion of coming back to Malakal, to this weekend's Thrilling Tale—how we defeated institutional adversity, and in spite of ourselves succeeded in getting another barge convoy to set sail upriver.

But First—Coming back. Not so easy.

The allure of Canada and Calgary and friends and family and good single malt whisky and good food all ganged up on me and pummeled me hard. They are a constant yearning—a draw on my attention in these first days and occupy my thoughts almost completely. The voice of a loved one, the indescribable heady aroma when you savour a glass of single malt, the realization that you aren't being eaten by flies or bugs or tiny invisible crawling things 24 hours a day, and so much more. And, most especially, the crisp dry Prairie air on autumn mornings. I miss all of that.

When you're here long enough, you forget—or block out—the unpleasantness of your existence over time, and you develop a new normal, an equilibrium, where the bad bits are just part of the physical and mental landscape.

My own deterioration is the same…weight-loss at a rate of a couple of pounds a week doesn't really get noticed because it's gradual. Then you wind up in Juba after a couple of months and everyone says, "Hey, you lost a lot of weight." Holy Shit. Really?

And I had lost a bit of weight. About seventeen pounds. Which puts me at a good height-weight ratio for the first time since I quit smoking several years ago. I can stand to lose more. I suppose if I drank Nile water I'd lose a whole lot more, and quickly. That's a bit extreme.

I digress. It's a common failing of mine…as is my overuse of ellipses.

On the one hand I tuned out a lot of the bad things about Malakal, or more accurately, I resigned myself to them. On the other hand, there are all the many good things about Calgary. And now I find myself in Malakal with the Calgary memories strong in my head.

It's conflicting.

The first day or two, eating freeze-dried meals, sorting through canned veg wondering if I was ever going to be able to eat that stuff and not puke in disgust, lying at night in that uncomfortable single bed (I didn't think it was uncomfortable when I left for leave) it's not hard to feel a little down. Self-pitying. Whine whine snivel.

And it's always worse at night.

In the day I can open my blinds and the sun comes in and it heats up the container to the point where the ancient air-conditioner, already straining, is taxed even further; It coughs and sputters alarmingly, shaking the whole cabin, before either returning to a dull chugging or gaspingly stopping for a few minutes. But the cabin is bright and maybe if it's not cheery it is at least welcoming, so it's easy to feel content.

But at night. With blinds down and fluorescent lights on. Oh, how the atmosphere changes. It's more confining, harsher, not welcoming. Outside, it's dark dark dark and every exit from the cabin usually involves being attacked and feasted upon by the insects—it's not a great feeling. It's a struggle to hoist yourself up and over that mental and emotional wall. But day after day, it gets normal again, or I become resigned to it again.

It hasn't rained in weeks, and the dry season is almost here…not fully here…but it looks promising. The daytime heat is in the high 30s and the sun on your neck feels harsher than in the oppressive humidity of September. The trucks throw up clouds of choking, blinding dust and the wind creates small vortexes that dance across the road in front of you. The dust makes the horizon's sky a light brown instead of blue, and it is darker than usual because this is the season where fields are burnt…clouds of white and sometimes black or grey smoke dot the landscape and the old brush and crops, and the inevitable burnt garbage, adds to the smog and stink. The dust gets into your eyes, and you can run your tongue along your teeth and feel the grit and taste the sweat as it beads on your upper lip.

As hot as the days are, the nights have cooled with the mornings being deliciously fresh for an hour or so after sunrise. It's welcome not only because of the relief, the ability to open the windows and air out the cabin, but because it keeps the morning bugs down. The dogs still lie in the road, and the dust coats their fur, permeates their skin, and must keep the fleas down somewhat. In the relative cold, they huddle together for warmth.

Today I stood outside near our office, surrounded by large piles of gravel meant to be used for road repair, and looked around. I walked a full circle, looking at each thing in turn, soaking in the memory. From the helipad where one Rwandan Mi-8 sat, to the surrounding berm, across to the sea cans and impromptu parking lot, which was rutted and potholed like every other place, with old crates and barrels and boxes and generic crap that littered the area, the water and fuel tanker trucks on the roadway, and the once-white now brown-tinged office containers. Dogs pantingly trot here and there between sparse and scraggly shade trees. But then, looking up—once past the brown dust smoke haze, I stared at a cloudless sky that was a perfect blue. I marveled at it. Beautiful.

I'm lucky to see this.

So, that's where I am. Every day Calgary fades just a little bit in the memory, and Malakal becomes more and more real. And I see that the good things, the unique things, never left. They were always there—I just need to sift through a lot of shit to see it.

But the Barge. Again with the Barge…

I learned on my return to Malakal last Friday that we were launching a barge convoy in the next day or two from BANFRU down to Juba. The route along the Nile transited both SPLA and Opposition positions. The planning had been going on while I was on leave, and the launch date was on a Sunday. With the last barge incident (also known as the Kaka Hostage-Taking Extravaganza) fresh in all our minds, we planned and took extra precautions and tried to put all the bits and pieces in place that would ensure both the safety of the convoy and (especially) our MLOs and Force Protection dudes who were on board. This was expected to be easier since we were basically travelling empty back to Juba. Not much point trying to loot stuff if there isn't any stuff to loot.

While we couldn't be expected to ensure the security of the convoy along the whole route, our main responsibility as the MLO planners was to ensure that nothing bad happened as the convoy sailed past Malakal. We are often our own worst enemy. Not everyone works weekends—actually, let's rephrase that. No one here works weekend.

The SPLA, I would assume, after a hard week of doing SPLA stuff (I really have no idea what that would be), might want to just have a day or two to hang out, get hammered, sleep in, and relax. I certainly know that the current SPLA Liaison Officers think that. Because they basically told us not to bug them on weekends.

So, here was the Game Plan.

My patrol of a single vehicle and another MLO would take the Barge MLOs to BANFRU and drop them off with all their kit. Then we would stay there and coordinate with BANFRU Operations until the barges started powering up. From that point—it was supposed to be 0800 but who the hell were we kidding—it would take a least 15-20 minutes to hook up the barges to the pushers, get everyone in position, and push off upriver. And it would take at least another 30 minutes or so to pass the first checkpoint. And that's if we're lucky.

Once the convoy started moving, putting barges into positions, and so on, we'd launch the second MLO team who would go into Malakal, pick up the SPLA LO from his accommodations, and head up to the first of two positions along the White Nile along the barge convoy route. This initial point was at a known concentration of troops and anti-aircraft positions just past the airport and at a bend in the river. The timing should work out. This was totally wishful thinking on my part—timings never work out.

The barges started moving; we launched the guys, blah blah blah. All good. At first.

We then heard that the SPLA LO (who is a temporary replacement and not from around here and he is a nice guy but super weirdly awkward when it comes to social interaction) decided he didn't want to get out of bed. And then he didn't want to go to the first position to liaise with the SPLA, so he went with the MLO team to the airport instead.

Which would have been awesome if the barges had been airplanes.

When we found out that this whole thing was going sideways, my patrol left BANFRU and went to link up and deconflict the situation (I was going to use another word instead of "deconflict"— it rhymes with "unstuck") with the SPLA LO and my teammates. And since the SPLA dude didn't know where the first liaison point was (but we did), I led, and the other vehicle followed us. When we

151

got to the designated location to the east of Malakal airport, we all dismounted, and the LO went forward alone to talk to the guy in charge. It was early and the soldiers were just stirring from their little one-man corrugated tin shelters.

After a while, the LO came back with a dude who was "sort of" in charge. He told us that his soldiers didn't know there was a barge convoy coming, and that he recommended we wait for a day or two to make sure everyone, especially other SPLA concentrations by the river, could be informed.

His face fell when I told him the convoy had sailed already. It was on the move, mate. And it was moving fast. And while he bitched and whined about our poor communication and timings, one of the MLOs pointed out that since a unit less than five kilometers from BANFRU hadn't been informed after a week of us repeatedly advising their leadership in Malakal, the SPLA lines of communication weren't all that great either.

Then a real commander showed up. He was in civvies but clearly carried some authority, and he and the LO got into various animated discussions in Arabic and Dinka where I am sure we were being brutally reviled and our parentage was being insulted. But the man in civvies turned to us and said, "Maafi Mushkila. No Problem." The LO confirmed that there would be no problem with the UN barge convoy…

Once the LO realized it was going to be cool, and after some ego-massaging by myself and the other dudes, and once he felt confident that he had done a damn fine job, he lit a cigarette, and we joked around and shook hands with the dude in civvies and a couple of soldiers. Less than a kilometer away, the wheelhouse of the lead pusher came into view over the foliage. Awesome. Right on time.

BANG!

BANG! BANG!

What the fuck?

Gunshots. Close. And all I could think was, "Oh great…here we go." Looked at my watch for the time, look at the shot direction (Northeast) and waited for something else to happen. There was a bit of rapid-fire chatter going on, and the SPLA troops were quick to tell us that some of their guys were out hunting birds for food. The shots were not directed towards the barge, and definitely not aimed at us.

Awesome.

From being a bit of an obstructionist earlier in the morning, the SPLA LO was looking more confident. He was being helpful and was doing what he was supposed to do as a Liaison Officer. And we were all pals again and I said we should go to the Malakal Port (our second checkpoint) to see the convoy through and would he mind getting us access there? Then, since it was close, we could drop him off at his accommodation in town for lunch and that would finish everything for the day. He nodded happily.

We set off down Alpha Route, the riverside road/track that paralleled the Nile, south towards the port. Past the large main mosque, impressive and desolate, turning into the small single lane road that led us to the port, we parked and waited by the vehicles while the LO went to coordinate and get us permission to stay there.

So. The port. Not what you'd imagine a Western Port with a capital P to be. Or a recreational boat landing for that matter.

It was a simple waterside with a paved area, with several long, thin wooden barges beached haphazardly on the bank. A lone donkey stood impatiently in the sun, harnessed to a homemade two-wheeled trailer which mounted a 55-gallon metal drum full of Nile water. The water sloshed as the donkey, bored and impatient, tossed his head and stamped a foot, waiting for his owner to return. Soldiers bathed along the bank, almost hidden among the reeds. Many women from the POC site, with matching faded yellowy-orange vegetable oil jugs now used to haul water, filed past us towards the river to fill the containers, balance them on their heads, and make the return journey back into the town, then onwards to the base.

It was blisteringly hot in the late-morning sun and we instinctively gathered under a tree to escape the heat. I peered intently at the waterside buildings, cement-walled and bullet-pocked, with twisted, green-painted metal doors or gaping empty doorways, all abandoned and emptied of anything useable. Brick buildings, of British-colonial construction. Small, neat, empty. Relics of the last century.

The LO, as talkative now as he was sparing with his words before, stood with pride and told us about the Nile River, the habits of the fish that inhabit it, the uses for the many reeds and grasses and the abundant papyrus found south as you travelled towards Bor. We stood there dumbfounded and amazed by his broad knowledge. He was not a stupid man by any stretch. Uneducated perhaps, but extremely knowing and aware of his culture, his history, and his environment. The conversation was very interesting indeed.

And then, slowly, fighting the Nile current, the convoy came into view. A couple of dozen barges, joined together in rectangles of four, or eight—each shoved upstream by a pusher craft, all flying the blue UN flag. Among the boats were relics of the Second World War—Landing Craft Tanks, old LCTs, repaired and modified and repainted but still cruising after many decades, moving at the convoy's slow pace but giving the impression of much more speed. We watched, impressed by the number of barges and the sheer size of the convoy. The lead barges and pusher were opposite to us. And then, waving from the armoured perch at the helm was Petros, one of our MLOs. We waved back in response and silently wished him a Safe Journey.

No trouble. No further gunshots. No checkpoints or blockades.

Happy that what had started out with unpleasant potential had instead become a successful day, we drove back to base. We drove quickly, before our luck changed.

The level of scrutiny on leave in Malakal and Juba was incredible, and you had to plan and submit your requests as soon as possible to get the dates that you wanted. If you waited too long to apply for leave, you would often be disappointed. And no one would care because it was your own fault. Several of us had a leave tracker that would calculate how much leave you had accumulated at a specific point in time. It was extremely useful!

It wasn't just applying for leave that was time-consuming. Getting out of Malakal was complicated, and you could spend hours comparing the prices and times of flights from Juba, or Entebbe, or Nairobi to your destination. As I mentioned, the UN ran a regular service to Uganda and Kenya.

Coming back from vacation, your first day was devoted to administration, because Juba needed something called a Leave Return Report, which required several scanned documents, including:

The approved leave request,

Security clearances, of which there were two. Internal for South Sudan travel—so from Malakal to Juba, and External for travel outside the Mission—such as Juba to Entebbe.

Copies of your passport showing the exit and entry stamps,

Copies of your boarding passes,

And I think one or two more documents…

Ponderous.

DAY 104

FASHODA/KODOK

IT TOOK A WHILE TO SHAKE the malaise of last week. Bits of it still linger. But day by day it gets easier to fall asleep and easier to wake up…and the sleeps are sounder. Or would be if the damn dogs weren't howling and fighting at zero-dark-stupid.

Malakal is still relatively peaceful. But Upper Nile State—of which Malakal is the capital—is still a tinderbox waiting to go up in flames. And I'm not saying this melodramatically, either. The West Bank of the Nile remains in Opposition hands from north of Kaka to beyond Tonga in the South, except for the blip around Malakal which was occupied by the government forces in September to secure the airport/lines of communication. That blip, which includes the villages of Lelo, Detang, and Warjok remain a source of constant frustration to the Opposition. They have been threatening to push the SPLA off that bit of West Bank for months now.

The other significant frustration—and likely the point that could start the war up again in earnest—is the Presidential decree creating 28 states from the existing 10. This means more governmental appointments, more administrators, and more gifts, graft, and bribery for the government to cement their support. If you want more details, read some of the news articles, but basically as it affects the Shilluk in the west bank area, this decision will give Malakal—seen as traditionally Shilluk—over to the Dinka. The issue is a Red Line for the Opposition.

On Monday, I knew I was going on a DAP later in the week to patrol with a bunch of UNMISS civilian folks to a place we hadn't been in over six months. To a place that I had an almost compelling need to visit.

Remember, many emails ago, when I talked about a crazy-brave French explorer who, from Brazzaville in the Belgian Congo, went East to link France's Western and Eastern African colonies? If you didn't, look up Marchand and Fashoda. After a very perilous journey with dangers most of us cannot even imagine, he was travelling along the Bahr-El Ghazal River, went Left at the White Nile instead of continuing east along the Sobat River, and—with the other lucky bastards who survived the long journey—set up at a little place on the Nile that had an old trading fort, and raised the French Tricolour.

Now, timing being what it was, the British military had just fought a battle outside Khartoum and defeated the ruling Mahdi, ensuring that Sudan would be under Anglo-Egyptian rule for another several decades. It was at this battle where a young Winston Churchill was involved in one of the last traditional cavalry charges in the 19th Century. Involved…ha…he was intimately involved.

I like Churchill. While it's easy to look at an older pudgy WWII-era Winston smoking a cigar and giving the V for Victory sign, it's hard to imagine that back in the day he was a young and dashing Army officer. During the cavalry charge of the Lancers at Omdurman, Winston was armed with a privately purchased Mauser broom-handle pistol (semi-automatic with a 10-round integral magazine). During the cavalry charge he shot several Dervishes, including one that was running at him with a raised sword. Winston fired as the Dervish's chest touched the muzzle of the pistol. An engagement distance of perhaps three feet.

That takes a certain coolness under fire…

After the battle of Omdurman, General Kitchener (the British Commander) heard that there were other white men in the south of Sudan. To establish who they were and what they were up to, Kitchener dispatched a gunboat and some troops. They found the French at Fashoda. Had a parlay. And the British eventually built their own small fort near the French one while the politicians in London and Paris rattled their sabers and got themselves worked into a frenzy. While relations on the ground in Fashoda were cordial—one would only expect the finest manners among the French and

British officers, of course—they were anything but pleasant back home. It played out in the press, the navies of both countries began to mobilize, and there was a very real threat of war until the French backed down. Over a collection of huts on the White Nile.

That's where we were going on this patrol. To Fashoda. To Kodok.

As I said, UNMISS hadn't been to Kodok for several months, and the plan was to re-open dialogue with the local authorities. Since the fighting had broken out again in Upper Nile State in the late spring, all the local authorities might have changed and obtaining current contact information was a big "To Do" as a task. We simply did not have a lot of information, but we did know that we would have to get clearances through the Opposition headquarters…which we did. There was regular communication by ourselves and some other UNMISS folks with the opposition, so I wasn't overly concerned—they would give us a flight safety assurance for the patrol, or they wouldn't. We'd fly or not. They eventually did give their approval—on the morning of the mission.

The patrol prep—for me anyway—included reading previous patrol reports and looking at maps and trying to figure out what was where. I just wanted a sense of the ground and where most of the buildings were, even if I didn't know their function.

Now, technically I wasn't in charge of the patrol. That authority defaulted to the Force Protection Commander for reasons that completely baffle me. But here's how reality works—I was running it.

Why?

Because I've participated in other patrols where the Command and Control is not clear, and I didn't like the "standing around looking at each other wondering 'Who is doing what?'" bullshit. So, while the poorly-crafted Patrol Orders may have stated that the Force Protection Commander was in charge, I took the responsibility upon myself because no one else would…oh, and because as a Military Liaison Officer it's my job to facilitate things exactly like this. We are the interface among the military and civilian agencies, and to facilitate interaction/liaison, etc. Not the Force Protection, not the civilian UN folks, but the MLOs.

The night before the patrol, I prepped my kit, as I always do. Checking and double-checking batteries, map coordinates, sat phone numbers, medical supplies, extra food, water, and the thousands of little routine things that you do. Attention to Detail—and I like doing it because I get a sense of knowing where things are, knowing my kit is good, and that something likely won't fail—like a sat phone battery—when you really, really need it.

I also didn't sleep well. My mind races every time we go outside the routine of framework patrols. These missions we go on are important, have good potential, and there are secondary and tertiary implications to the questions you ask, the assistance you can provide, and the deals you strike. And the endless possibilities and parameters of "What If" run through my already over-alert brain and make sleep difficult. But I eventually did get some sleep. Just not soundly or particularly well.

And woke at 0500. Got up. Made coffee. Did my morning routine, but more quickly than usual. Got to the office painfully early with my loaded pack and helmet and plate carrier. We needed confirmation on some things, and I wanted to get to the office early and make sure we were good to go.

I thought we were gripped on all the details. We weren't.

Trouble started at Air Operations and MOVCON. The manifest was over-full…the add-ons were essential (seriously essential) for the mission, so I bumped a couple of guys. I did make the effort to walk to the Sector HQ and talk to someone (there was no one in the office that early), and then to the State Operations Centre (there was no one there either). Awesome. I chose who got bumped. I didn't like doing it, but priorities are priorities. As we boarded the vehicles to take us to the airport, I introduced myself to the UN civilian lead for the patrol, gave him a copy of the orders and agenda I had put together (he didn't bother attending my final coordination meeting), and chatted about the objectives and main effort for the interaction with the Kodok authorities. Then I sat quietly in my seat as the bus lurched its way down the road to the airport, which has since been graded and smoothed by the Indian Army engineers (Hurrah!)

Once at the airport, the bus drove past the Rwandan Force Protection for the airport. Beside the gate two off-white and beat-up Mambas with heavy machine guns stood parked, soldiers in the turrets. Driving along a dirt track, we got onto the apron and—being asphalt—the ride smoothed considerably. The bus lurched to a stop close to the helicopter, we disembarked, walked over to the bird, and climbed the narrow ladder into the interior. This is easy if you're not carrying anything. If you're carrying your backpack (with 24-48 hours' worth of supplies) and a small bag with your plate carrier and helmet, and if everyone else is doing the same, trying to find a spot, putting the personal protective equipment under the seats, it's a bit chaotic. The Mi-8 seating configuration isn't at all like comfy chairs in a real commercial airplane. They are basically bench seats running the length of the aircraft's hold. Ten seats on either side. But it isn't a seat…it's a bench. Your seat is aligned with the seatbelt location.

Yes. There are seatbelts. They are spectacularly useless.

Eventually we all got seated, and before the big overhead fan started turning, the UN civilian chief said a few words, then the Force Protection Commander (a nice and efficient young Captain) spoke, describing how the disembarkation from the helo would proceed when we got to our destination. Basically this—Helo stops, Force Protection secures the site, then the rest of us. I would be first out the door after the troops and start shepherding people to where they needed to go.

The flight crew handed out ear protectors (I had my own high-quality ear protection) and the rotor started clunkily turning with a whine. You could hear and feel the straining motor and gears, and through the window see the shadows as the blades turned slowly, then more and more quickly and the shuddering and shaking of the fuselage made clear picture-taking impossible for my smartphone. Then, almost imperceptibly at first, we were airborne. I started the timer on my watch.

As soon as we were airborne, normal conversation became impossible. I took out my ear buds, plugged them into my phone, and cranked some tunes to get me through the flight. Rammstein's "Mein Land" seemed apt.

The flight was circuitous for a number of very good security reasons. I gauged our direction by seeing where the sun shone through the porthole windows. I had already done a rough estimate on airtime off the map before we took off. I like to know details like this. I was sitting mid-way in the guts of the Mi-8, which although is a beast can still be tight when you jam 20 people inside. The issue was that the windows in that part of the bird were blocked by the external fuel tanks, so to get a look at the ground you needed to reach over and crane your neck back or forth to get a glimpse out the window behind you. Not much point…it all looked the same. Swamp. Green or brown grass. That was about it.

There wasn't enough room to stretch out and my shoulders were crammed uncomfortably with my neighbours. So, I leaned forward, elbows on knees, and I rested my chin in my hands and closed my eyes. I might even have dozed slightly. And after a while, the changing pitch and sound of the rotor told me that we were starting to land.

I tried to get a view out the window as we made our landing approach, and saw a small twin-engine civilian plane parked to the side of the dirt strip…it was offloading humanitarian aid. In a swirling cloud of dust, we hovered, descended, and finally settled on the ground. The rotors slowed, then stopped, and it grew quiet and hot inside. The crew chief was already outside placing the chocks under the wheels, and the Force Protection did a very rapid dismount to secure the site.

I was next out the door because I would be the one advising the senior UN civilian. I looked around…all clear…bunch of local civvies standing around gawking at us…there was not a soldier in sight…okay, there were two. They were waving and smiling at me. There were also two civilians with them.

Signalling the passengers to come out of the helicopter, I walked over to the civvies and introduced myself. They had some English but were clearly more comfortable in Arabic. A couple of UN folks on our patrol were fluent Arabic speakers, so they made their own introductions. In short, the conversations took off, everyone was shaking hands and saying Hello, and clearly no one needed me to stand around and get in their way. I stood off to the side of the crowd for a second and did a quick scan to get a sense of the place.

Looking west towards Kodok, there was an overwhelming dustiness. In the air. On the ground. Everywhere. It was a fine white-grey powder that curled up in a small cloud around my boots after every step. In the near distance was a narrow creek with a small bridge, on which several children were fishing. Beyond that was the town itself, and while there were many brick-walled and more modern (1920s-ish?) buildings placed haphazardly, there were also hundreds of tukuls, the common round reed and thatch huts.

This was a well-populated place.

With the Force Protection commander, who told his dudes to provide a wide perimeter around the team, we walked slowly towards the town. Slowly, because everyone was talking and everyone was friendly and in a place that didn't have television, having a helo land and a bunch of people emerge was kind of a big deal. Having a tall white guy in the group (that would be me, if you were wondering) was just icing on the cake.

As we crossed the bridge, the kids ignored their fishing and stared at me. I waved and smiled—as I tend to do, because courtesy costs nothing—and one of them piped up "Khawaja!" and the rest of the kids laughed and pointed at me, repeating the word. "Khawaja" can be interpreted as "Stranger" or "Foreigner". It is also used as "White Guy." I smiled, greeted them, and received big smiles in return. We walked on towards the town, past girls and women with 20-liter buckets of water balanced precariously on their heads, heading back into the village. The women were in a typical garb in these parts, a shirt or t-shirt, with a long robe of material gathered and tied off at one shoulder. The materials can be plain or colourful, or ripped and soiled, depending on the place, the person, and the circumstance. Although they ignored us, their eyes followed us.

We walked past the Red Cross facility (Humanitarians were working here) and the old hospital, which had been abandoned after an alleged attack in the mid-summer. I noticed the trees sporadically growing here and there, individual and scraggly, but still over three meters high.

The buildings were more clustered and orderly as we approached the County Commissioner's office. Brick, generally. Some structures more worn and decrepit than others. They all looked like a British colonial bungalow. Thick walls and narrow doors. Some with a verandah. Old. Very old. In some cases, just the main foundations and part of the walls remained.

We waited outside in the sun while our escorts went to get the Commissioner, and the Force Protection expanded their cordon around us. We were the subject of interest and waves from the several civilians, who with a few military folks and police (surprise! Hadn't expected to see them) had marked our progress as we walked along the dirt dust track towards them. A few of us walked over and shook hands with them, said hello, introduced ourselves. There was no point standing out in the sun doing nothing.

We were ushered into the Commissioner's office and waited for a few minutes in a covered verandah while the scraping of chairs and tables told us that this would be a fairly formal meeting. There was a slight stir as the commissioner arrived, a large man in height and girth, well-dressed, unsmiling, who shook hands with us and let us take our seats in the main room.

The room was not large, and our chairs were laid out in a row before a small, raised area where two tables had been placed end to end. Behind these tables sat the commissioner and two others. To the side were two other men—interpreters and key local staff.

Once we were settled, there was a bit of confusion about who wanted to speak first and who was translating. A few nervous laughs but it got sorted. There were a few seconds of anticipatory silence. And the meeting kicked off.

We discussed a lot of important topics in a short time, but to go into detail would probably put you to sleep. Here's the rough outline—Introductions. Discussing the UNMISS mandate, talking Human Rights issues and violations, Child Protection, Civil Affairs, Military Liaison (yours truly), and finally IGAD, the brokers of the latest peace agreement. From them, we received their names, positions, contact information, preferred lines of communication for future contact, some serious allegations, the local security situation, the local economic situation, humanitarians working in Kodok, and so on.

Our ground time was running out. I was sitting behind the civilian leader and gave him a tap on the shoulder and a reminder that we were 30 minutes from launch. There is no such thing as a short goodbye in South Sudan, especially when both sides believe that the meeting was valuable. There is chatter, and follow-up, and further information, and plans for a future meeting.

Eventually, we got everyone out the door and lined up for a

couple of pictures by the side of the building. About three meters up the wall was a plaque that read "Marchand 1898". To honour Jean-Baptiste Marchand—explorer and soldier.

Throughout the patrol, but especially at that point, the historical significance of the place just welled up and slammed into me. This was a place that was in many ways untouched since the 1920's (architecturally). There was no urban renewal of Kodok. No demolition to make way for a new mall or highway. This was literally walking into the past. And I felt it. Imagined it without hot weather gear or malaria meds—I tried to envision what 1898 or 1928 or 1958 would have looked like here...

While continuing to herd, prod, and otherwise coerce the group towards the airfield, I walked with the Force Protection Commander and discussed his disposition, how his troops performed, a couple of points for improvement, and to scout out the path with him by being slightly in front of the group. This was another opportunity to look at the town...and I marveled that there were no soldiers in sight (well, very few) because they were nearby, but not in town. For the first time in Upper Nile State, I patrolled in a place that felt civilian-ized. The kids fished, the cattle grazed in the low swampy area where the grass was greenest, women fetched water. It was calm. Peaceful. More reminiscent of my previous deployment in its tranquility.

Then my mind kicked me—Get your Eyes and Ears open. Never let your guard down. Be suspicious. Patrol's not over until it's over.

Part of the Force Protection had stayed to guard the helicopter, and they were patiently standing there as we approached. The pilots and crew lounged in the shade of the Mi-8, bored. Waiting to get back.

As we walked up to the helo, I asked the crew if they would have left without us if we had been late. They smiled at my lame joke (I blame the heat), then boarded the aircraft and started going through their pre-flight drills. The Escort Commander and I discussed how we would fold up the perimeter, and then I spent my time doing mundane things, like counting passengers to make sure we didn't inadvertently leave someone behind. Sometimes civvies are like cats—they never listen, and they sure make a fuss if you leave them in a warzone for no good reason. Okay, that second part really isn't applicable to cats, but you get my meaning.

The local leadership had walked with us to the aircraft to continue the conversation—mainly trying to line up a future visit, but in some cases just idle chitchat. Relationship-building is critical to any interaction in these societies. The result of this, however, was that trying to get the civvies on the damn helo was turning into a challenge…but it slowly got sorted out. They got on board while I stood at the bottom of the ladder. Then I hopped aboard, followed by the last few force protection troops.

There was silence after everyone had selected a seat and strapped in, just before the rotor started its turning, and several of us made eye contact and smiled or gave thumbs up. We had started the dialogue with Kodok again. To my mind, we need to go back within a couple of weeks to do some focused assessment and investigation, and—this is important—to listen to what they needed. This initial meeting was a great start, but it was like rolling a grenade into the room—there's lots of noise and stuff flying around—but for an enduring relationship, we needed a smaller group to deal with specific issues and conduct a proper key leader engagement.

As the helo raised its ponderous body off the ground, creating a rising cloud of dust, all I could think of was the town and the plaque on the side of a building. A small monument to a man long dead in a place unknown to most of the world.

I remain in awe of people like Marchand, and of the British who followed. Of the missionaries. The traders. The brave and devoted and foolish wanderers. The Adventurers.

We don't make them like that anymore.

———————————

Fashoda/Kodok was fascinating. And the history student in me was running overtime on that patrol. When Marchand made it back to France from Fashoda, he'd been away for four years on his exploration. Four Years. He continued to serve France and was present for the Boxer Rebellion in China and was wounded several times during the First World War. He survived the war, retired, and died in France in 1934.

Back to the present—I was supposed to go back several weeks later to conduct a follow-up patrol and do an analysis on the old hospital which had been allegedly bombed (or perhaps strafed) by SPLA helicopter gunships. This would constitute a war crime if we could verify it. I think the word got out to the SPLA authorities, because we never got that patrol off the ground. The SPLA stopped us at Malakal airport and refused to let us take off. I filed a Freedom of Movement violation report up the chain…where it disappeared.

a Cenotaph
Porter un
cérémonie
minute de
ec Facebook

Thak you
So much!
for leaving Canad
and going to
another Countr
to keep peace
Love Maya

DAY 109

HONEY WAGON BINGO

I HAVE MORE FOOD THAN I KNOW WHAT TO DO WITH.

This is not a common phrase in Malakal.

Several UN cargo flights had come in last week, and some the week before, and at one point, The Kiwi and I were driving by the sea-can where the inbound cargo is stored. It was open and a couple of the local employees were in there. Taking advantage of the opportunity, The Kiwi and I popped our heads in to say Hi and scout around for our stuff and—Hey Look!—There were a couple of Gold Bags for me. I call them Gold Bags because the good folks in Juba put my boxes into huge heavy-duty gold-coloured plastic bags (I think DHL?) …seriously big bags. And they hold many valuables. As a result, the MOVCON guys know that if there's a gold bag, it's for The Canadian. This is particularly good when I don't have a copy of the Cargo Move Request form, or the reference number on hand. Which, to be honest, is most of the time.

The complication was that I was supposed to do a patrol in town with Claude around 1400, and my gut said that there was no way I'd make it back in time before they shut the sea-can for the day, and I am an impatient guy when it comes to stuff…especially my stuff. The Kiwi, as a good mate, offered to pick it up for me. Honestly, one white dude looks pretty much like another around here, and the MOVCON guys do sometimes get us confused. I gave The Kiwi my keys so he could drop the stuff off in my container.

The patrol into town was shitty. Literally. We were responding to a request to pump out a septic tank in advance of a Very, Very

169

Important Person, "VVIP" visit scheduled for some time in the near future. The SPLA do not have that capability and requested it from UNMISS. And we obliged.

Why? Simple really. If the VVIP was to visit Malakal but stay inside our camp, it suggests that Malakal isn't secure. But by staying in Malakal town, austere as it is, it sends a loud and powerful message that Malakal is safe and secure (mostly), and that the civilians should be encouraged to return to town from the POC and IDP camps in Upper Nile State. Which is exactly what the Government of South Sudan, and the civilian Governor of Upper Nile State is trying to do here. The broader political implications are huge, and the State Coordinator wasted no time getting this request turned into (for the UN) quick action. Of course, an MLO team would accompany the team doing the work, to liaise with the SPLA, and to give a sense of security to the Engineer guys who would actually do the work sucking out the tank. It was just Escort duty for our MLO team.

We were to link up with the Water & Sanitation guys in their… specialty vehicle… (I referred to it throughout the afternoon as either the "Honey Wagon" or the "Shit-mobile") at 1400 hours just in front of Alpha Gate. An SPLA Liaison Officer would lead the convoy. We'd follow him, and the Engineering dudes would follow us. Except…I didn't have a point of contact or phone number for UNMISS Engineering. And when I did get the info, it was almost noon. And the number was wrong.

Remember when I once said you couldn't get hold of anyone between 1200 and 1400 hours? Yes. That happened. And that wasn't good.

Claude and I decided to be at Alpha Gate no later than 1340 hours. We had told the SPLA LO our plan, and he rolled up behind us around 1350 hours. And we waited. Then two trucks of JAKLI Force Protection showed up and stopped behind us. I walked up to the lead vehicle and spoke with the patrol commander, "Uh, Hi! What's up?"

They were tasked to come along as our protection detail.

In our planning, we specifically didn't request Force Protection— we were doing the SPLA a favour. They'd make sure nothing went sideways. I chuckled thinking about Force Protection troops using lethal force to defend a Honey Wagon. That would be awesome to read in the papers…

I gave the Indian Battalion's Operations Officer a call on my radio and let him know that I appreciated the initiative, but that we didn't need his soldiers. They could go do their own town patrol, but their presence with us would probably give the wrong impression. Ops agreed, and as I walked over to talk to the Force Protection commander, he was already on his radio getting the same message in rapid-fire Hindi. I thanked them for showing up, of course, and then off they went into town.

It was 1400 hours. And still nothing. No sign of the Engineering guys. I was getting antsy. The SPLA LO was starting to look really worried, mainly because I think he had a lot of personal credibility riding on this one task. So, what does one do? I called my boss and said that we might have a problem. Then I called The Kiwi and we decided to give it ten minutes then he'd go hunt people down.

1410 hours. Two vehicles pulled out of our gate onto the main drag and up to us…a Honey Wagon led by an SUV. They made it! The LO was visibly relieved and broke out into a wide grin. We gathered together and had a quick chat to confirm the order of march, and then we rolled out the gate and into town.

The rest of the patrol was frankly boring. I noticed that they had cleaned up a lot of the derelict cars that had littered Charlie Route and had pushed them into various courtyards…mostly out of sight. The tall grasses had been burned off from the graveyard and the sports field, and around many homes. The place was getting a Dry Season cleaning. Well, bits of the place anyway. Especially the route the VVIP would take from the airstrip into town.

Once we got to the accommodations—quite a nice place relatively speaking, with good security potential, decent fields of fire if you needed to defend it, easy to limit vehicle and personnel traffic, and so on. The two-storey house was also within sight of the SPLA Division Headquarters and they had quite a few troops to ensure that nothing bad would happen. We all looked around the courtyard and the Engineering guys opened manhole covers and hatches and determined that—yup—the septic tank was full. Completely full. They got the pump out, backed up the Shit-mobile, and most of us decided to go somewhere else—upwind seemed like a good option—to stand around and chat.

Because none of us was leaving until the Honey Wagon was full, we had nowhere to go and nothing to do. The SPLA driver—who was tall and lean, of course—started talking to me in broken English. I spoke to him in broken Arabic. His English was far better—and here's a surprising thing—while he didn't have a broad vocabulary, his pronunciation was excellent. This lad has the potential to be perfectly fluent in English. He had spent time in Khartoum as a refugee, and had been educated there, as had many of the South Sudanese diaspora. His primary spoken and written language was Arabic.

But he knew about Canada. We talked specifically about the large South Sudanese community in Alberta. Especially in Brooks. And other soldiers in the area came and joined in the conversation, including some dudes who sauntered past, AK held by the barrel and resting on the shoulder, looking with surprise at seeing a Khawaja, shaking each others' hands, and showing even more surprise at the fact that I was able to piece words together into rudimentary sentences.

And we joked around, and talked about history, and education, and how Canada has many immigrants from around the world. One of the soldiers said Canada was a great country to be so open that even black people could move there and be welcomed.

That was a different and striking perspective for me.

Our chatter—over the hour or so while the chugging of the Honey Wagon's pump told us that the work was still in progress—was unforced, honest, enjoyable communication at a basic human level. No bullshit. No agendas. No bargaining or jockeying for a power position. Just a bunch of guys hanging out and getting to know each other. That was a rare moment in this place.

The conversation ebbed and flowed depending on the topics. We talked about Malakal, the fact that I had picked up Arabic in Bentiu, and we talked about Unity State and the issues there. They wanted to know what the mission and people were like almost a decade ago. Then the driver asked me why I came back to South Sudan....

And I had to stop and think about that—why did I volunteer for this mission? Was it the money? The escape from the office routine?

The adventure? The medal? The adrenaline? These are all factors, I guess.

But the deep down, no bullshit reason is this—I like the people of this country. I liked them in 2006. I like them now. I'd like for them to benefit from the great potential here. Whether Dinka, Nuer, Shilluk, or of whatever tribe…. I've never met people of such great contrasts or such great promise. When they are good, they are everything you could want in a friend—Loyal, Happy, Caring, Funny, Hospitable, Curious, and Intelligent. But when they are bad…Oh Lord. They are the worst sort of bad. Vicious and Cruel.

The driver stood there, patiently waiting for my answer, and I told him I came back because I like the People of South Sudan. From his expression, my answer came as a surprise. I don't know what he had expected, but my response wasn't it.

We talked for a while longer, until the Engineer let us know that the container was almost full, but that the septic tank would only be half-full. We all figured that half-full was good enough and that the VVIP wouldn't be able to fill it back up in only a couple of days. We said good-byes to all, hopped in our vehicles, and slowly led the full, slopping Honey Wagon through town, past the airport, and back to camp.

Camp. State Support Base Malakal. And my container…M-22. Where there were three gold bags of stuff for me. I was in Heaven.

The four boxes I had sent myself while on leave had arrived. Food—Freeze-dried meals, snacks, pudding cups, pepperoni sticks, squeeze pouches of applesauce, cans of tuna, and spices. Maintenance supplies—Duct tape, packing tape. Useful things—US poncho liner, Magic Door to keep the flies (mostly) out.

So much food. So much snacking deliciousness. So much stuff. I have more food than I know what to do with…

Inside one of the boxes was a letter from the Canadian Forces Postal Unit…they had X-rayed my packages (distrustful bastards) and removed prohibited items. That's right. A can of Febreze and a small can of WD-40. Apparently, the cans were taken and destroyed. I bet the destruction smelled like "Fresh Linen."

Another care package was from an old Marine Corps comrade—snacks, some other goodies, and a USMC T-shirt with John Wayne's "Life is Hard. It's Harder if you're Stupid."

A small box from my Headquarters—with all sorts of great gifts, including some magazines, pictures from their Trip to Canmore, and a Thanksgiving card from a bunch of the HQ folks. Thanks!

And, from Operation Santa—a gift box for deployed troops. Filled with goodies, presents, and some decorations, too. A mixed bag of stuff and I want to wrap some of the items and give them as presents to the MLOs who are staying here over Christmas.

Tossed into the bags was a stack of Remembrance Day cards from school kids—A pile over two inches thick. I love these. Most of them are very similar in the message, a bit boring, and plain. But I read them because someone took the time to write it, and it's the least I could do. And I had plenty of time. There were some absolute gems in that pile, either special and worth keeping because there are drawings and designs and the children took the time to colour them in, or because of the joyous and hilarious simplicity of the messages…

"Thank you for sacrificing your life for me" (uh…wait a second! What?)

"Hopefully you do not die and you survive the war and see your family again" (No Shit. Me too.)

"Thank You. When I grow up I wanna be a soldger like you guys even though I'm a girl. Thank you for giving your life for us. My great grandpa did too but he died by a bomb." (Poor guy)

Fantastic and funny.

Most importantly, though…in the cargo was a case of Heineken from the fine folks in Juba. Thank God. Nothing like a cold beer or two in the evening after PT. It's a chance to socialize and relax at the end of the day…and since beer has significant nutritional value (just work with me on this), it's even more important given my limited diet (that whole lack of fresh fruit, veg, dairy, or meat thing).

My morale is high. Morale is important. Beer is importanter…

That patrol was funny as hell, and strangely satisfying. It was an amazing opportunity to engage the SPLA troops individually (when their NCOs or Officers weren't getting in the way) and get a bit of an insight into their world. The troops weren't from around Malakal—they were from Equatoria in the south of the country—so I don't know if they hated being garrisoned there. They were bored and edgy most of the time, so this chance for interaction was definitely an eye-opener for me.

Getting a gold bag was like Christmas-time every time. It lifted the spirits and made you feel so much less alone. And you could share—especially with The Kiwi—who also had his supply network of New Zealand-specific items. We could trade items and compare taste and nutritional value—most of our packages were food. Or beer. Or boxed wine.

I always referred to the box wine as "Cardbordeaux."

DAY 117

THE BREAKS IN ROUTINE

THE ELEMENT OF ROUTINE is a predictable pattern that really hasn't changed a whole lot in the past several weeks. Malakal is—by and large—peaceful. And while there are occasional bad things that happen because sometimes you can't fix stupid and soldiers will get hammered, or stoned, or start fighting, or whatever…and maybe let fly with an AK, institutionally—and this is where it counts—it's quiet. The civilian administration of Malakal is coming (or has come) back from Renk and is trying to build the conditions that will generate the confidence to pull the people out of the POC camp and get them into the town.

And while that's really, really great, and pretty darn essential (that Peace objective is the whole point, really), it means that, especially for the MLOs, we are only doing some very routine patrolling. Especially the framework patrols, which are boring as hell—it's not as if you're heading 100 kilometers outside of Malakal and you need a lot more planning, long-range radios, supplies, and recovery, and force protection to reach your objective. The normal run of the mill drives through Malakal and out to BANFRU were a little soul-crushing and it's easy to get blasé.

To be fair there are many things that require regular and mundane attention. Things that need to get done because if you don't do it, they won't happen. This also applies to personal chores and maintenance.

Dishes and cutlery, for example—some folks pay their cleaning ladies extra to do the dishes. Not me. The cleaners use the regular ablution water (non-potable) and I use drinking water for washing up. Never been a fan of intestinal parasites.

Laundry—I pay the cleaner 200 South Sudanese Pounds a month (about $12.00 Canadian) to do my laundry. Of the three or four washing machines on our living area at least two are broken at any point, and you only ever have time for laundry on weekends, and everyone has the same idea, so no matter how early you get up to find an empty machine some sneaky bastard already has a load in. And then there are higher levels of asshole laundry behaviour—someone once stopped my washing early, dumped my clothes on top of the machine, and put their own wash in. Initially mine looked okay and it was only when I was hanging the clothes up to dry that I realized they hadn't been through a rinse…I didn't bother seeking revenge (yes, that fact surprises me too.)

Here's a fun laundry factoid for South Sudan—never leave your laundry out to dry overnight. Flies can lay eggs in the seams of your clothing and in the case of some insects (the Bot fly comes to mind) they will hatch, burrow into your skin, and thrive as larvae until they exit your flesh. And I always thought the movie Aliens was an original idea…

Cooking. Washing. Shaving. Laundry. More cooking. All these little things you must do. All of these boring routine mundane time-killing and horrible little tasks made longer and more agonizingly painful by our austere existence. At least the patrols—boring as they might be sometimes—gets you out of the camp. But it's not as though you're really seeing anything interesting. "Security situation is calm but unpredictable" tends to describe it.

But occasionally, there are some breaks in the monotony, such as the superb and informative visits to the outlying Team Sites to get a sense of what the security environment looks like outside of Malakal. The opportunity to hop out on a regular resupply flight, request an additional two hours on the ground, and spend that extra time getting the lay of the land, inspecting the local camp, and getting a detailed understanding of the security and humanitarian situation is invaluable. My recent trips were eye opening and preconception-shattering in that both Melut and especially Renk (our most northern outpost in South Sudan) have markets, functioning civilian governance mechanisms, a civilian population that is not oppressed, not living in constant fear, and co-exists peacefully with the military presence. Absolutely amazing. Malakal—South Sudan's second city—isn't there yet and has a long way to go.

But talking about Renk—that patrol took a lot of flying in a Russky-contracted Mi-8 helicopter to get there, with only a couple of hours on the ground, but it was a worthwhile whirlwind tour. The town. The straight paved road that went up to the Sudan border. The briefings from the MLOs who lived there. Very informative and insightful. A whirlwind of information being fed to us—bang bang bang. It was my kind of patrol!

And the best part is that I bought bread in Renk. The delicious smallish round khubz—slightly smaller and thicker than a pita; heavy, moist, fragrant—that I used to devour in Khartoum and Bentiu years ago. Fresh from the baker. Still warm. I bought ten pieces for $0.75 Canadian. I immediately ate one and stuck the rest in my pack. I finally finished the last two almost a week later. They may have been starting to get a little moldy.

Bottom line—If your view of Upper Nile State is only based on living in Malakal, conducting the routine and dismally boring town patrols, or maybe driving to BANFRU, you are getting the wrong impression of the entire area of Upper Nile State.

Malakal town hasn't had anything exciting happen in quite a while, and it's been months since I searched for a corpse with Human Rights folks along BANFRU road. This place is slowly improving. At least it is on the eastern bank of the Nile. The west bank—with the dominant Shilluk tribe and being mostly under the control of the Opposition—has different challenges and a different dynamic.

But overall, that should be pleasing, right? That the situation is improving. That you aren't hearing shelling or rifle fire. Or looking for bad things. Or following up on abductions. Or finding bullet holes in your container one afternoon.

Of course, I'm pleased.

But lurking deep down there—in a place I sometimes don't like to think about—is a desire for excitement and confusion and a mental and physical surge when nothing is known but everything's rumoured and based on fragmented snippets of information you jump into the Land Cruiser and drive through Alpha Gate. And it's confusing for me, because when it's exciting, I wish it was boring, but when it's boring, I wish that it was exciting. Funny, isn't it? Chaos and excitement breaks up the routine—the fastball situation where Boom! You're out the door in minutes. Those patrols get the heartrate up.

For example…

A couple of days ago we got a call that the SPLA had detained a Force Protection patrol at a checkpoint in Malakal. Holy Shit! There was lots of high emotion and excitement. We were all scrambling looking for info, details, something to verify all this.

This was a very, very big deal because the Force Protection is armed and they were new and the SPLA were armed and they'd been around a long time. Sometimes it doesn't take much for tempers to rise and force to escalate and then one guy tries to be a hero and then it all goes horribly wrong. Let alone that this is a clear violation of both the UN's Freedom of Movement and the Status of Forces Agreement with the government of South Sudan.

But what did we know? Apparently, our dudes were stopped at a checkpoint. Somewhere in town. Not much to go on. Information flow was a trickle, then nothing. Silence.

Screw it, let's just go and we'll figure something out on the way—so with one of the SPLA Liaison Officers we hopped in the Nissan and barreled down the road through the main gate and along Airport Road…racing (relative to the potholes and ruts in the road) to get to town as soon as possible. No words in the SUV—we were all silently wondering what the hell had happened to cause this incident? And where? And who is holding our Force Protection? New troops? SPLA militia instead of SPLA 2 Division? Couple of drunken dudes? Who knew?

And as The Kiwi drove (I sat in the back while the SPLA LO occupied the passenger seat), the radio crackled and we started getting fed some useful information from Base. The key points were:

• The Force Protection Patrol had been released from the checkpoint and allowed to return to Malakal Base.
• The patrol would meet us in front of the airport.
• No one was hurt.

Their patrol hadn't arrived when we pulled up to the Airport in a cloud of red road dust, but they showed up a few minutes later. The patrol consisted of a couple of pickups with the troops sitting along benches set in the rear that allowed them to face outward. In the centre of the truck bed a soldier stood with a pintle-mounted Machine Gun. The young Rwandan Force Protection commander came up to us and we all shook hands. He appeared nervous but quite calm considering the circumstances. We all looked at each other for a second in silence, and then I spoke, "Okay. Tell me what happened…"

And he started talking. And it all sounded normal until he described the area he drove in, and the location where he was stopped and where they were harassed. The checkpoint location wasn't making any sense to us. The Kiwi and I looked at each other and shrugged, and the LO shared our confusion. I asked to see the Patrol Commander's map.

He didn't have one. Hmmm…. Okay. That's your first problem.

Right then, I'll draw a sketch map. We moved to the hood of the truck so I could write on something solid, and pulling out my notepad, I drew a quick overview of Malakal and area. The Base, the Airport, Airport Road, Alpha, Bravo, and Charlie Routes, China Road, Market Street…and when I drew further south, towards the edge of town…the Commander was able to point out the checkpoint location.

The LO, Kiwi and I all gave a collective "A-ha!"

It was in an area we didn't go to without prior SPLA consent. We figured—correctly—that it was an area of SPLA troop and heavier equipment concentrations. We didn't go unless there was a specific reason, and only then with authorization and with an SPLA Escort officer at the very least. And sometimes even those measures were no guarantee of not getting stopped and turned around.

We all slowly and calmly explained the Why, the Where, and the How to Not Do That Shit Ever Again to the Force Protection patrol leader. It was a miscommunication I guess, but one that could have ended quite badly. I told the Commander to come by my office for a coffee anytime and I'd show him where he could patrol without any issues. Hell, I'd even print him his own reference map.

We drove back to base and re-entered the world of The Routine…

Malakal, BANFRU/POC site, Malakal, BANFRU/POC site. Cooking, laundry, cleaning, PT. Blah blah blah. Back to Groundhog Day, where everything is the same and the only difference in the pattern is that on Saturdays the Morning Brief is an hour later and maybe if the "Hard Rock Café" camp bar has any beer, you can buy a couple on Friday night and listen to loud repetitive music. And Sunday is the day to get your stuff together for the next week and have the evening poker game. But even the occasional DAP to outlying areas gets routine, and that's surprising because I really love helicopter rides. The frustrations become routine. The bullshit about getting Flight Safety Assurances from SPLA and/or the Opposition becomes routine. And time dragged…until the next surprise.

It was a good one.

There was last week's patrol, where "UNMAS," the UN Mine Action Service came by and let us know they were heading to Malakal to pick up some Unexploded Ordnance. This could be any mines, grenades, shells, or anything explosive that hasn't exploded—we called them "UXO". Apparently, the SPLA had requested some UXO disposal expertise in town. Now, liaising with folks is what UN Military Liaison Officers are supposed to do (including yours truly), and never passing up a good chance to look at things that go Boom! we offered to come along…you know…to support. And that's what we did. We knew our SPLA Liaison Officers, we were known quantities in town, and there had been a past incident with UNMAS where they didn't bring force protection or MLOs in support and they were harassed and robbed by local troops. So, even more incentive for us to come along for the fun.

Long story short—apparently someone said there was a mine somewhere. Maybe. In the past, a "mine" has turned out to be a plastic cap with some wires on it. Or a hubcap. Or Nothing. We weren't getting our hopes up.

We drove to the suspected area with an SPLA escort (a Toyota Hi-Lux pickup painted camo with the Divisional symbol on it and half a dozen troops with AKs in the back). We finally stopped in the south end of Malakal town, introduced ourselves and chatted with a couple of the local Brigade officers, and one dude pointed to a fenced grassy area behind a house and said, "It's over there."

So, I strolled "over there" to have a look in the courtyard.

Holy fucking shit!

Scattered haphazardly in and around a hollow—possibly old fighting positions—was a wide and deadly collection of UXOs. Anti-tank mines, artillery shells, RPG rounds, boxes of ammunition, mortars, and recoilless rifle rockets. My God, things I'd only read in a book or seen during pre-deployment training, all sitting there… corroding, tossed away, deadly…and as I looked, I could see that there were more shells buried in the deeper grass, and that this area was completely strewn with ordnance. Jackpot!

Then the reality of the situation, and the significant number of shells and mortars scattered around, and the very real danger of being vaporized into a pink mist hit me. I slowly backed out of the area and let the demining guys do their thing.

We went back there two more times…to collect most of the ordnance, and then to do a controlled demolition on a hefty anti-tank mine located several klicks south of their perimeter. Seven kilograms of explosives leaves quite a crater.

That whole episode was valuable and interesting—it broke up the monotony. And then—yet again—it was back to the routine. It's just the way it goes around here.

The small breaks—the good patrols, the surprises, even the bad experiences (nerve-wracking as hell)—achieve something. They make you feel like you're adding value for achieving the mission mandate. They provide a platform where you can take advantage of the experiences (if you want to) and pass on those lessons to the next team going into the hopper. The good and bad chaotic interludes do more than just serve as a break in the routine. They make the routine tolerable. They energize you.

They make you want to go back out again.

———————————

The work with UNMAS was incredible, and I was thankful for the Explosive Threat training I'd received at the Peace Support Training Centre in Kingston prior to deployment. I had a minimum grounding in mines and explosive things, but honestly, it should have been pretty evident to the most uneducated person out there that these things were dangerous.

It was, it seems, the season of finding shit that went Boom. Because the locals burned the fields every year (to help the crops) a lot of UXO were discovered after the grass was burned off. Many of them were fused—meaning they were fired and didn't explode when they hit the ground, or maybe they'd been fused and dropped before they could be launched, but they were dangerous and deadly. And a fire had rolled over them, which couldn't have helped their stability.

It was a bit of a circus when the local troops realized that we were looking for mines and mortar bombs and stuff and would take them off their hands. One SPLA dude started running at me holding a fused mortar bomb in each hand (they were pointing downward) with an ecstatic "look what I found, Dad!" expression on his face. Panicked, I put both hands up in a "Stop" gesture, then lowered my hands to indicate to him that he should put the bombs down very gently (and flat on the ground).

I laughed about it later.

DAY 127

ESCAPE FROM MALAKAL

I'M IN ENTEBBE.

Happy Boxing Day! The beer is cold. It's sitting in front of me now. It's a Nile Special…half liter size. Dark brown bottle. Cold. Did I mention that? Condensation and beads of moisture on the bottle, and on the glass when it's poured.

Yes. Entebbe…calm. Peaceful. Nothing to do but Nothing. Especially while on leave. I stare at the blank screen wondering why I don't feel like writing.

It isn't that there aren't stories to write. There are, and good ones, but the urge and the compulsion to write something is waning today. It shouldn't be too much of a surprise I guess, since after four months Groundhog Day has become the norm, and while the differences are fun, and zany, and keep me wanting to go out the door, the small things don't seem noteworthy, because I live it every single day.

And maybe it's that I'm relaxing right now and part of this might be processing the past few weeks. There is so much to tell—the small things, the petty annoyances, the things I take for granted—and maybe it's not that I don't want to write, it's more likely the case that I don't know where to start. The enormity of what I want to tell is slightly paralyzing. More to the point, I want to give a real view of what I'm doing here, and it's not all exciting.

I guess I don't want to bore you.

There are a couple of fun anecdotes or short tales…let's share those. The shit stories can wait for another day, because they will need to be told,

Okay, blank screen. Game On. We'll order one more beer and then we'll dive in…

ESCAPE FROM MALAKAL

As I have learned in my several months of travel in South Sudan… the first truth is to give yourself extra time in case of delays. This is essential. Especially when you're going on leave.

So, my plan was—22 December departure from Malakal to Juba. 23 December was National Administration at Canada House. 24 December—Fly to Entebbe. But why would I want to spend Christmas alone in Entebbe? Believe me, I didn't. But because of the holidays, the UN flight to Entebbe on the 24th was the very last flight until the 29th. And that just wasn't going to do, not at all! And that pre-supposes all the flights are on time, mechanically sound, etc. Oh, and that war or something doesn't break out. So even if there was a delay of 24 hours, or maybe even more, I'd be okay to get to Entebbe.

The second truth is to always pack accordingly. Especially with food and water—going to South Sudan? Bring Snacks! By the way, "accordingly" means for the worst-case scenarios. Well, maybe not worst…but definitely second or third worst.

Look, if there is a delay for 24 hours, and we are stuck in the middle of nowhere and have no access to food, I will likely help feed you (with maybe a cracker or something), not only because I'm a kind and generous guy, but also because I don't want to hear your stomach rumbling beside me or feel your eyes hungrily following the spoon as I scarf down a Canadian ration pack of Montreal Smoked Meat (which is awesome by the way).

You don't plan ahead? My friend, you don't eat. And don't think I can't be a cold, heartless bastard when it comes to food.

Sorry. I digress. I do that a lot.

So—back to the flight leaving Malakal …with check-in at 0930 hours. I was at MOVCON early with all my stuff. The flight was (of course) delayed. MOVCON dude would give us updates on our radios as information was available.

1030 hours—delayed some more. "Come back at 1245 hours." Screw this—I went back to my container to make lunch and have a nap. Woke up, went back to the waiting area.

1245 hours—More and more delays. "Maybe 1400 hours. Plane is still on the tarmac in Juba." Wait wait wait. Listen to tunes. Fidget.

1430 hours— "Flight cancelled. Come to MOVCON and grab your luggage." Bloody hell.

1431 hours— "STOP!" We all listened attentively "Maybe the flight is not cancelled. Exercise patience and we will let you know".

1445 hours—OK. Still waiting. Maybe someone somewhere pulled a horseshoe out of their ass, and a magical aircraft will appear. Or will it?

It did.

Twenty of the passengers (based on priority) were now taking a helicopter to Juba. I was number five. Yee Haw! I broke all speed records racing back to MOVCON.

Our weight limit was now 15 kilograms instead of 20 kilograms (Jesus Christ please don't weigh my small pack…It's seriously loaded down!) So, an Mi-8 ride with just me and 19 of my closest friends jammed like sardines inside. With our luggage placed in the centre of the aircraft and held down with a cargo net.

Flight time of two and a half hours. Dear God, it was agonizing.

Most of us listened to tunes, or watched a movie on their tablet, or dozed…I went with the "tunes and snooze" option and listened to some Philip Boa and the Voodooclub—a brilliant band, by the way. There was almost no room between my feet and the luggage in front of me, so I rested my small pack flat like a pillow, leaned forward as much as possible, and napped for minutes at a time. And sweated. And became very aware of being pressed up against my neighbours because we were so tightly crammed together. Agony. Lower back hurt. Legs cramped. Loud whup whup whup of the blades.

A bit turbulent. I was hoping that the dude beside me didn't throw up. We had spoken earlier in the day, and he mentioned he was a nervous flyer and got sick quite easily. In turn, I mentioned that I was a sympathetic puker—if someone hurls near me, I'm not far behind. We laughed about it at the time because we were on the ground, and I certainly didn't expect to be flying beside him. He probably felt the same way.

When we did finally land in Juba (vomit free, thankfully) and after being jammed together for hours, with no ability to move or stretch, we stumbled and staggered out of the Mi-8 like old arthritic men until our legs uncramped. It must have been quite a sight for the folks at the terminal to witness. But, despite the stiffness in our joints, we were smiling like crazy. We had made it! We were in Juba and the first step of our various journeys was now complete. For some of my Malakal friends, we shared a handshake, a warm hug, and a "Merry Christmas, brother" before we parted ways.

My pickup from our National Support Element was ready for me at the Terminal, and we drove to Canada House…a veritable oasis. My home away from home. For a day anyway.

The 23rd was spent doing laundry, relaxing, going out for pizza at the Rainbow Hotel (I ordered the Veggie Pizza with Extra Meat—yes. It's a real thing) with a friend of mine, and eventually sleeping. Sleep is never over-rated. I love sleep. I just tended not to sleep soundly in Malakal. When I slept anywhere else, I slept well. This was despite the panicked wakeups in the middle of the night "where the hell am I and is that a light? What happened? Was there a sound? Okay, okay, calm down. You're in Juba. Go back to sleep."

One funny example was the night of the 23rd, after I'd handed in my pistol to the Ops Officer that day (because I can't take it with me on leave, obviously). I had one of those snapped awake heart-racing moments because I didn't feel the pistol under my pillow, and I freaked out in my dreams because I thought I'd lost it somewhere…

Yes. That's funny all right.

On the 24th, things were smooth-ish, apart from showing up several hours too early for check-in at MOVCON, which meant a ride back to Canada House so I could hang out and enjoy the awesome bandwidth for a few more hours. For once, I am not being sarcastic. The bandwidth is freaking brilliant compared to pretty much anywhere else I've been in Africa.

Around noon, I got a drive back to MOVCON and checked-in within five minutes. If you have ever experienced the UNMISS terminal in Juba, you'll know that's a damn miracle. It was amazing. There were no issues at all. No line up, no crowds, nothing. And it would be great if there was a bar, or a lounge, or something other than a big container to hang out it. The waiting area had a TV playing some blurry, obscure, and random show in one corner (might have been a TV station from Sudan), and a coffee bar (which makes a damn fine Americano and sells vouchers for a trickle of Wi-Fi) but not actual alcohol-serving bar. There weren't many passengers that day. We all sat and waited. And waited. And waited. If you didn't have something to distract you—like a book or tunes—you would likely go quite mad.

Part of the delay is that all our UN ID cards and passports were collected at check-in and brought over in bulk to South Sudanese Customs for stamping. Sometimes it takes a while. They have a lot of things to do, after all (doubtful). But you aren't going to leave unless you have your ID and passport, right?

I didn't know anyone on the Entebbe manifest, so I sat quietly, listened to music, and burrowed into my thoughts. Eventually I stepped outside to an open waiting area that was fenced-in but covered with corrugated iron sheets. At least I could look at airport stuff going on. This open area led to the apron and boarding area. Growing impatient, I kept looking at my watch.

Eventually, UN airport staff drove up in a van and started yelling people's names and handing out passports. We boarded. We took off. And as we climbed over Juba, as has happened every time in the past, the weight lifted from my chest and shoulders. I stretched my arms and took a deep breath.

The arrival into Entebbe, the customs stamping, and luggage collection was very smooth, followed by a quick cab-ride to the Lake Heights Hotel (which I highly recommend) and an easy check-in with friendly staff. I dumped my kit in the very clean and modern room and had a quick look round the hotel before I zoomed up to the rooftop bar. A bar that has a great view of Lake Victoria, and an amazing menu. Large portions, delicious fruits and veggies (kick-ass salads!) ….and beer. And the beer is cold. And good. And cheap. I'm prone to the Nile Special.

THE DRY SEASON

I want to talk about Malakal for a bit, mainly because the dry season has kicked in and there are differences from when I arrived there. Certainly, the biggest change is in the nighttime and morning temperatures.

Mornings are cold! Seriously chilly. Around 16 degrees Celsius, and maybe even less if there's a decent breeze. It's strangely smile-making to open the door every morning and realize that it is cold outside. It's dark too. Really dark. Doesn't start brightening until around 0645-0700 hours…

As I once said, I'm up at 0545 or earlier every morning. And for some reason my internal clock—intestinal clock might be a more accurate term—gives me a warning around 0600. So, donning some clothes, socks, boots, and a t-shirt…grabbing the essentials (including a flashlight), I dash over to the ablution container. At 0600, it's dark! The dogs aren't so fond of the cooler weather, and rather than curl up in the road beside my container, they seem to have found another place to sleep.

Oh—and there was a cull of the dogs some weeks ago. Poisoned. That's another reason why I don't see as many dogs now. Well, I saw a few dead ones. And one that was in the earlier stages of poisoning—poor thing was frothing at the mouth, stumbling, and trying to defecate. It's not pleasant to see, but it's necessary. But I think they killed Sparky the Wonder-Dog.

The race to the ablutions is always rushed, with a certain sense of gastric urgency. The stroll back to my container isn't rushed at all. I enjoy the cool weather feeling. The goosebumps on my arms. The cool crisp air, free from the smells of dust and burning garbage. It's wonderful. You can actually breathe!

More importantly, the cool temperatures keep down the many stinks and odours for the mornings anyway. But by mid-afternoon the temperatures are back to the mid-30s or more, and the dust is up, especially if there is a breeze, and the combined smells of staleness, unwashed bodies, garbage, and stagnation permeate the air.

But for an hour or so, it's glorious.

RESUPPLY

Finally, there was what I call the "Angel of Mercy" flight. That was a lot of fun, and it was a laugh and it's surreal. Which fits the bill for entertainment in Malakal.

One night a couple of months ago, when I was in Juba to vote in the Canadian Federal Election, we had karaoke night at the

Task Force Commander's accommodation in the Canada House compound. Yes. Karaoke. Don't judge me.

It was a lot of fun, especially because I only do one karaoke song ("Mac the Knife" a la Bobby Darin—Remember, you aren't supposed to judge) and Mark, our National Support Operations Officer, tried to sing Eminem's "Without Me." For the most part, it was good clean fun and we had a lot of laughs. One of the visitors is Canadian, and a pilot for an International Organization. Val was a hoot—she sang karaoke with the best of us, was very entertaining, and got along very well with everyone (which is important). I asked about her work and the type of plane she flew and what got her started in aviation—I've always been fascinated by flying and she was a wealth of knowledge. Fun night. We even let her try on the boss's helmet and flak jacket. So—Meet Val. Canadian Pilot in South Sudan (her second time here!)

While chatting briefly a few weeks later, Val mentioned she was flying into Malakal. Me—joking around—asked her if she could bring me a beer. As an additional part of the discussion, I mentioned that the Base was only a few kilometers away, and if she was ever delayed at the airport, we'd make sure she would be taken care of at the camp. It isn't as if we have a whole lot of Canadians kicking around South Sudan, and we take care of our own!

I had talked about maybe bringing her a coffee, because Malakal Airport remains closed due to ongoing renovations caused by civil war and chaos. Calling it an airport now is a joke. It's an airstrip. The buildings are unused, plundered, and derelict. There are no functioning systems—no tower, no ILS, no crash response, nothing.

On the day Val was to fly in, The Kiwi and I had a patrol on the go that day in Malakal town and farther south—mainly supporting the de-miners as they detonated an anti-tank mine. But I let her know that if we got back to the base early enough, at the very least we'd stop by and see if she was still around.

We supported the demining thing with no issues at all—the mine blew up as planned with a rather satisfying Boom and large plume of smoke—and once the mission was complete, we drove up Alpha Route back into town, along Market Street where we dropped off our SPLA escort so he could have lunch, then up Charlie Route to Airport Road.

As we were pulling up to the airport, we saw the tail of an airplane behind the perimeter trees…not a big Ilyushin or Antonov cargo aircraft, but a smaller prop-driven plane.

"Yes, that's Val's number on the tail, let's pull in and say Hi."

We turned a final corner around the abandoned terminal building and could see the plane sitting alone on the apron. We backed the Nissan into a convenient gap about 100 meters or so from the aircraft and switched our engine off.

We noticed the force protection cordon around the plane. Seemed odd, somehow. We looked more closely and then did a quick double take—What the hell? The Force Protection wasn't UN, it was SPLA.

They had a ring of soldiers around the aircraft. What the hell is going on? The soldiers were facing out, away from the plane. That's a good sign. But they had surrounded it—Why? And there were a lot more soldiers than usual kicking around the airstrip.

So, we're thinking "Hey. Maybe they don't want a couple of MLOs just waltzing over to the plane." However, if there was a problem, we absolutely needed to find out what's up. As we sat for a second and pondered the options, we saw Val standing by a group of UN civvies. She waved, reached into the cockpit, talked to her co-pilot, and strolled over to our vehicle past the cordon of troops.

Well, it would be rude to sit here cowering in our Nissan. Out we went and met her on the tarmac mid-way between the plane and our SUV. Quick introductions of Val to The Kiwi. Of course, we asked about the SPLA guys, "What the hell is happening?"

Val explained that she was dropping off some women who had been separated for months from their families, and they were all being reunited in the Malakal POC camp. Through a miscommunication, the SPLA thought that she was dropping off some injured soldiers who had completed their recovery. Some pretty major wires got crossed…and the troops, perplexed that elderly woman instead of their comrades got off the plane, asked Val "Where are our Soldiers? Did you kill them?" Yes. Because that is exactly what humanitarian agencies do. Especially the Red Cross. We laughed and shook our heads in disbelief.

With that detail out of the way, some more typical chatting ensued—how was Juba, how was everything, what are the Christmas plans, what's the security situation, and so on? The SPLA guys kept staring at us and were looking confused, and I guess we had been talking for some time. Quickly, and without ceremony, Val handed me a small plastic bag.

"Sorry, I only got you four." she said with a smile. Only a Canadian would apologize for not bringing enough beer!

She wouldn't accept any money for the beverages because I think she just loved the idea of bringing a gift to another Canadian in the middle of nowhere. Grinning, I thanked her, ripped the velcro Canadian flag off my shirt, and handed it to her as a token of appreciation. With that, she said a quick goodbye to us, smiled, turned, and walked back to the aircraft through the ring of gawking SPLA troops.

We went back to the vehicle and returned to the base. The beverages went into the fridge. I shared them that night with The Kiwi (of course).

And that's how I got the Red Cross to bring me beer.

———————————

Getting out of Malakal was always an adventure—something always went wrong, there was always a delay, there was always solid reason to panic and expect that all my careful travel plans would be chucked out the window. This was the worst delay and I'm so happy that someone used their initiative to get us (well, mainly me) the hell out of there!

There is a lot to love about Entebbe. I enjoyed the history, the feeling of safety, and especially the fact that I didn't have to have the same level of apprehension that I did in Malakal or Juba. The tourist accommodations are first rate, and since it was a place I could relax, it was easier to sit back and write with a bit of distance from the day-to-day activities at the Team Site.

As for Val—Several weeks after this story took place, some random SPLA dude fired an RPG at her plane as she took off from Malakal. Never got reported. No one took any action. Just another day.

She eventually left South Sudan and still follows her love of flying.

DAY 145

HELLO! HELLO! IT'S GOOD TO BE BACK

I'M BACK IN MALAKAL for the home stretch. Put one foot in front of the other, keep the head down, and don't focus on the finish line.

I flew back to base on Monday after an outstanding leave in Uganda. It was a two-week extravaganza that included a couple of days in Entebbe (Oh Favorite City of East Africa!) at the Lake Heights Hotel. Yes, this is a shameless plug for a hotel where you will likely never ever stay, but if you are ever in Entebbe, spend the coin. The service is first-rate by any standards, the Wi-Fi in the rooms is fantastically stable, the food portions are massive (even for North Americans) and the food flavour is remarkable. Chef is a genius. Finally, the view of Lake Victoria from the top floor bar/restaurant is superb, with a cooling breeze to make the evenings even more comfortable.

The holiday started at the Lake Heights—a couple of days to de-jetlag for Jacqueline after her insanely long flight from Canada—followed by a week-long safari in southwest Uganda, and a couple of final days in Entebbe to relax before her return to Canada, and mine to South Sudan.

It was brilliant. Simply brilliant.

But this isn't a travel monologue, although the leave certainly started that way—the whole trip was to really see the wild animals (and the not so wild ones, since they'd been habituated) but it quickly turned into a series of conversations and rewarding human interactions. Political discussions (upcoming Uganda election in February), education, the past troubles and future potential for

Uganda, of stories and histories. It became a trip where the human factor was primary, within which the natural scenery and fauna served as an essential background. But make no mistake. The animals were magnificent, and numerous. But there were only a couple of moments that really stood out, and I'll talk about those as we get farther into the story.

But first, an interlude…

As I was about to start writing tonight, there was frantic banging on my door. I unlocked and opened it and peered out into the darkness. One of my mates was standing in the shadows in front of my container. I leaned out of the open door… "Hey Brother, what's up?"

"Here. Hold onto this." and he passed me a loaded AK-47 and a bandolier of four magazines.

"Get inside," I said.

We quickly stepped into my cabin. As I removed the mag and cleared the weapon, he smiled with embarrassment and explained, "My friend is really drunk and stupid right now and I don't want him to have it. I'll pick it up tomorrow morning."

"Sure, mate. No problem. Enjoy the rest of your evening."

Just another night in Malakal.

Back to the story…

ON SAFARI—FIELDCRAFT

You civilians suck at fieldcraft.

No offence meant—well, that's not true—but you stamp and stomp and get caught on vines high and low and Jesus, if there was a branch to step on and break, you'd break it. You all sounded like a herd of Elephants. No, Pachyderms would be quieter, and so would drunk circus clowns. Also, you're lucky there were no trip wires because you would have found them with the same unerring accuracy that allowed you to find every single ground vine. If this was a Patrol School course, I would have failed every single one of you on your complete lack of noise discipline.

Frankly, you are all terrible.

We went chimpanzee trekking. I cringed and tried not to lose my mind watching the tourists' "Shhhh. Be very stealthy, we are going to find chimpanzees" gong-show. Thankfully, nobody was wearing camouflage—I was sporting a robin-egg blue shirt, for example—and most folks had reasonable footwear, which is critical for trekking around the hills. Our guide was in dark green. With an AK. It was actually a Chinese Type 56. And the safety was on. Yes, I checked. I notice details like that.

The day started at 0545 with my alarm. Neither of us had slept well—different bed, lifeless pillows, claustrophobic mosquito netting, and unique sounds. My alarm roused me, and with a weary groan I rolled over, grabbed a headlamp, and scanned the floor (don't want to step on a slithery thing), found the two overlapping sheets of the mosquito net, and spread them to step out into the room. Making my way to the light switches, I clicked them repeatedly, and apart from clicking, nothing. There was no power. That's a reality on safari. We had a lantern, and I had a headlamp and a couple of flashlights. And I'm used to doing ablutions in the darkness.

The cottage at the Chimpanzee Lodge in Kibale was beautiful, pristine, and something out of a movie from the British Colonial era. Our place—self-contained for the most part—was a thatched cottage with a large bed in the single room covered by an overarching white net, a wardrobe (sort of) and a tiny bathroom with western-style commode and a small shower. Water was heated a few meters away from an elevated clay tower about two meters high. The water reservoir was on top, and underneath was a wood-fired opening. The staff would get the fire going—heat the water—water goes to a reservoir near the bathroom—and Hey Presto! Hot water in the morning (After a few minutes of running the tap.)

All this was done in the morning—I showered with the lantern sitting on the (closed) toilet seat, and the hot water was glorious. Feeling much cleaner, I put on my pants, socks, t-shirt, long sleeve shirt, and boots. While I was prepping my kit in the main room, Jacqueline was in the shower and getting herself ready for the day. Same deal—high socks, shoes, long shirt. Wanted to avoid the mosquitos, ants, ticks, and any other ground-based bitey things. We had DEET cream and bug spray. We used them both liberally. And we took our daily Malarone pills, of course. Because malaria sucks.

We did these actions in the semi-dark. With lantern and flashlights. Army-guys chuckle mockingly at this, because we can do damn near anything in pitch black, while hungry and sleep-deprived. When civvies can do this without completely falling apart, it's pretty damn impressive. Jacqueline did very well.

Brekky at 0630 was awesome. And too much. And if there's a complaint I could make about all the food and meals I've had in Uganda…there is too much damn food. Seriously, the portion sizes are more than I can handle. Which might be me drawing a false conclusion after four months in South Sudan, but I couldn't finish the meal. Where I come from, that's a sin.

And believe me, the quality was superb—the fruits are local (mango, pineapple, banana) and are like nothing you have tasted back home—fresh, succulent, firm, perfect. The bread was homemade, freshly yeasty, and aromatic, and heavy…the way bread should be. The eggs richly yellow and scrambled. A feast.

We scarfed down the food, and Morris (our guide) was ready to roll, so we hopped into the Land Cruiser and drove along bumpy, red-earthed roads. These paths were strangely reminiscent of South Sudan, except that here there were tall trees and forests, interspersed with tea estates—the leaves short and brightly green, and palm trees, pineapples, mango trees, and vibrant and lush greens and flower colours across the hills. Unfamiliar birdsong echoed around us. Even the breeze was fragrant with flowery scents and a peppery, leafy smell. Lingering everywhere, though, especially while on the roads, was a scent of dust. Red, ochre-coloured dust. A fine powder, which penetrated windows and air-conditioners to rest in your skin, hair, eyes, and nostrils.

After less than an hour of driving, we arrived at the chimpanzee centre, and after signing in, received a quick briefing. This friendly chat involved a large amount of common sense—don't surround the animals, keep your distance, don't mimic their vocalizations, and so on. Basically, all the things that remind you that these are not cartoon characters, and if provoked they will rip your face off.

In my early-morning wandering imagination I thought of chimps in bow ties and tuxedo jackets, balancing silver platters, wandering the grounds and offering us martinis. For this ridiculous image, I blame a childhood spent watching far too much cartoon television. And seriously, who would even think that this could be remotely realistic? No one drinks martinis that early.

And then, mid-briefing, The Americans showed up. Late and Loud. Everyone visibly cringed. There were valid reasons for this. First, someone was actually wearing a pith helmet. Secondly, they were louder than shit through our introductory briefing.

"Let me tell ya, Phil…I didn't even hear ya get up this morning, Har Har Har!"

One of the German tourists had enough of their behaviour and publicly jacked them up for their rudeness, lateness, and volume. The Americans quieted down for the rest of the briefing.

No offence, America, but you need to seriously screen who is allowed to leave your country. These folks were The Ugly Americans. In khaki. With a pith helmet. (Where the hell did they even find that?)

Anyway, after the briefing, we broke into smaller groups, led by a guide with an AK, and stumped, stamped, and crackled our way into the jungle to find Chimps. There was no way we could have snuck up on them—they would have heard us several hundred meters away.

The hiking was fantastic. The foliage was green and butterflies of vibrant yellow and red and green hues flitted between the leaves. The trees themselves were tall, so tall, more than ten meters high, but interspersed with this were lower canopied trees, shrubs, and vines. They made the forest a dim, damp, but very alive place.

And I flashed back to my decades-old Infantry training, and all the other places I'd experienced where being in the woods meant listening and thinking more tactically. I walked differently—lift the feet, move around the small saplings, duck under vines, use the back of the hands and arms to move branches out of the way so you don't grab thorns, look all around. And none of my efforts mattered. Because everyone else was crunching and stomping…Sigh.

Damn, you are all so loud.

But we finally saw the chimpanzees. In the trees. Quite high up in the fig trees and we stood there looking. The other groups came up to look too and with their cameras and massive freaking lenses they snapped a zillion pictures and as the chimps moved we manoeuvred to find better spots to see them.

The chimps were quite wonderful to look at—a dominant male,

a female with a baby on her back, an adolescent wandering around. Sometimes we'd hear fruit falling down the layers of leaves and branches as the chimps were finished eating them…and we made an effort to stay out of the way to avoid getting brained with a pit. Occasionally there would be a sound of rushing leaves, sounding like rainfall, and in the sunlight filtering through the leaves you'd see a mist. You would hear the patter of water as it fell from one layer of leaves to a lower layer, and finally to the lowest foliage. Chimps have large bladders, it seems.

After an hour or so, our necks were stiff from craning upwards, always upwards, but this was a community that had been habituated to tourists…after an hour or more, first one, than another chimp clambered down trees. They stayed high enough for safety, checking us out. Maybe two meters off the ground, three to four meters distance. Looking at us, and us looking at them. They were calm, but they go through this routine every day.

Then one dropped down to the ground. Then another. The tourists went crazy with the cameras clicking (no flashes thank God) like Paparazzi. Getting closer, filming, moving, better angle, better picture.

I wanted to scream, "Stop! You're missing everything!"

The battery in my camera had died a bit earlier, and I was strangely thankful for that. Because rather than burrow into a viewfinder, I could really observe the activity from a broader perspective and appreciate it even more. We had wild primates within three meters of us. Why not study them? Look at what they did? Look at the black-grey of their fur? Enjoy their facial expressions? See how they interacted with each other? Wasn't that the whole point?

I took some awesome pics on my smartphone because they were close enough and it was convenient. But the rest of the time, I stood back looking at the behaviour of both the chimps and the other tourists. They did their thing, sat, ate, rolled on their back occasionally, and then moved on (the chimps, not the tourists). Finally, having had enough, they effortlessly climbed a couple of trees, and disappeared from our view into the high leaves.

It was an Experience. And it was Magnificent.

That was the start of it. More than a week in Uganda that

explored some of the natural beauty, the animals, the tourism, the roads, the villages. A small glimpse into a country that—we used to joke with many locals—most North Americans only know from the movie "Last King of Scotland."

ON SAFARI—KASENYI SAFARI CAMP

No-one likes to tell you that a lot of your time on "safari" is spent in a bumpy vehicle on poor roads—from dusty and rutted sometimes to paved and occasionally smooth-ish—spent in silence looking at the scenery zip along beside you. Villages (which are usually poor) interspersed with towns and small cities (which are slightly less poor) slide past you one after another.

Usually, the market area lines both sides of the main street, and you can see everything from bicycles to beef carcasses on a butcher hook, to old tires, to fruits and vegetables, bright in colour, laid out carefully in symmetrical piles. Tomato, mango, beans, jackfruit, pineapple, bananas, potatoes, and much more. A rich soil, with enough rain to maintain the fertility throughout the growing season.

We stopped at the Equator to take pictures. Standing with one foot on each hemisphere. Joking around. Fun times.

The safari camp—which contains many more permanent structures than the name might suggest—was set up just at the border of the park, overlooking a saltpan crater lake. Higher altitude and much drier. Reminiscent in some ways of the Southwestern United States…sun-bleached animal skulls adorned the walls. Cacti that were the size of large trees. Bleached wood. Dry and damn hot in the searing sun.

Because there was no fence or barrier between the park and the camp, the animals didn't realize that Queen Elizabeth Park ended and regular human habitation began. For our safety, between sundown and sunrise, we had to be escorted from our tents to the main lodge by a guard with an AK. While the local fauna recognized that we are the top of the food chain during the day, the nighttime reality is slightly different. You do not wander at night. Things will easily hunt, kill, and eat you.

Set on the slope of a hill, our tents were enclosed by a high mud wall with a wooden door, high and secure enough to prevent entry by wild animals. The tents were technically "Tents", but within the tent was a king-sized bed, a permanent bathroom with shower, and a patio which was high enough that at night you could stand outside and hear or maybe even see nocturnal animals (I spotted a Cape buffalo on the second night). It was damn opulent—with a solar lighting system so that you would always have some interior lighting twenty-four hours a day. There was a trickle of Wi-Fi at a hotspot by the bar (how convenient!)

Two points stand out here at Kasenyi—the encounter with a lion, and the Safari Camp owner.

We briefly met the owner after we checked in. The camp had only been in operation for just over a year, but it was brilliantly laid out. The amenities were excellent if a bit austere. Paul was pleasant, engaging, and promised to chat with us at dinner. But first, we had an afternoon game drive planned.

Our guide was extremely well trained, with excellent eyesight and an innate ability to know where the animals were or were most likely to be. He had worked for decades with the Uganda Wildlife Authority prior to being a tour-guide, and I suspect this is where a lot of his knowledge was acquired. We set out on a tan-brown, dusty road to see what we could see…and the area was rich with wildlife. Many different birds, a couple of warthogs, the ubiquitous Dik-dik (a small antelope weighing maybe six kilograms), and a couple of hippos wallowing in a muddy patch of soil. We kept driving and circling for something more interesting.

The Lion was resting, head cradled in his foreleg, in the boughs of a cactus-like tree. Morris had spotted him from a distance, and we took the Land Cruiser off-track to approach the tree and get a better look. We drove to within five meters of the tree, and I stood up in the open top of the vehicle to look more closely. Initially, the lion's head was hidden by his foreleg and massive paw, but sensing our presence, he lifted his head and looked up and over to the left and right before settling his gaze on us.

I had the camera out and zoomed in to capture his face as he looked around. When he turned his head to look back at me, I was held frozen in fascination. Such power. Such confidence. Such majesty. And completely Free…and gazing at me just meters away. Spectacular.

I can't explain why this particular experience mattered so much. But it did. It was the single best moment of the safari. We returned to the camp, happier for what we had been lucky to see.

Getting to know Paul, the owner, was an unexpected and pleasant surprise. He fled Uganda in 1979 after Idi Amin's ouster, settled in the US, worked hard, and got into the ground floor of the biotech industry in 1981. Over the next few decades, he advanced professionally, raised a family, and became the epitome of the American Dream. Then, upon retirement, moved back to Uganda, purchased land, and built the Safari Camp.

He and I talked about the differences and similarities between Uganda's and South Sudan's past, political issues, ethnic-tribal issues, history, and many other topics. And in these few hours of conversations at the bar, some interesting conversational threads were woven.

One of the first was the actual story of Uganda during the Amin regime. Paul was quite open about discussing this country's troubled past. The disappearances. The friends and family members abducted and never seen again. The horror of the State Research Bureau, where thousands were tortured and killed. It was a tragic time.

The second was his interest in South Sudan. The history, the land, the descriptions of Malakal and the differences I'd observed between my first and second deployments. At one point in our discussion, Paul said, "I'd like to invest there." And I (understandably, I think) responded with a bit of surprise and skepticism. He was the first person who ever talked about investing in South Sudan, maybe setting up a lodge in the Malakal area. I told him that I was a bit taken aback—it was a bit premature to be doing that sort of thing, wasn't it?

"John," he said, smiling. "It took decades for the strong investment in Uganda to happen. Look at it now. Give them time."

I appreciated that statement and his perspective very much. I was looking at the past in Upper Nile State, and I was certainly focused on the present. While we discussed an abstract future for that country, we never really thought of it in terms beyond the timelines of the current peace agreement. Here was a man who thought positively and with a longer-term vision. And he's right—maybe not this generation. Maybe not even the next generation. But maybe the one after that? There's hope, I suppose.

The final point was made during our frequent discussions on South Sudanese culture. We talked about the history and the different factors and potential barriers to a successful and enduring peace. I asked him a pointed question—how did he see himself? By tribe or nationality?

"I am a Ugandan," he responded. That is an important statement.

My view for South Sudan is that when national identity supersedes tribal affiliations…when Murle, Fertit, Bari, Dinka, Nuer, Shilluk, and the many other tribes see themselves as South Sudanese first, and tribal second, we will see progress in that country.

ON SAFARI—PUCE

The last night of safari, we stayed outside Kampala at a very eclectic resort hotel on Entebbe Road. While talking with the owner of the lodge, we met an elderly Belgian man who had recently retired, was recently divorced, and who was planning to live permanently at the lodge. The last decades had been successful for his career, but not for his health. Having grown up in what is now Rwanda and Uganda, where his father was a doctor and expert on tropical medicines, he was determined to move back to Africa for his remaining years.

In his short time in East Africa, his health had improved significantly. Better flexibility, better diet, less discomfort, reduced medication. The climate was a tonic for his chronic pain…

Yves had a vision and a dream to save chimpanzees. And he told us this story from his youth, more than 70 years ago…

As I noted, he had grown up in Africa, and his mother had taken in an orphaned baby chimpanzee. Naturally, over time, the chimp became habituated to people, lived in the house with Yves, his parents and sister, and was greatly loved. The chimp was a member of the family and was Yves' best friend. They named the young chimp Puce, and she thrived with her adopted humans.

Then the family made ready to return to Belgium for several months of home leave. They could not take Puce to Europe, and she didn't understand that they would be returning in a matter of months. So, the family departed for home, leaving Puce in the good care of a trusted friend.

From the first day she was alone, Puce wouldn't eat. She used to sleep with a blanket and would cast it aside every night, several times a night. The caretaker would sleep near her and replace the blanket as often as possible. He would hand Puce her food and she would reject it. Within days, she died.

At this point, The Belgian, eyes welling with tears as he told us this story, broke down sobbing. He stopped, flushed and embarrassed—removed his glasses and wiped his eyes—and apologized for his emotion. For his entire life, he had never forgiven himself. Puce had chosen to die because his family had abandoned her. She died of a broken heart.

Yves' desire was to create a charity that would save abandoned chimpanzees, rehabilitate them somehow, do something for them. He would call it the Puce Foundation.

I hope he succeeds. He deserves that.

MALAKAL—AGAIN

After all those adventures, it was time to return to Malakal. To get through the next few weeks and start thinking about thinning out the container, contemplate my handover notes, and send baggage back to Juba. Also, to continue to perform the usual duties of a Military Liaison Officer, even up to the final days.

It sucks to be back, but not as difficult as when I returned from Canada in November. Maybe knowing it is near my end of mission date that makes it easier to endure…and it is just a matter of endurance.

This whole damn mission has been about endurance.

I flew from Entebbe to Juba on a UN flight with two fresh and sparkly-new Canadians who were going to be working at UNMISS HQ in Juba. Good guys and we spent hours talking about the mission from my hilariously sarcastic perspective. Juba for the weekend was Juba. Nothing new or surprising. Retrieve my pistol. Have a couple of beer, lots of sleep, lots of time by the water reservoir (pool).

My flight to Malakal from Juba was—due to a technical issue with the aircraft (it was damaged and being replaced)—via another Mi-8 helicopter. It was a lot less fun than when I flew from Malakal to Juba, mainly because I was going the other way and I knew that

Malakal wasn't going to be a zany thrill-ride of awesome-ness. My guts twisted as I flew back up-country.

I landed at the Base, went through the usual routine of grabbing baggage and accessories at MOVCON, and strolled over to the MLO offices to say Hi to the Team. Kei, our female South Korean MLO, was so happy to see me she ran up to give me a big hug. I think she surprised herself because she then stepped back, bowed, and shook my hand more formally. She had managed the Operations shop by herself for almost a week, ever since The Kiwi had departed for his leave, and it clearly had been a bit hectic for one person to manage. Normally four people are engaged in Ops duties.

"Hey! I'm back! What's new?"

Oh…the usual…

A grenade had gone off inside a pickup truck outside the camp on Saturday. Several dead and injured.

An unattended cooking fire inside the POC site led to a massive conflagration that displaced over 1,000 people and resulted in numerous burn injuries and the death of a toddler.

And a guy just handed me a loaded AK to keep it away from a crazy-drunk dude.

Ya baby, I'm back.

The holiday was brilliant. But apart from the natural amazing beauty, the hospitality of the Ugandans, and the wildlife, it was the engagement and interaction with people that made this trip so special. You learn a lot by sitting down and just chatting—listening to their experiences and points of view and gaining a bit of knowledge and a different viewpoint in return. And the people we met were happy to share.

The owner of the lodge was eye-opening in terms of his enterprising spirit. "Whatever you want to do, John," he said one evening over a drink, "You can do it in Uganda. Run a small school to teach English, or start a business, or anything at all. You can do it here." Interesting perspective. It gets you thinking.

Throughout this trip, and every other time we've travelled, I was always very aware that we were rich and white doing very touristy things, and that we were living with a high degree of artificiality. We knew we hadn't even scratched the surface of the people or their culture.

DAY 161

CRISIS (BARELY) AVERTED

IN A MONTH, I'LL BE HOME.

There. A definite fact in a tour that has had bloody few of those truths lying around. The routing is Juba—Addis Ababa—Toronto—Calgary. I'll be home on 23 February. Unless the UN screws up.

And with that comes the shocking reality that I need to leave this place. That there are things to do. Pack up my kit for shipment back home, mostly, but also sorting through items I'm not taking back to Canada and are too dust-infused, contaminated, or otherwise worn out but which might still be of value to someone...running shoes, walking shoes, towels, mosquito net, and so on. So, it's started. I am putting my barracks boxes together with stuff I need to send to Juba this week so that when I get back from leave, I can then send it via DHL to Calgary. This could take up to 3-4 months. Just the way it is.

And Yes. I have one more leave. Here's the plan—I leave Malakal on a Thursday (4 February), leave Juba for Entebbe on Friday (the 5th), and then after a few days on leave, I arrive in Entebbe on the 10th. I fly to Juba on the 11th, and then up to Malakal on Friday the 12th for a final blowout weekend of farewell parties (and a shit-load of administration) before I punch out on the 16th from Malakal to Juba. In Juba, I perform some administrative contortions for Check-Out before finally leaving South Sudan on the 22nd.

"But John, you haven't told us where you're going on leave! We need to know!"

I don't know myself. I was really, really hoping for the Netherlands, and from there ideally hitting Munich and Bamberg (I realized

211

that the Rauchbier in Bamberg is really worth going back for!), or a diversion to Copenhagen to hang out with my Hjemmavaernet (Home Guard) buddies…but the timing just isn't going to allow that. Today I have looked at everything from Dubai to Cape Town, to Madagascar, to Zanzibar. And right now, Zanzibar might be a winner. But if you know me, you know that until the decision is made, I could end up buying a ticket to anywhere!

Wait and see. I need this leave, this final decompression, this break. I need to sit, explore, eat good food, and drink good wine and beer…and write, I think. While I need to let Malakal go, I have stories to tell first.

Last week sucked. Hard.

Without going into too many details, last week we narrowly averted an incident that would have guaranteed a return to the last 20 months of war. It was a result of complete ineptitude and horrendous communication on the part of UNMISS HQ in Juba.

A UN aircraft with leading members of the Opposition was flying from Juba and was due to land in Malakal airport (which is controlled by the SPLA, not the UN), transfer onto UN helicopters, and fly to the Opposition Headquarters near the Ethiopian border. Nobody was told about this in advance. The result was that we in Malakal had about three hours' notice to react. The military side in Juba was given about the same amount of time. The SPLA had no idea this High-Level thingy was happening until we told them. They were not impressed, they were definitely not happy, they figured the UN was trying to screw them over, and they were prepared to arrest and detain the passengers as soon as the plane landed. The SPLA in Malakal were pivotal to the success of the mission, and the UN had pissed them off. This was not a good start to the day.

We scrambled. Well, some of us scrambled. The civilian part of the mission here was more active than I had ever seen them, and I was completely engaged with our SPLA Liaison Officers, putting a plan in place, trying to give a robust presence without being so feisty that we escalated tensions. And when we got to the rendezvous at the airport it all looked surprisingly routine. Our patrol consisted of three MLOs—two of them branched out to do some coordination and find out what was happening on the flanks. I was the central point of contact as the Patrol Leader and walked over to our State Coordinator (civilian UNMISS leadership for Upper Nile State) and let him know what I knew, and to find out what he knew at that point.

Our Force Protection was on the ground as was a modest SPLA presence. It felt calm although we were told tensions were high. It all looked good until a half-dozen or more Toyota Hilux pickups loaded with troops came screaming down the road, pulled into the airport parking area and the SPLA dismounted and spread out fast across the tarmac. More Hiluxs followed with 100 more troops that we could see. They were armed with everything from the ubiquitous AK-47 to larger machine guns and RPGs. Oh, shit.

Now this is an appropriate reason for tension—we had a strong Force Protection presence of Rwandans and a company plus of SPLA occupying exactly the same terrain, and in several places, their perimeters overlapped so you had SPLA and UN troops within feet of each other. Yes. That was just bad for so many reasons.

I kept feeding info back to Base on my Tetra radio, just for their situational awareness if nothing else. We were eventually told we had the Green Light from the SPLA to land the aircraft and none of the delegates would get arrested. Nice of them, but I wasn't sure I trusted the message. We had been lied to before, and frankly, with the tensions running as high as they were, who knew what would happen? I could hear a plane's engines in the distance.

Showtime.

Base kept asking me if we should abort the mission, and all I could honestly say was that there was a very strong SPLA presence on the ground and that we had been given authorization to proceed. We could see the aircraft in the distance as it banked to final approach. Cancelling would have severe implications. Going forward and having it go kinetic would have severe implications. Was I confident? Not at all. But I recommended we proceed.

Ian, my UK mate (The Kiwi being on leave and missing all the fun) was wandering around with a worried look, and I expect I had exactly the same expression on my face. Nothing about this situation was good. We were both near the parked vehicles and standing close to Rwandan Force Protection, because if it went bad (and that's what

Ian and I were expecting) we could pick up an AK or two from the Rwandans and bug out. (If you're remotely interested, our plan was to cut across country avoiding the roads and SPLA anti-aircraft positions until we got to BANFRU. Anyone planning to drive out in unarmoured SUVs would have been mown down fast). The other MLOs and UNMISS personnel around the airfield watched and waited.

Things were moving fast and we finally passed the point of no return. We were committed. The plane descended rapidly, finally touched down, and the roar of the engines' reverse thrust was momentarily deafening. Tensions were heavy throughout…

I leaned over to Ian and said, "Hey man. If it all falls apart, it was great serving with you."

"Ya, Mate. Likewise. Well, 'ere they come."

A hush settled. It felt as if the wind paused, the birds stopped singing, and a pall of silence fell on all of us. The aircraft began to taxi to our area. It was tense. We knew, at that point, that all it would take was some idiot to trip and accidently fire a few rounds to kick off an epic shitstorm of bullets…my stomach hurt. I had to break this stress.

I leaned over to Ian again and said, "Okay…cue Horrific Bloodbath in 5, 4, 3…"

He glared, "Not bloody funny, mate." He was right.

Minute by minute, the situation calmed down. The Opposition delegates disembarked from the aircraft, and a few of the SPLA leadership went over to greet them—it appeared that some knew each other from before the civil war. The tension dropped. A couple of smiles. Conversation. It felt like we could exhale. Waves of cramps hit my lower guts and I leaned against our vehicle for a few seconds until they passed. Stress release or something…

Since it didn't really seem like we would be caught in a crossfire any time soon, I wandered across the tarmac to a group of SPLA senior officers standing near a derelict firetruck and saluted the 2-star general. He smiled at me and shook hands. "Canada?" he asked.

"Yes, Sir." I responded with my most jovial "Hail Fellow Well Met" demeanor.

We chatted for a few minutes. Extremely pleasant. And everyone was smiling. That post-tension release caused us all to be a bit giddy.

I saw Manyoun, an SPLA bloke I worked with on the demining mission, and we shook hands and hugged. I asked about his health (he'd been sick with an intestinal bug) and we made small talk. There were others that I spoke with. Recognizing me, laughing.

From crazy stress to stupid casual in minutes.

By the time we got back to the office I was tensed up again, and I reported everything to the Senior MLO, and let him know how close the morning had come to being a complete disaster. We had been within 30 minutes of re-starting the civil war, with international repercussions. Once that debrief was completed, I went back to our office, where the rest of the team was hanging out, chatting, playing tunes, and being too loud, loud, loud. I sat at my desk and tried to work on my patrol report, but the chatter was grating in my mind like a fork on a chalkboard. Cacophony. Dissonance.

And it hit me. Apart from the three of us who went out on the patrol, no one else had done a damn thing to coordinate and plan and they didn't understand the implications of today's events. Our job as MLOs was to always have situational awareness and a detailed understanding of what was happening in our area. This knowledge prepared us when we had to go out the damn gate to make things happen. And in this case, to prevent bad things from happening.

But some members of our team weren't interested in knowledge or improvement or taking action. They didn't get it, and they didn't want to. They avoided work. And then—bastards—they would take a share of the credit. They were a threat to themselves and the other MLOs, it was near the end of my tour, and I had enough. Despite showing no interest in working, in the midst of their yammering, a couple of the MLOs were quick to tell me exactly how that patrol could have gone better.

I left the office. It was all too much, and I was about to lose my shit. I needed to be alone for a while. I was livid. Standing out alone near the helipad, I felt something break inside me. I got truly angry for the second time this deployment…and the ripe spreading of rage through my body felt good. I was on a hair-trigger and wanted any excuse to throat-punch someone. Then, along the perimeter, I watched some asshole driving an SUV almost run over a stray puppy.

Seething, I stormed back to the office.

A couple of the MLOs were discussing how the next phase of the operation should go ahead, and I shut them up by saying, "Everyone wants to do Ops stuff until it's actually time to do Ops. If I want your advice, I'll ask for it." I sat down at my computer to plan the next series of patrols. And somehow, everyone knew I was mad. "Somehow" …that's funny. The atmosphere in the office was heavy and there was a storm cloud over my head. The Team started to give me space. At least it seemed quieter in the office.

Abby and Samirah from Human Rights showed up to chat and after a few seconds knew something was very wrong with me. Samirah jokingly tried to give me a shoulder massage.

"Don't touch me," I snapped.

They left the office.

After months of busting my ass, I'd had enough. I was done. You can't do anything about the lazy, the stupid, and the weak MLOs—the Floppers. At least most of them shut up and might even do one or two of the things you tell them. But they are frustrating—giving suggestions but won't do an ounce of work to see the final result. They will happily watch you go into the high-risk missions and will sit back under the flimsiest of pretenses, then brag about how much they contributed. God, I hate them.

But what to do? For the last weeks of the tour—be angry and biting and blisteringly sarcastic? I'm actually pretty good at that and it honestly would have been cathartic. No. I decided that the Floppers were going to continue to be the target of my complete disdain, but the newer members of the team and those MLOs with good potential were going to get as much of my experience and mentoring as possible. I only had a couple of weeks left in Malakal, and I was going to generate something positive out of this anger.

We had a couple of new MLOs come into the mission while I was on leave, and I realized that nothing had been done to get them up to speed so they could actually function in their jobs. So, we slotted them on patrols. We taught them how to get paperwork completed quickly. We took them around to meet the people who could stamp and sign things and speed the administration process. (Why had nobody else done this?) More about them a little bit later…

I put Claude—a relatively experienced MLO—to lead an Air

Patrol instead of myself. Smart guy, West African, charismatic, hardworking, incredibly fit. He had the potential but needed to be pushed a bit. Claude and I worked through the Operations Order, we both informed the SPLA of the flight, I sat in on his Orders Group where he nervously delivered his patrol instructions and stammered a bit while answering questions. But he did it. And he had thought about it. It wasn't bad, actually.

On the day of the patrol, we both dealt with SPLA suspicion and threats to forbid the flight. He stressed. It was in his body language, his facial expressions, and in his whole demeanor. I knew I made a good choice letting him lead it because he had taken personal ownership of the patrol and he clearly wanted it to succeed. With Air Operations working some magic we got things right, and the SPLA let the patrol go (mostly). Claude went out to the airport, got his team on the helo, and led that team of UN military and civilians. It was a good group that flew over to the West Bank, they got some great info and made some progress with the Shilluk.

After the patrol returned late that afternoon, I had a debriefing with Claude. I asked how he felt in the preparation and the scramble that morning, then in the execution and return of the patrol. He admitted he was nervous and stressed, and that he hadn't relaxed all day until the patrol landed safely back in Malakal.

"Claude," I said, "it means you cared. You put your heart into this patrol and worked your ass off to make it succeed. Everyone saw it. Good Job."

He's going to be alright.

The two new MLOs that showed up when I was on leave are on their first deployment—Ahmed is from a country with a long history of peacekeeping. He was young, energetic, and very keen to do well. Decent English, curious and active mind, and well read. Kato's country is a newcomer to the UN peacekeeping game. He was an older, quiet, and thoughtful officer. He had a natural calmness and charisma that garnered respect. They had strong potential and were very good to work with.

I took them both out to BANFRU on a Saturday to look around. See what we could see. Get a sense of the traffic and trade between Wau Shilluk and Malakal POC camp. To do this, we strolled on the earthen bank of the barge loading area, and then clambered up the Hesco bastion defences to the Guard position on the northwest corner of the camp. From here, we could get a better view of the activity on the civilian landing area, where about twenty of the low, pointed, dark-wood canoes sat beached amidst the Nile reeds and water hyacinth.

The Bangladesh Navy guard in the tower saluted us smartly, and then watched us peering over the sandbags at the activity below on the riverbank. A half-dozen men with AKs, half in uniform, were questioning a group of civilians sitting in a group by the canoes. Building materials, including panels of corrugated metal sheeting and metal poles, were lying in piles. Clearly looted from Malakal town. Around the corner of the berm, locals were boiling water and had set up a little tea or coffee stand under the shade of a tree. Beside this tree sat a long row of wheelbarrows, empty, waiting to transport goods from the West Bank to the POC site.

I turned towards Kato and Ahmed and described the Nile. The history of the area. The importance of Malakal for any lasting peace in South Sudan. I didn't know what else I was going to say but felt that I needed to say something. Whether they understood it, whether they would apply it, wasn't important. I needed to get something off my chest, and like it or not, they were going to hear it. I leaned back against the sandbags and stared at them both.

"Guys. You've been here for a couple of weeks. You've been on a few patrols. You've seen what happens day-to-day in the office."

Nods.

"There are two types of MLOs. There are those that sit at the computer all day, do nothing, learn nothing, and are happy to collect UN pay. They have no interest in improving themselves…."

I paused, unsure how to proceed.

"You're MLOs. You need to know how to train your brains to Observe. What you report is important."

I turned and faced outside the camp, towards the civilian and military activity at the waterfront,.

"What are you seeing right now in front of us? How many canoes? How many armed men? How many in uniform? Did you see the guy with the Rhino Division patch and the white lanyard around his shoulder? How many civilians at the tea area? How many wheelbarrows? You need to know this to make accurate reports. This is critical. Just saying 'Calm and normal activity' means nothing because no one else knows what "Normal" means. Do you understand what I'm telling you?"

Nods and acknowledgement.

"Decide which type of MLO you want to be. If you want to sit back and do nothing, that's your business. You will collect a lot of money and a medal that you have not earned. You will never learn anything. But if you want to be the other kind, you will learn a lot in your time here. You will make connections and friendships that will last for the rest of your lives. People will rely on you. You will have earned respect. That decision is up to you."

I stopped at that point for several seconds to let it sink it. What else could I say?

I snapped them back. "Right then. Seen everything? Let's go."

We climbed down the defences and walked back to the vehicle in silence.

The UN almost re-started the civil war. Because the UN civilians don't trust the UN military and vice versa, but the military will always get screwed over by the UN if push comes to shove. The civvies are the professional career folks and the people in uniform are seconded to the UN for a short time and are absolutely expendable.

That patrol, My God, I have no idea how we snatched victory from the jaws of defeat, but we did. Despite me slagging the UN civvies in my earlier paragraphs, I must give much credit to the State Coordinator, who was caught as much by surprise by the goings-on in Juba as the rest of us, and who was out at the SPLA Division Headquarters and then on the airfield showing some real Leadership. I think his actions are what turned it around.

But after the stress of that patrol, furiously standing at the helipad with my hands balled up in fists, feeling so enraged and yet impotent to do anything, I felt something break. The breaking felt physical. Like picking up a dry branch in autumn and snapping it in half.

DAY 172

ZANZIBAR LEAVE

AH ZANZIBAR!

Islands of spice. Saffron and cloves and chilies and wonderful fragrant delights. Cultural mix of Arabic, East African, European. Delightful winding narrow alleyways and Indian doorways, with shops and merchants and sales of everything from "TinTin in Zanzibar" T-shirts to wood carvings, to coloured cloth, to spices, to anything you can imagine.

Freddie Mercury was born here. Yes. I was also surprised at this discovery. I was wandering around on my first day and not sure where I was and tired from being awake since 0300 and having a bit of sensory overload when I stopped in front of a building and thought, "Why the hell are there all those pictures of Freddie Mercury on the door?" I read a sign that proclaimed that Freddie (not his real name) was born in that very house in 1946.

I came to Zanzi with three firm objectives—to sleep a lot, to eat a lot, and to drink a lot. To maybe push away the bad shit and replace it with good things just before going home. And I slept... Lord How I Slept! In bed by midnight, up around 0800 for a 0900 brekky. Wander around, shop, explore, then maybe lunch and a pint followed by an early-afternoon nap. Then a shower and an afternoon of finding a bookshop or coffee shop for a decent Americano and a quick read before wandering back to the Hotel for an afternoon shower (and pre-dinner nap) before changing for dinner.

I have loved this. The wanderings. The getting lost in the narrow alleys. This was deliberate—I would wander with a sense of

221

aimlessness to stop and try to figure out where I was and how to get back to the hotel. It was like a fun mental maze game where you're the mouse looking for that piece of cheese. It was distracting and pleasant in that there were little gems of shopfronts throughout the town that you'd never find as a tourist.

The strong Arab influence in architecture, culture, clothing, and food, injected a weird sense of being in Morocco, or Tunisia, or Algeria…not Africa. The feeling of being compressed in walkways and by crowds, which was so different from the open savannah of Malakal. Oh, there were many differences between Zanzibar and Malakal!

And now the staff at the hotel all know me. "Hallo, Mistah John!" they say at the entrance and front desk. I am the guy who wanders in and out of the hotel at all hours. Usually sweat-soaked. But I always say hello, and ask how they are today, and I am interested in their answers. And I smile. Because I'm happy and relaxing and getting decent sleep and eating good food and why not share some of that joy with the folks who make the hotel such a welcoming and clean place?

The weather. Hot. Humid. Dark in the morning with low-scudding clouds that leave a lingering moisture on the ground from an early morning drizzle, which only makes the day more oppressively humid. So different from the dusty dry heat of Malakal. An afternoon sun that bakes and sears the Wazungu, who, with sweat-drenched shirts, find the nearest shaded rooftop bar or waterside restaurant to enjoy the breeze and a beer. For those preferring local beers, there was a fine selection. Kilimanjaro, Safari, Ndovu.

Zanzibar is an island off the coast of Tanzania, so it's no surprise that the seafood was amazing. Hell, all the food was amazing! Indian, Swahili, Arabic, European cuisine. Fish, crustaceans, mutton, goat, beef…no pork though. This place retains a significant Muslim influence. But the delicacies of squid, calamari, prawn, and fishes. The many curries. The buns, naans, and chapatti. I'd close my eyes and smell each forkful of deliciousness, inhaling to get the full sensory overload before eating it. Chewing slowly to enjoy the texture. The happiness and joy in experiencing the tastes was a time of such crazy pleasure for me. Flavour was sorely missed in recent months. Coming from Malakal, this was a feast of flavour—food isn't freeze-dried. It isn't eaten out of a bag with a spoon. It isn't eaten in a sea-can.

Visually stimulating and interesting. To be in Stone Town, with narrow winding alleys. Local women in traditional Arab clothing, local men wearing anything from pants to jellabiyas, and (of course) tourists in shorts, sandals, t-shirts. Herd upon herd of tourists. Especially off-putting were those touristy women wearing those God-awful baggy African-theme print yoga-pants and spaghetti-strapped T-shirts. Not to be judgmental…who are we kidding, you know I'm judgmental…but that horrendous fashion statement justifies every negative stereotype the locals have of rich white Europeans. But wait—it gets better. A few of them (or I saw the same woman three times in a row) wrapped a scarf around their head to clearly demonstrate their "cultural sensitivity" while wearing the baggy pants and skimpy t-shirt. Because showing your bare shoulders and cleavage is somehow respectful of the local culture?

You get approached by every dude around here looking to be your guide for an hour or a day. Just trying to make a shilling or 10,000. One guy wouldn't take my usual "No" for an answer, and he was really funny and not offensively pushy and actually pretty cool. So, I hired him. 10,000 shillings (about $5 Canadian) for a tour of Stone Town and the Spice Market.

My guide's name was Mohammed Ali. He was a small, thin but compactly built dude with a broad smile. I pointed out that he has really let himself go since he retired from boxing. He chuckled but I don't really think he understood the reference.

We navigated through narrow streets, alleys, and courtyards and I knew he was rushing "Because Time is Money, Man," but he was alright. As we walked, we chatted about politics and an election that didn't happen and all sorts of stuff, and he is married with small kids (aren't they all) and spent a bit of time working the sympathy vote. Nice try, dude. Not my first rodeo.

After ten minutes or so, we arrived at the bustle and noise of the market. Crushing crowds interspersed with the white or red sunburnt faces and necks of tourists, seeing the sights. Ali and I wandered through the spice market, and he randomly (roll eyes) took me to two dudes in a stall, where I picked up some saffron. Yes, I tried to haggle. Yes, I didn't try all that hard because I sort of didn't give a shit about a few dollars either way. And I like to think I got a decent price but who am I kidding? The Mzungu price is a million times more expensive than the local price.

Ali wouldn't have been a tour guide in Zanzi if he didn't try to take me to places I didn't want to go and sell me stuff I didn't want. He asked if I had seen This Palace or That House and, to his surprise, I said "Yes" to all of them. "Dude, I researched it all on the internet and figured out where to go."

An aside…All the street vendors wandering around with things you don't want will zone in on white couples and families like seagulls on a sardine. These vendors tend to leave single white guys alone, but they would still usually make the effort, because you never know… maybe I want to buy something.

My response to any sales-pitch was always something like this, "Hey man. These things are awesome and totally worth the price. But I know how this all works. So, I don't need a guide, a disco, tanzanite, or a woman. But hey, there are probably LOTS of Wazungu who need your help today. I'm not one of them…"

Usually, they laugh and move on.

One guy was insistent while holding a whole bunch of little wooden stick-figure men. He just wouldn't accept No for an answer. I finally looked at him and said, "Seriously? What am I supposed to do with those things?"

He stopped and paused. "Uh, I don't know…gifts?"

"I work in South Sudan. Do you think they need gifts?"

He walked away.

Let's jump back a bit. Remember my reasons to come to Zanzibar?

LOTS OF SLEEP

Ten hours a night. Add in morning and afternoon naps. Sometimes an evening nap. Almost 12 hours a day. Easy. I clearly needed this. Soft bed. Minimal noise…except for the construction crew at 0730 daily working right beside me. That is a minor distraction. Who cares? Sleep and plenty of it.

LOTS OF (GOOD) FOOD

In addition to what I've already described, a couple of places stood out.

A bar on the seaside with a seafood ragout which had delicious flavour if a bit too much tentacle and squid-ish-ness. Had a decent view of the ferry and container port, so you could sit and watch boats go by.

The Spice House had a chicken tikka masala that was freakin' brilliant. The butter naan was also freakin' brilliant. The combination of too much spice and too much grease wasn't quite so awesome. The result was a night of rumbly guts and a number of frantic trips to the bathroom. But completely worth it. Now that was a curry with authenticity! And my skills of recovery are pretty good. Pepto and Imodium are my friends.

LOTS OF DRINK

Beer. Clearly a result of the German Colonial Influence. Kilimanjaro—adequate at 4.5% alcohol per volume. Safari—more adequate at 5.5%. Ndovu—awesome at 5% but contains Crystal Malt which I initially misread as Crystal Meth and freaked out a little bit.

Alex and the wait staff on the upper floor of the hotel are awesome. They continuously feed me beer. I type on my laptop. The manager came over and said, "You are always so busy writing, Mistah John!" That could be because I am wearing my bitchin' Special Operations Command t-shirt and look totally badass with my beard and I am busy trying to type and drunk-call friends.

But right now, Alex the Bartender is slicing limes and the gals are serving drinks and everyone is doing okay. There's a low hum of people from the alleys below the hotel. And I'm happy in the afternoon heat at the bar with my beer and my words flowing freely and easily. Malakal is a million light-years away. And here I am. Tipsy on my third Safari, sitting contentedly at the bar, in the shade, loving the freedom of nothing. I don't want to leave this.

Tomorrow brings changes and travel. First to Entebbe, then Juba, then Malakal (the thought of this makes my stomach twinge). A repeat of my first journey to South Sudan so many months ago. I return to Malakal for a weekend of farewells and out-processing and other shit and as much as I hate that place and all it represents; I will miss the people. The good ones at least, because no one misses the assholes.

The misery and sadness and desolation of South Sudan exhausts me. The sheer volume of crap, then adding to it the attitudes that prevent peace and progress. Throw in institutional myopia, laziness, ineptitude, and finger-pointing. Whatever. I go home in two weeks.

Leave it. Stop thinking about it. Stay present. Stay here in Zanzibar….

Tonight? Seafood. Beer. Sleep.
Tranquility.

Zanzi was a treat. And a tonic for the soul. I flew from Entebbe at zero-dark-stupid to Nairobi, where I had no Kenyan shillings and couldn't even get a cup of coffee because the airport shops weren't opened yet. And then the flight from Nairobi to Zanzibar was awesome because we were able to fly over—well, almost over—Kilimanjaro. The summit was uncharacteristically clear and snow-white blinding and absolutely awe-inspiring in its sheer magnificence. And it was yet another link to Hemingway's time in Africa and his exceptional stories.

While in Zanzi, I stayed exclusively in Stone Town and didn't really wander farther out for touristy things. But I walked and walked for hours on end. So drained and exhausted on the one hand, and so much energy on the other. Tired and Wired.

In contrast to the trip inbound, I have absolutely no recollection of the trip back between Zanzibar and Malakal. How long it took, how I got there, who I spoke to, where I stopped en route (I assume Entebbe but can't recall if I even stayed overnight). It's not even a blur. It's just a blank.

DAY 184

JUBA - CANADA HOUSE

FLIGHT HOME IN APPROXIMATELY 30 HOURS. And with that the end of my (second) time in South Sudan. And here I am trying to sort the jumble in my brain because there is so freaking much to tell and share and talk about and I think I've missed everything important.

Why is there such a cacophony of ideas and images and sounds and thoughts in my head? I think a big part of it results from the fact that I'm out of this Mission in a few short hours, and maybe I need to tell everything in the time I have left in South Sudan, but I simply can't. This is a way of grasping onto the memories and visual images in my head before they fade. Because they will fade with time, and people will become indistinct and names will be forgotten and stories will shift and warp in the telling because time does that to memory. I must keep clarity of thought and word. I have to keep this true and honest.

And where am I in my body and mind? How am I? There is a natural self-analysis that goes on at a time like this. An accounting of all your physical and mental bits to call the roll and make sure everything is accounted for.

Fingers and toes? Check.

All the other bits? Check.

No chills/sweats or bug bites or weird fevers? Check.

Sense of humour? Like my coffee, dark and bitter. Check.

The other mental parts?

…Good…

229

I have to admit I paused before writing that. I'm good, but saying that, there's some stuff I need to get rid of. The stressors have been powerful and constant, and there is some (okay, a lot of) cumulative stress that has built up over the course of the tour, despite my best efforts to smooth it away in Uganda and Zanzibar. Not a showstopper.

But the tour changes you. Every tour should in some way. For the good, ideally. You've had an Experience. To not bring some of that back with you, absorb it into yourself, embrace it and be better for it, seems unfair. You leave some of yourself back where you were and bring something new back home with you.

So, yeah. I have changed. How much? No idea. I just know it's there. Being the most isolated Canadian Armed Forces member in the world didn't help, I think.

Yes. You read that right.

Let's look at the stats—where was the nearest Canadian support? Juba—over 500 kilometers and an hour (plus) flying time by fixed wing. Closest Canadians? In Bor—over 350 klicks away, and the only way to get there was via Juba. Or on a barge (which would take 14 days, by the way). No one was as isolated as I was. It's a distinction I wear with some pride.

But I digress—separating myself in both time and space from South Sudan will certainly help to regain some clarity and perspective. But that's for later.

I want to desperately, but cannot, put you with me in Malakal. There is simply too much to tell, and the enormity of description would cloud the really important things—the most important points—of my story. Thoughts and memories and wishes collide right now. I wish I had fished the Nile. The unsettling feeling of flying over the West Bank of the White Nile, seeing the SPLA defensive lines, and knowing that this area was so contentious to the Shilluk. What if I had negotiated more forcefully with that annoying little SPLA Sergeant at the airport– the little shit with all the damn power of the State to stop our flights—for that second Kodok patrol? Maybe I should have bought a goat at BANFRU and asked the Indian Army cooks to prepare some curries for me. Remembering the surreal feeling while on patrol and eyes on swivels to anticipate what might happen. And so on.

There is no single-story thread. There are snippets of tales. Of successes, of many disappointments, and of a nagging continued prodding in the back of my brain that I have set something aside and don't quite know where it is. And I think I know where part of it lies. In an intense yearning to find something good here. To end the tour with something positive, something beautiful. Something to counter the massive amount of shit that was Malakal. I don't want to remember only that.

Sorry about the ramblings. It's where my head is right now.

Let's pull back from the jumble and start where everything in the UN starts….

Administration—Leaving any mission, especially a UN mission, isn't easy. There is a set bureaucracy….an Order (with a capital O) to things and enough paperwork to denude a small forest. But make no mistake; the administration is tedious and boring. Why would I even waste time telling you about it? Because it is critical to get it done right. And there is a lot of stress in compiling all the bullshit information the UN wants. Even more, if you don't do it right, if there are outstanding charges against your pay account, or you owe some equipment (like a car or computer), you aren't going home until it all gets sorted out. That is stressful. Especially when you want to get out of Mission and on a plane to Happy-Land…

"But John, if there are established rules it should be easy, right?"

(Maniacal laughter) "Oh God, No! Don't be naïve!"

There might be rules, but the application of these rules changes minute by minute. Depending on who has the power. And in the UN, having a Stamp is power. The Stamp is sacred. And if the Stamp Wielder is not in the office, nothing gets stamped.

Yes. It is the Holy Grail of bureaucracy.

So, the Out-processing—the scavenger hunt of running from one office to another with the all-important "Check Out Form" (requiring around ten signatures and stamps), smiling in my best "Super-Friendly White Man" demeanor at the all-powerful people behind their specific desk—transport, computers, supply—who will sign and stamp the paper. Without this being completed, you will not be allowed to leave Malakal.

The all-powerful signers and stampers know their power. They are well aware of their worth in your world. They will remember whether you were nice to them throughout the mission or not. They can turn a minor error into a major problem. Or not. Depending on how you act, and how they feel that particular day.

Luckily, I am jovial, and funny as hell, and really quite polite. As a result, my little Stamping ritual went quickly. Also, because I'm not an idiot, I started out-processing before I went on my final leave to Zanzibar. I wanted to make damn sure I had as many signatures as possible before my return. Clever, no?

It took a couple of days' work in Malakal until I received my final stamp…on the morning I flew out.

I went through exactly the same sort of thing in Juba at the two UN Bases here. In Malakal, finishing the form got you on a plane to Juba, and completing check-out in Juba will get you on a plane home. And they are clever about it. After all other signatures (and stamps. don't forget the stamps) are on that magical check-out form…the nice man takes your packet of forms and hands you a printout with your flight information. That's it. You are Done!

Euphoria!

With that, being completely checked-out of the mission, I stayed in Canada House until my flight home. Spending my time relaxing (okay, lots of naps), packing for the return home, snacking incessantly, and collecting my thoughts and feelings. Trying to make sense of Malakal, and of this deployment, and by extension, of myself.

I don't feel that I achieved anything.

I bashed my head against walls of myopic thought and glacier-like initiative. I tried to carry forward some of the things my predecessor had done, but I knew that the minute the competent MLOs left, any progress made in procedures or processes or documentation or liaison would slide right back to zero.

I went on poorly planned patrols and lived the consequences by being stopped, or turned around, or harassed. We planned good patrols that never went anywhere because of terrible weather and road conditions. We tried to execute air patrols and while a few were successes, most were horribly planned, or stopped at the airfield by SPLA Security just "because."

I saw good people in Malakal worn down. Souls beaten. Pushing too hard against the system. Many people gave up. Others still fight hard for concepts like "Human Rights." To counter every dedicated and selfless humanitarian were the lazy, self-entitled, overpaid shitbags who did nothing, because doing nothing carried no risk. Well, not for them anyway.

Risk aversion—It was endemic throughout the mission. I was guilty of that, I must admit. There was almost no way of getting a Casualty Evacuation Flight Safety Assurance from the SPLA and Opposition on weekends, and with only a medium-level medical facility in Malakal we did nothing important or risky between Friday and Monday. We figured the average time to get a severely injured person from Malakal to Juba would be at least eight hours once we cleared all the bureaucracy. Oh, and Juba airport was closed on weekends. For Canadians, used to extensive aviation and medical resources from the war in Afghanistan and a "Golden Hour" for medical care, this is a shock. It should be.

Our rule to mitigate the lack of evacuation capability was simple, "Don't get hurt on Weekends."

The mix of cultures, languages, and values, while a positive hallmark of the UN, is also its greatest weakness. Think about the many language issues, communication issues, and more importantly, cultural issues. If you take people from hundreds of countries around the world and stick them in an organization like the UN, there are going to be differing views on subject like gender, sexual exploitation, and sexual orientation—and not all in alignment with the stated UN values. There is also the endemic careerism and lack of accountability from both civilians and troop contributing countries. If your culture doesn't admit mistakes, tries to blame someone else or gloss over failures, and won't consider an after-action review to decide what needs improvement, and actually work to improve them, you are part of the problem.

Negligence—A local had cultivated a tiny plot of soil outside the POC site where he tried to grow a few veggies. He stayed out there at night to stop pilferers. One night, not long ago, he caught two thieves. They were armed (he wasn't), so he fled down the road, through Kilo gate (which was unguarded and unlocked) into the UNMISS Base where he was shot and killed 57 meters from the nearest guard tower. The guards saw nothing.

One reason they saw nothing is that their guard tower was behind and below the level of an unfinished berm and newer guard tower. The new tower blocked their view. They couldn't see outside the camp if they'd wanted to. To reiterate this point—a civilian was chased by armed men inside the UNMISS base and was killed 50-odd meters from a guard tower, and they saw nothing. I mean, they saw the body and took pictures after the fact. But they didn't see who did it. By the time the UN wanted to interview them, the guards had already been rotated back to their home country.

Our Special Flight Requests for air patrols were consistently screwed up. Wrong coordinates, wrong location, wrong place name, wrong date or time. Almost every single time there was an error. The forms were all filled in by the same guy. Accountability? None. Ramifications for ineptitude? None. Why is this even important? Because when we made appointments for meetings and had to cancel at the last minute because the time, date, location, or route is wrong, we collectively looked like idiots.

Local "Authorities"—The airport is a classic example of this. The local SPLA airport dudes would randomly change the rules to screw over the UN—they seemed to make shit up as they went along. Today your patrol is no problem and can go ahead. Tomorrow the same circumstance is totally a problem and you're blocked. The next day, it's not a problem. And the day after that? Who freaking knows? South Sudanese nationals (and UN employees) have been prevented from flying on UN missions in UN aircraft…sometimes. Other times it is okay for them to fly on patrols. On different occasions, the national staff are interviewed then allowed to travel. The next day, they are interviewed but aren't allowed to travel. Every day is different, just Because. And was there any support from UNMISS HQ in Juba? No.

UN Inaction—Freedom of Movement violations happened often and would occasionally get reported up the chain as I did with a follow-up Kodok patrol at the end of December. But these reports would disappear in the ether of UN bureaucracy. We never get feedback. Speaking of UNMISS not doing anything about critical issues, I don't think Riek Machar or anyone in the Opposition ever got the bill for the 56,000 liters of diesel General Angoy pilfered during the hostage taking incident.

Tribalism—Blind historical hatreds. Killings, abductions, rapes. Weekly, sometimes daily. Examining murder scene photos with Human Rights trying to figure out what happened. How many bullet holes? What caliber? Size of blood pool? Once, a body without a head. Once, a disarticulated skeleton with just a pelvis and part of the spine remaining. Tribal hatred was so endemic that the POC camp was separated along tribal lines to mitigate the violence.

Good Times.

Personal protection—Who would have had my back—or would know how to help—if something went wrong? The Kiwi, the Brit, the Germans, Norwegians for sure. Zambia, Nepal, and Fiji would try as would some others, I guess. And that impacted every single day of the mission. My First Aid training was extensive, but who covers me if I'm hurt?

The reality of being armed is quite comforting, by the way, yet I patrolled outside the camp unarmed. There was an irony of being armed for threats inside the camp—every night with my loaded pistol under the pillow. Why? Because the POC camp perimeter wire was 50 meters away from my container. And with 46,000 IDPs in an 800-meter by 800-meter square—frustrated, hungry, bored, and angry—it was a powder-keg. I've said that before. No one listened.

Regrets—Never having the frank and open discussion I wanted with Adam, one of the SPLA Liaison Officers. From him of all people, I needed to know that he—an intelligent man who had spent time in Canada—knew what Right Looked Like. I really regret that. I wished he had admitted that the Bullshit was just Bullshit and he really didn't believe all the crazy propaganda spouting from Salva Kiir and his cronies. But I'd never know now, would I?

Insomnia—Waking up several times a night with my flashlight on, first seeing only the white shroud of the mosquito net until my eyes adjusted to the light and saw into the container beyond the netting. Snapped awake by dreams, imagined sounds, or real ones. The dogs howling at night. Always at a spot just outside my place, across the dirt road. Until they poisoned the dogs. Insomnia sucks.

The Dogs—Hating them but relenting once. I fed a timid bitch who was clearly nursing some pups. I gave her a whole container of canned cheese, spoonful by spoonful. Dropped far away from me at first, she would crane her head forward to grab at it and move back a pace or two to wolf it down, only to wait patiently for the next morsel. Dropped closer and closer each time until she was on my doorstep. It felt good to feed her. Gratifying. I am very aware that I fed a feral dog while thousands of hungry people lived less than 100 meters away.

The Pee-Bottle—A 1.5-liter water bottle that saved me trips to the ablution containers 50 meters away. At night, this was a godsend. I didn't much feel like running into a pack of local hounds at zero-dark-stupid. You learn a lot about your bladder capacity after a while.

Sad and Tired—The buildup of mental and physical callouses. The small things that sustain and nourish you enough to drag your tired ass out the door for another day of…who knows what? Every day could run the spectrum between Nothing and Everything. Between Lazy and Frantic. This isn't just caused by the factional fighting and generic bullshit. The environment wears at you. The heat, the dogs, the bugs, the boredom, and excitement. It all grinds you down piece by piece.

Food—boring and predictable. Granola bar and coffee for breakfast, noodles, and canned tuna for lunch, and usually a freeze-dried meal for dinner. Shipped from Canada because you could not buy fresh food—or any food at all—in Malakal. Although there was the camp cafeteria, we nick-named it Café Dysentery and avoided it completely.

Social Life (kinda)—Happy memories of the "Hard Rock Café" on Friday nights with the other MLOs for a couple of pints (if available), or a glass of wine (if available), or water (you get the idea by now). Sit down and laugh and tell stories together and get deafened by the DJ playing African tunes and some of the crowd of UN military and police and civilians trying to dance. When fully deafened and bored, I would take my leave. Wishing my mates Good Night, I would walk the dark road back to my container, the music loud but fading behind me, small flashlight looking to avoid dogs curled up in the road, hearing the pad pad pad of my own steps in the dirt.

Shock—Memories of our car being swarmed by twenty to thirty SPLA troops at the south end of Malakal town, where they had a concentration of heavy armament, and they clearly didn't want us there in spite of the fact their General knew about our patrol and had authorized our mission. Angry faces, indistinct, yelling, gesticulating, armed. Feeding on each other's raw emotions and you could smell the Mob Mentality escalate. It took some time to calm everyone down.

The highlights of the tour replay in my head. A series of contradictions—Frustrating, satisfying, happy, sorrowful, frightening, safe, surreal, insane.

If I close my eyes, I can still smell Malakal. It's the dust. Red parched soil that hasn't seen rain in months, mixed with ash and trash and who knows what. A swirling mist in the searing afternoons and it's unavoidable. It permeates clothing, buildings, and air conditioners. Eyes get scratchy, throats get hoarse, and the dust coats your teeth. It has a distinct smell—a dead earthiness.

It smells desiccated. Of a nation wasting away in madness.

———————————

Those last hours in theatre felt surreal. Sitting in Canada House trying to empty my full and swirling thoughts onto the blank page was a challenge, but I felt that the minute I left Juba all the memories and details and emotions would fade, and I'd lose my grasp of the tour and never be able to tell the story.

The memories were bizarre—they were not displayed in my mind as complete stories, but small, short vivid vignettes of a few seconds' length, jumbled in a random order whenever I closed my eyes.

This was the End of Something, and while I wanted to leave it, I wasn't ready to let it go.

UNITED NATIONS

This is to certify that

Maj John Karl VINTAR

Has been awarded

The United Nations Medal

In recognition of the duties and the service of peace as a Military
Member of the United Nations Mission in South Sudan.

UNMISS

Awarded on this 20th Day of November 2015

The UNMISS Medal was established on 09 July 2011.
Light blue of the ribbon represents the United Nations. Black
symbolizes the people and the state of South Sudan. Green represents
the fertile land of the state whereas the white symbolizes the hope of
peace and prosperity brought to South Sudan after a long struggle
for independence.

YOHANNES GEBREMESKEL TESFAMARIAM
Lt. Gen.
Force Commander
UNMISS

23 MARCH, 2016

ONE MONTH HOME

I'VE BEEN HOME A MONTH NOW. So, what do I tell you?

The homecoming at the Airport was perfectly understated. One or two family and friends (a total of four) to welcome me as I got off the plane…a hug and kiss from Jacqueline, and hugs and handshakes from my mates. Grab the baggage and head home.

The first days were numb. Or rather, I was numb. Overwhelmed by the vast amounts of sheer bloody everything that exists in a first-world country. So many cars on the road, so much food in the grocery stores, so many rooms and so much space in my house, so many white people everywhere. So much, so many, too much. All far too much.

I'm jumping ahead of myself. All that explosion of sensory overload happened days later.

I landed on a Tuesday and didn't have a chance to take off my desert boots and start relaxing before I knew that I had to go back to work the next day. Yup. You heard it right. Don't slack off yet, John. There's shit to do. Army Shit. Now go find your damn green uniform and black boots. And for God's sake, shave.

Here's the way our military system works, you report for duty for three half-days as soon as you get back from a deployment. There are a number of reasons for this, including some administration and generic paperwork, but I always felt that the real reason was to allow the folks at your unit to check you out, and for you to see them.

I spent those days talking to my mates, handing over my files, and signing a bunch of papers, working out at the Headquarters gym, drinking coffee and chatting and learning a bit about what was going on. I also spent a day travelling up to Edmonton and back to complete an initial dental, medical, and administration check. This was absolutely necessary, especially since I indicated some illness/injuries while deployed, and it's an individual's responsibility to see the clinic within 48 hours of return. Makes sense.

Remember that I had to deal with a ten-hour time change, so I was a bag of hammers and there was no bloody way I was going to drive the 300 kilometers north to Edmonton after less than 48 hours in Canada. I hadn't driven faster than 40 kilometers per hour in six months, I was jet-lagged as hell, and although the weather was unseasonably warm, this was February in Alberta, and I was not prepared to drive in case of a snowstorm. As a result, the Headquarters kindly ordered a car and driver for me. We linked up on Thursday morning at 0700 hours and started driving north.

The driver was a good lad and extremely conscientious and stuck to the speed limit. Exactly to the speed limit. This is not a common practice in Alberta. To be fair, he was a Military Policeman, so getting nicked for speeding probably wasn't a good idea for his career. I wasn't talkative, which is rare for me. Usually, I am chatty, but I didn't have the energy to talk. I was pissed off for no reason, and I fell asleep a lot on the road, and really just wanted to get all the shit over and done with. My first appointment was at 1000 hours and I kept checking my watch as we drove, hoping we'd make it on time. We rolled onto the base about 15 minutes late and pulled in front of the clinic.

I was used to functioning on UN time, which is never on time, but I still hate being late for anything. I was antsy and tense and ready to jump out of my own skin. And I stayed quiet because I think my mood went from Zen to Rage with no middle ground and I honestly didn't want to start giving the driver shit. So, I shut up.

As soon as we got to the clinic, I hopped out and told the driver, "Right. The Tim Hortons is left at the lights if you want a coffee. I will be at least an hour so take your time. But be back here waiting no later than 1130 hours, okay?" And I walked briskly through the front door…

So, how was it, John? Are you as healthy as a tractor? Mostly, yes. Here's the summary:

Dental—gums are a little soft. Might be a cavity. The dental assistants asked if there was a reason for that. Didn't I floss? I commented that I had run out of floss months earlier and there was no floss resupply in South Sudan, and for good measure I addedt that I had gone several months without fresh fruit or vegetables. But I would be sure to floss regularly from now on. They were understandingly sympathetic and set up a cleaning for me in April.

Medical—as I noted, apart from six months of insomnia, some rotator cuff and lower back issues, and a sinus infection, I was physically fine. Some pills for insomnia, physiotherapy appointments for the back and shoulder, and a Mental Health check in 90 days. I was good to go!

Administration/Pay—no problem. Signed some forms. Was informed that my leave was good until April 5th (almost five weeks! Hurrah!) and my Reserve pay would kick in on that date. (In case you didn't know, the Reserves receive 85% of Regular Force salary for reasons that really don't stand up to scrutiny. This doesn't apply when you are on operations, where you receive full Regular Force pay.)

Once the administration was completed, that was it. Finished. Just over three hours. But there was one last task…

Before the deployment, I had been issued a party-pack of Surgeon General controlled items, like narcotics, anti-retrovirals (remember, HIV/AIDS in Africa), and other goodies that needed to be returned to the pharmacy. No-one had yet informed me that I had to return them (they would have thought of it eventually) but I figured that everyone in the military would get really pissy if I lost my Fentanyl and Tylenol 3s.

After my dental check, and before the medical review, I walked to the pharmacy to let them know what I wanted to do. It seemed like the correct thing, after all. I waited politely in line. When it was my turn, the nice lady behind the counter said, "Good Morning" and asked how she could help.

"Hi. I just returned from South Sudan on Tuesday, and I was issued a number of Surgeon General controlled items. They are in my possession now. I would like to return them, please."

She paused…a look of panic spread quickly…and she fetched her supervisor. As I waited for them to sort themselves out, I maintained a benign, contented smile, thriving on the flurry of activity. As it turned out, the Pharmacist who had issued me the drugs before my tour wasn't around anymore, and it would take a while to find the paperwork, and could I come back when they figured out how to receive the items?

Still smiling, I responded, "Well, of course. I'd be happy to. But there is a time constraint as I'm only here for the day. Is that an issue?"

It wasn't an issue. I will say this, the folks at the pharmacy are damn good. I showed up after an hour and handed over the goods. I assumed after six months in South Sudan all the drugs would be destroyed and not re-issued, but the important factor was that they weren't on my charge anymore.

Once I walked out of the clinic, the driver and the vehicle were standing by (good lad!) and we started the drive back home to Calgary. All in all, it was about seven hours of driving for three hours of administration. But it was a requirement, and now it was a check in the box. Finished.

Now Leave was within reach. Glorious, Glorious Leave.

During leave, there were a couple of things that stood out and stuck in memory after being away for so long. Some small and inconsequential, but vivid in contrast to the tour. I made a list as the days went on, because I had to re-learn being in a first-world country.

There were a couple of nasty surprises.

WHERE THE HELL AM I?

One of the first nights back home, I woke in a sweat-soaked panic. The shadows and lights and smells were different. I didn't know where I was and I felt I had missed a flight or something and I panicked and where am I holy shit frantic scramble where's my pistol holy shit holy shit find the gun holy shit…. Then I heard a snort from the floor.

Brandy was in her doggy bed and she's a pudgy little thing and she snored or snorted or something and it was enough to stop my rising panic and suck everything back into a space I could understand at 0200. That little pup stopped me, brought me back to Here and Now, and let me get back to a fitful sleep.

TRAFFIC

Freaks me out. I'm used to not many cars on the roads. When I used to encounter vehicles in Malakal they were usually UN or SPLA. If they were SPLA, they would be bombing down the roads at 80 kph with a half-dozen dudes in the back and you pulled over and waited until they passed. They did not give way. They sure as hell weren't going to give way for you.

FOOD

Bloody Hell how much food do we need to advertise? There is so much. And how much goes to waste? Thoughts on our concepts of Plenty. On Excess. On Waste. On taking all the amazing shit we have for granted. I came from a place with nothing and want and misery and now I can wait in line at the grocery store to buy fruits that don't even grow in Canada. Mind completely blown. And everyone assumes this is the normal state of affairs.

COLOUR

Not like a colour palette for house-painting. I'm talking skin colour. I look around and think, "Wow. There are a lot of white people here." Not to be insulting. A statement of fact. I was the minority for several months and frankly, I'm far more comfortable with a bunch of East Africans right now than with white guys from my unit. We were a lot more honest and open about colour and race in South Sudan than I could ever be here in Canada.

MOOD

My nerves are sitting close to the surface. Pretty easy to set me off. I don't do crazy rages, but I get sudden bursts of intensity, and there aren't a lot of warning signs. Lots of ups and downs. Small things that would never normally even get me interested become major points of high emotion. I get sharp, stern, angry.

I almost lost my mind at a store a few weeks ago where the sheer lack of goddam common courtesy got me pretty wound up. Move your damn shopping cart to the side, don't leave it in the aisle. At the checkout, don't engage in idle conversation and bring twenty outdated coupons with you. I kept my mouth shut because I didn't know how angry and vocal it was going to get, but my hands were shaking with rage as I was bagging my groceries.

Something's different this time.

Something's not right.

LETTING IT GO

IT'S TIME TO LET IT GO.

It's time to stop wearing Malakal like a pair of mud-caked boots. It dragged me slowly down into a deep vast pit from which I could only look up, forlorn and aching, at the light that shines above. I have been many things, including my own worst enemy. That is slowly changing, and step by tentative step, I am crawling upwards. Towards a goal, but what?

I don't know. Nor do I care because it isn't where I'm going that carries any weight, it's what I'm escaping from. Once up at ground level I will be able to see a farther horizon and find my path again. The grand fallacy, as I realize it, isn't that Malakal won't release me. That's wrong. The pit is of my own creation because I'm the one holding onto Malakal. I'm the one not letting go. Or wasn't.... because I am now.

How do I put this clear in my own mind and recount the path of the last few months in a way that you'll feel it? I have no doubt the tale will wander here and there; it always does as you should know by now. The path is ultimately one of time. Time is a fickle beast. Sometimes it grinds sand and salt into the wounds as you replay the episodes over and over in your head. Time reminds you of many failures and of places you'd rather be and things you should have done. Time heals all wounds, they say. That's seriously funny. Because I think it's bullshit. Time is making it all hurt more.

Within the first month back from my tour I completed another interview at The Military Museums in Calgary. It was a project to trace my transition through a series of video interviews. The first was conducted in August 2015 before I went over. The second was in November 2015 when I was back on leave after the hostage-taking. This was the third interview which took place three weeks after my return.

That interview reinforced that I wasn't mentally in Calgary. My mind and soul were still in South Sudan. As we talked, my rate of speech sped up and became more clipped as I spoke of the last months' frustrations. The interviewer was skilled and compassionate and a dear friend, but her inquiries drew me out more than I had prepared for and put me back in the dusty heat and gut-knotted days in Malakal. My gestures became more animated, my face more flushed. There was a familiarity and beauty in my hatred of the mission, and it showed throughout the interview. I was too used to feeling viscerally alive, because it was only a matter of time before the soporific of Western Civilization's excess numbed me. Made me comfortable and sleepy. We couldn't have that.

An offer came from PSTC in Kingston to sit on a writing board to revise the United Nations Military Expert on Mission course. Formerly known as the United Nations Military Observer Course, also known as the Peace Support Operator's Course. Because putting "Operator" in the name makes it sound all bearded and aggressively door-kicky. Not like the reality of sitting in a stifling office with shit-slow internet while being acutely aware of one's own body odour. This UNMEM course is the month of training for folks heading off to UN missions in Lebanon, or Congo, or South Sudan. I wanted to go on this writing board because I was desperate to find meaning in what I'd done and giving back to the institution was one path that I thought would help me. I needed to cocoon for a while. The Brigade Chief of Staff was supportive, and I expected to spend a glorious month in Kingston—clearing my head, writing, drinking, and doing lots of PT. Or so I thought.

The writing board was a trial to my focus. We examined training objectives in minute detail, wrote and re-wrote and questioned everything to the point where I started to doubt myself. And rightly so. My mission-specific biases were flushed away, and we approached the material from a pragmatic point of view. And oh Jesus, my brain hurt. I would be exhausted coming home at the end of the day, and

I would try to work out, and eat, and drink. But with the exhaustion was a mental energy and renewed focus on the subject matter which snapped me awake at night more than the bad dreams to ask "What if we tried this? Or that?" It was a good month, also because I had the chance to see my parents, who lived outside of Toronto.

Mom and Dad were in their late-80s, and Dad's cancer had become more aggressive. It was initially expected that old age would have killed him first, and although the cancer was spreading rapidly, he still stood straight and tall, if thinner than I liked to see. Maybe he wasn't as clear in speech or as sharp in thought as he once was, but I still saw that strong, able man despite his age and illness. Because his spirit was strong.

My last visit to their house involved Dad and I planting fir trees in the front yard by the house. I dug the holes, set the trees, replaced the soil, and tamped it down. Dad's efforts involved using the hose to water the hole and the trees, and to provide sound advice while I shoveled and dug.

"Jesus, Jesus, Jesus" he said, head shaking and eyes laughing, "They're not straight."

"Dad, the holes are straight enough. And deep enough."

He smiled, "You know my father would never have accepted that. He'd have made me re-dig them until everything was perfect. And I think this one is too far to the left."

"Your father never served in the infantry," I retorted, sweating. I leaned on the shovel, "I can dig a goddam hole, Dad. The trees won't care how straight it is."

Throughout this exchange, our eyes met, and we suddenly burst out laughing at our own banter. How warm and easily relaxed to joke together. It was comforting for us both.

I flew back to Calgary a few days afterwards. But to what?

I didn't know. I had expected to find a civilian job somewhere so that I could command one of the local battalions. The incoming Brigade leadership insisted that I had to be a part-time Reservist to be promoted and take a command position. In order to do this, I would have to give up my full-time Reserve status and find a civilian job. So, I tried to play the game and applied for various civilian positions. Repeatedly. Without any success despite a couple of call-backs. And increasingly with less and less interest. I had a lot of other shit on my mind—my father's increasingly deteriorating condition, the fact that I was bored senseless as the Brigade plans officer, and that it became easier for Jacqueline and me to hide at our computers or phones and not communicate in our large house that seemed vast and empty.

I couldn't speak about the tour or what I was going through because no one could relate. And sometimes I talked far too much about it, but always recounting the superficial and unimportant details and zany events but never the real emotions of fear or sadness because I didn't think the very serious topics would be fun to listen to, and I wasn't able to be that honest with others. Or myself.

I was isolated in a small headquarters among peers who would have tried to understand but couldn't because they had no frame of reference. I needed to feel heard, but I was afraid of sounding like a Whiner, and didn't want to burden my colleagues with my shit. That was a self-imposed barrier because I know damn well that if I had made the effort to tell them I was hurting, at least one or two would have listened, given me a hug or a slap on the shoulder, or their time, and they would have been part of the healing process. That was all my fault. I still feel pretty shitty about it.

My refuge was in morning coffees, and in moments spent walking among tall trees speaking in the breeze along the Bow River. A deeper understanding of myself was discovered in reading—Hemingway's Nick Adams stories stood out, since I related to the protagonist's internal and external solitude. Scrawled concepts pouring out effortlessly as words and feelings and ideas crammed together in a mixed mental jumble. How joyous to create. To write and then read the words aloud, listening for rhythm and alliteration. To appreciate the product. This helped ground me.

There was—once, maybe twice—an email from my leadership asking "(business, business, business). Are you doing okay?" That was funny and I shut down because my belief was this—if you really, really gave a shit about how I was, you'd have called me. You'd have chatted with me on the phone or brought me into your office and asked me face to face. The most impersonal means of asking about my mental health did the exact opposite of the intention. With the impression that nobody was particularly interested in my well-being,

I isolated further. I became less inclined to reach out. Why bother? Fuck it. My rages grew along with the empty bottles in the recycling bin.

Yet bright spots happened in the summer of 2016 that gave me hope that I wouldn't be stuck in this pit.

I was a guest lecturer at the University of Calgary to discuss the mission and the role of peacekeeping. It felt good. I was energized again. I researched and prepared extensively, and I felt that spark. It was excellent. There was an article in the Brigade magazine about my mission, and apart from a couple of factual errors it was not too bad. Again—Validation.

Finally, upon my return from Kingston and the writing board, I went through the mental health check-up with a social worker in Edmonton via video conference. At the end of the interview, she took a deep breath and said, "So. Here's the thing. You don't have PTSD."

"Well, I know that. I mean, I'm not perfectly fine, but..."

She continued, "But you are processing a lot that has happened over the past several months. Would you be willing to see a counsellor? Think of it as preventative maintenance. Better to deal with issues now than in a few years when we may have a real problem."

I hesitated for a second, then said, "I am feeling strangely defensive about this, but sure. I'll do it."

"Okay. Someone will be in touch." She ended the call.

End of teleconference. Beginning of self-doubt and wondering if that was just a ploy to get me in to see a shrink or...thoughts swirling and self-confidence eroded because if a professional thinks you have a problem, maybe you do. But something was certainly not right. I felt it. A bunch of folks probably saw it, too.

I started my counselling sessions. And it was the best thing that I could have done. In a forum that was open, non-judgmental, and kind, I found compassion and understanding. And I was challenged, too. To be honest and not "game" the sessions by saying what I thought was expected. I opened myself, was willing to be vulnerable, and it hurt. It was necessary to not avoid the issues but acknowledge and try to accept them. And then work through them.

I really felt the first session or two were getting past that exploratory stage of verbal and intellectual sparring with the social worker, and we were establishing a foundation of knowledge and history from which to move forward. Things were starting to look positive. And despite some setbacks, I was starting to feel positive. I took some tentative strides forward. Then my Dad passed away on August 1st.

My father's condition had worsened significantly since I had seen him a few months earlier. He had been in palliative care for over a month. I had flown to Toronto to see him a week or so before his death, and our last meeting was still sharp in memory. His death, such a small thing in some ways, left a larger emptiness and greater void in the world than I could ever have known. A rock was removed from the pond, and although the balance and equilibrium will always return, my heart felt the difference.

Just as I was climbing up and recovering from the tour, his death was another hit that hurt me deeply. Stopped me. I felt myself sliding back down.

I flew back to Toronto to attend his service, and to give his eulogy. I felt that duty strongly. It was a good service, well-attended by friends and family, and representatives from Dad's (and my) former unit, The Royal Regiment of Canada. The Royals have always understood and followed the tenet that once you have served in The Regiment, you are part of the Regimental Family, and you are part of its history. And when a member of the Royals passes, members of the Regiment will be there to grieve with the family. We take care of our own. This was an extraordinary comfort to us, and especially to my mother.

Two months later, I received another request to teach at the Peace Support Training Centre. My Chief of Staff's indulgence had run out, and as he approved the request he said, "It's time for your friends to cut the umbilical cord." Message Clear—no more going away from my regular job to teach. But I was prepared to go to Kingston even if I had to take leave to do it. I wasn't going to miss this opportunity.

The Kiwi was there as an instructor.

We hadn't seen each other since February 15th, 2016, in Malakal. And our reunion was epic. Epic like a Viking Saga. It was glorious and booze-swamped and reflective and cathartic. Make no mistake, we did work, too—we delivered a presentation to students from a couple of universities where we broke down the Kaka hostage-taking incident in minute detail to illustrate how the UN can make simple tasks difficult. We acted as directing staff on the final exercise. We gave lots of advice to the folks heading to South Sudan. In our off hours we compared notes about counselling and mental health, we drank and drank and relived our time together and it felt purging and good. I think we realized that Malakal was with us but also behind us. We had lives and homes and shit to do.

We commemorated Remembrance Day together at Battery Park in Kingston followed by a whisky at the Tir Nan Og pub and then another. Then he was off to the airport—back home to New Zealand. That evening, I sat alone at a pub and nursed a pint before making it an early night. It had been a punishing week with lack of sleep and excess alcohol, and I was worn out but happy. Kingston always made me happy. Focused, energized, valued.

I knew it was time to move on. Military career options in Calgary were limited and completely uninspiring, and frankly, I didn't like what I was turning into. I was becoming angry, petty, and jaded. I knew that I could be better—I needed to be better. My sessions with the counsellor reinforced that I was in control of my life, and I was the one who was going to make the changes necessary for my long-term health.

So, how do you make a fundamental change? By making a fundamental change.

By the spring and much of the summer of 2017 there had been many stressors and challenges and I had overcome them one by one. I had tried to move forward spiritually, emotionally, and physically. But it wasn't easy and there were low points.

One of the lowest was saying goodbye to Brandy, our loving and loyal pup. She had been ill for a few weeks in the spring, and in some pain, but the initial prescription from the vet seemed to work. For a while, she was her usual playful self. But late one evening, her condition worsened, and we took her to an emergency clinic. It was liver failure. The chance of any recovery was zero. The vet gently broached the subject of euthanizing Brandy, and Jacqueline and I were absolutely gutted. Now? Tonight? This was a brutally hard and yet simple decision to make.

It was time to say goodbye.

Jacqueline and I held our little doggy in a soft towel as the vet prepared the injection. As a final, loving gesture, Brandy gave my nose one last lick. Then she was gone.

We cried for days.

Without Brandy's energy, the house felt so empty. Occasionally, we'd find a worn and chewed-up dog toy in the house and burst into tears. And then everything felt even emptier as Jacqueline moved to Kingston to start her new job, and I prepared for the property sale and my own move to join her in several weeks.

At the end of July, my social worker and I met for the last time. It wasn't emotional, but it was poignant. I was moving to Kingston, I knew there were mental health resources available if I needed them, but in some ways, I was in better shape than I had been in many months. It took time, but things finally came together, and I was ready to hop into the car and make my way East. But there was a final flourish on my last day at the Brigade Headquarters.

The Division Commander was coming to Calgary to have lunch with the troops, say a few words, and share some information. This conveniently coincided with a summer BBQ lunch. And I couldn't be happier, because I knew the General from our time at the Headquarters in Edmonton many years ago and he is an exceptional leader that I would follow anywhere. There was an added bonus.

The Brigade Chief of Staff had taken me aside the day before and asked, "You're going to be at the BBQ, right? As you know, the Division Commander's going to be there. Apparently, there's a presentation for you."

I was taken aback at this news, "Sure, I'll be there. It's my last day in the office. What's the presentation?"

"I have no idea. Just be there."

"You realize my next eighteen hours will be spent agonizing over what this could be, right?"

He smiled, "Yes. I'm very aware of that."

Right then. No clues. No hints. Just show up.

The presentation was a Command Commendation for the Kaka Incident. Brigadier-General Cadieu read the citation as I stood before my comrades and my mind went back to Malakal and those frantic days in October 2015. I was surprised and humbled that someone thought that I had done something deserving of recognition.

For months I had felt useless and under-utilized at work. I was still feeling pretty low and had just expected to walk away from the Headquarters un-noticed. I would have been okay with that. That award, on my last day, lifted my spirits. It let me leave the Headquarters with my head up. With pride. It made a difference.

So, I loaded up the car and drove to Kingston. Jacqueline had already set the groundwork for us. We had new jobs and new challenges, new experiences to live and new friends to meet. It was wonderful. She had bought our house before I left Calgary, and we couldn't wait for our furniture and effects to arrive to make it our home. Kingston was nourishing for the soul. It was a time of learning and growing of course, because recreating your world into something you want is never easy. But an essential element was still missing, and I felt the absence more and more as the time passed.

In the fall of 2017, I attended a retirement lunch and ceremony for a military colleague. He had also recently returned from a year as the Commander of Canadian personnel in South Sudan. A very large number of friends, family, and colleagues were at the event, and maybe it was purely accidental, but seated at my table were several veterans of various African UN missions. I didn't know all the people, but we made quick introductions. As everyone spoke and shared stories during the lunch, there was a palpable connection and an easing of barriers— because whether you were in Sierra Leone or Democratic Republic of the Congo, Rwanda, Sudan, or South Sudan, there were similarities in the storytelling and circumstances that we could all easily relate to. At times, and with familiar smiles, we'd nod and laugh as a tale came to its often-comic conclusion. There was a collective understanding around the table that made me smile.

This retirement event solidified the idea of getting some Africa veterans together for a few drinks to share our experiences. I mentioned this to a few folks, and they thought it was a good idea, so I sent out a quick invitation to a local pub, not really expecting a lot of interest. Six of us came to the first gathering. We all had fairly recent South Sudan tours from times when the situation was bad in the country no matter where you were. The pub was quiet except for our banter and over the next few hours we had a couple of pints and some snacks and went around the table telling stories and putting timelines to our tours and playing the "where were you, and who was there with you?" game. And it was good.

Actually, it was better than good. It was light-hearted and fun and while there were some very serious moments, this was just the first step in getting to know each other. With that knowledge comes trust, and from that, sharing, and then perhaps resolution or healing or acceptance or whatever is needed. Maybe that will come later, because not everyone needs the same thing. Everyone was changed by their tour, but not everyone was damaged by it. That was a valuable lesson.

The camaraderie reinforced something significant. Because each of us had deployed as one-offs on our missions, and these missions were small and irregular, we came home with unique, life-changing experiences that our colleagues at our units couldn't relate to because they hadn't lived it with us. We didn't have the forum to share our stories truly and honestly. It was so wonderful to talk and to listen to those who had similar encounters—they understood me and more importantly, I understood them too. I had missed this collective energy. This true sense of family. I felt lighter somehow. It was like slipping off a heavy rucksack. It was like I was finally home.

CONCLUSION

ONCE YOU'VE HAD A BROKEN BONE, you're far more aware of it when the weather changes. It aches when the humidity builds, the towering clouds form ominous and black, and storms linger on the horizon before sweeping over you with sheeting rain.

That's how this tour felt. How it still feels.

The memories and impact of South Sudan stay with me. Sometimes the feelings they evoke sit faded and grainy in the distance, and at other times are sharp and vibrant and present. But it's always there, more or less. You get used to it.

I started the tour with optimism and joy at getting out of the damn office and back onto a deployment. Because I had already been to Sudan on a UN tour, I felt completely ready. I knew how to train and prepare myself. I thought I knew what was going on in-country, and I thought I'd be able to hit the ground running. No surprises. Easy days, right?

At first, each experience felt vibrant and memorable and so easy to write about. I felt an overwhelming desire to share this Great Adventure with those back in Canada. Even the inconveniences were all part of the fun. But as the stressors and friction points became more frequent and unpredictable, my ability to bounce back was strained. The hostage-taking, the roadblocks, the bad things, the incessant uncertainty of each day was lumped on top of the incessant boredom of diet, weather, and environment. It was both exhausting and exhilarating. Hating the fear of the unknown but loving the adrenaline afterwards. Eventually, everything wore me down and although I wrote constantly, it became more an escape and outlet rather than as a fun zany travelogue. Thank God for those few amazing moments of happiness and joy and exploration, because it was so easy to get jaded and angry.

Coming home after the tour should have been the best time of all. The happiest return and the reconnections and all the perfect moments you see whenever the troops come back from overseas and get on with their lives. That wasn't me. There I was, angry and dislocated, pushing away everyone who mattered and being completely self-absorbed and drinking too much and always wanting to be somewhere, anywhere else—except where I was.

After all you've read, what I'm about to say might sound screwed up, but I never regretted deploying. I would not ever do it again, but I wouldn't trade the experience for anything. I loved the fact it was austere, and difficult, and chaotic. I loved pushing myself and being challenged. I loved the good times, and the friendships, and the many heartwarming moments. And as much as I hate to admit it, I loved that twisting knot in my guts when we left the camp, and the relief when we returned.

But all that comes with a price.

Accepting mental health resources was difficult, but not that damn difficult. It was a lot easier having it offered to me rather than screwing up the courage to walk through the door and ask for help. But I knew something wasn't right, and I'm glad I got the support I needed. That was a significant step forward. But it was only one step of many.

Another long-lasting step was connecting with a community of veterans who had deployed to Africa—who had been there and sweated through it. The ability to be with others holding similar experiences was extremely powerful because you're denied this post-tour camaraderie when you go overseas as an individual. This was one of the only outlets I had, because deep down, nobody really knows about South Sudan or the UN missions. And you can't begin to care about something you don't know about. As I wrote once before—these deployments are invisible.

Those of us who served on those tiny forgotten missions don't need recognition. We get that officially in medals and extra pay and benefits. To my mind, we need acknowledgment. We need to be seen, and know that our actions, our time, and our deployments mattered somehow.

We also need to be heard. And this comes from collective experience, from shared pain and hardship, from the stories told among your brothers and sisters-in-arms who can relate deeply. They'll understand you and will take your burden and make it theirs, too. They'll do it willingly, knowing that you will do the same.

If there is healing, it is with them.

POSTSCRIPT

As of 28 February, 2023, Canadian Armed Forces personnel were serving on the following United Nations missions:

- United Nations Mission in the Republic of South Sudan (UNMISS). South Sudan – 10 personnel.
- United Nations Organization Stabilization Mission in the Democratic Republic of the Congo (MONUSCO). Democratic Republic of the Congo – 8 personnel.
- United Nations Multidimensional Integrated Stabilization Mission in Mali (MINUSMA). Mali – 4 personnel.
- United Nations Troop Supervision Organization (UNTSO). Israel, Lebanon, Syria, Egypt – 4 personnel.
- United Nations Peacekeeping Force in Cyprus (UNFICYP). Cyprus – 1 person.

INDEX

IMAGES

All photos by the author or in the author's collection, except for those taken by Andrew Thornton (page vii) and Tony Klaeboe (pages 26, 74, 80, 93, and 146).

Pg v. Melut. Abandoned UN vehicles at our base in Melut, north of Malakal.

Pg vii. Malakal town. On patrol several klicks south of the city, waiting to blow up a landmine.

Pg 5. Calgary. Packing for the tour, including lots of food. It's like a big game of Tetris.

Pg 6. Calgary. Final packing completed – putting six months of your life into five barracks boxes.

Pg 13. Juba. Canada House. Front view of the main house showing the bars on the main floor, and outside floodlights. All part of our layered security.

Pg 14. Juba. Canada House. Vehicles in the Canada House compound. Note the height of the compound walls topped with razor wire.

Pg 20. Juba. Canada House. Our chickens provided many eggs. A welcome and necessary source of protein.

Pg 26. State Support Base Malakal. This picture is facing south. The Protection of Civilians site is in the background while the UN offices and accommodations are in the foreground.

Pg 33. State Support Base Malakal. Despite being banged around and crushed, my Care Packages survived with the contents intact.

Pg 34. State Support Base Malakal. My container. The Kiwi reading a letter from one of his care packages. These were huge morale boosts!

Pg 39. State Support Base Malakal. My container. Helmet and flak jacket (and patches) always accessible.

Pg 40. State Support Base Malakal. Accommodations and an oncoming deluge in the background. The living areas were a warren of containers and narrow paths.

Pg 48. State Support Base Malakal. The Kiwi. The best mate you could ever ask for.

Pg 55. Tonga, Upper Nile State. Force Protection commander (12th Battalion, Jammu & Kashmir Light Infantry) and me.

Pg 56. Tonga, Upper Nile State. General Johnson Olony towers over IGAD representative (L) and the Senior Military Liaison Officer (R) during a patrol.

Pg 65, State Support Base Malakal. Delivering the intelligence report as part of our daily Morning Prayers.

Pg 66. State Support Base Malakal. A pack of dogs relaxing outside my container.

Pg 73. Bangladesh Force Riverine Unit (BANFRU). Local canoes outside the defensive wall. These were the main mode of transport across the White Nile.

Pg 74. Malakal town. Feral dog and buzzards. They ate well during the fighting in Spring 2015.

Pg 80. Malakal town. Meeting with SPLA 2 Division (Rhino) leadership at their headquarters.

Pg 86. State Support Base Malakal. A UN vehicle in the ditch less than 20 meters from our parking area. I didn't ditch it.

Pg 93. State Support Base Malakal. Muddy vehicle after a patrol.

Pg 94. Between Malakal and Baliet. Our patrol stopped by kilometers of mud.

Pg 101. BANFRU. Final preparations before barge sailing. Loading and preparation always seemed chaotic and disorganized but got sorted out eventually.

Pg 102. BANFRU. UN barge convoy leaving the dock. We would typically have a couple of MLOs and a dozen or more Bangladesh Navy Force Protection.

Pg 105. State Support Base Malakal. Bangladeshi sailors verifying returned weapons and ammunition.

Pg 106. State Support Base Malakal. The return of the military hostages, including our two MLOs. We recovered the civilian hostages a few days later.

Pg 123. State Support Base Malakal. A Red-cheeked Cordon-bleu (Uraeginthus bengalus) in front of the MLO offices. Small, almost unnoticed, and delicately beautiful.

Pg 124. BANFRU. Looking south along the White Nile River towards Malakal town. This is a view that has not changed in centuries.

Pg 132. State Support Base Malakal. On the minibus to get us to the Malakal Airport and on a flight to Juba.

Pg 133. Between Bentiu and Heglig, July 2006. Four UN Military Observers (including me) escorted several hundred SPLA troops from the north to their new garrison location in (then) Southern Sudan.

Pg 137. Entebbe. Random sign for a primary school with a very Canadian connection. Always happy to see the Maple Leaf!

Pg 138. Entebbe. The Lake Victoria Hotel was a great place to stay when transiting back to the mission.

Pg 146. Malakal town. Burned out and abandoned houses built in the style of the traditional mud and thatch "tukul."

Pg 156. Kodok, Upper Nile State. A plaque dedicated to Jean-Baptiste Marchand, French soldier and explorer, placed in Kodok by the British after Marchand's death in 1934.

Pg 168. Remembrance Day Card from Veterans' Affairs Canada. I don't know who Maya is, but I wish she knew that this card still makes me smile.

Pg 176. Malakal town. A small part of the large quantity of UXO that the SPLA wanted safely removed, and the UN Mine Action Service was able to deliver.

Pg 185. State Support Base Malakal. Waiting for the bus to get me to the Malakal Airport. The UN teaches you patience. You get used to waiting.

Pg 186. State Support Base Malakal. The ubiquitous Mi-8 helicopter. The workhorse of the mission.

Pg 196. Queen Elizabeth Park, Uganda. On safari. Capturing this picture was the highlight of our Uganda trip.

DOUBLE‡DAGGER
— www.doubledagger.ca —

Double Dagger Books is Canada's only military-focused publisher. Conflict and warfare have shaped human history since before we began to record it. The earliest stories that we know of, passed on as oral tradition, speak of war, and more importantly, the essential elements of the human condition that are revealed under its pressure.

We are dedicated to publishing material that, while rooted in conflict, transcend the idea of "war" as merely a genre. Fiction, non-fiction, and stuff that defies categorization, we want to read it all.

Because if you want peace, study war.

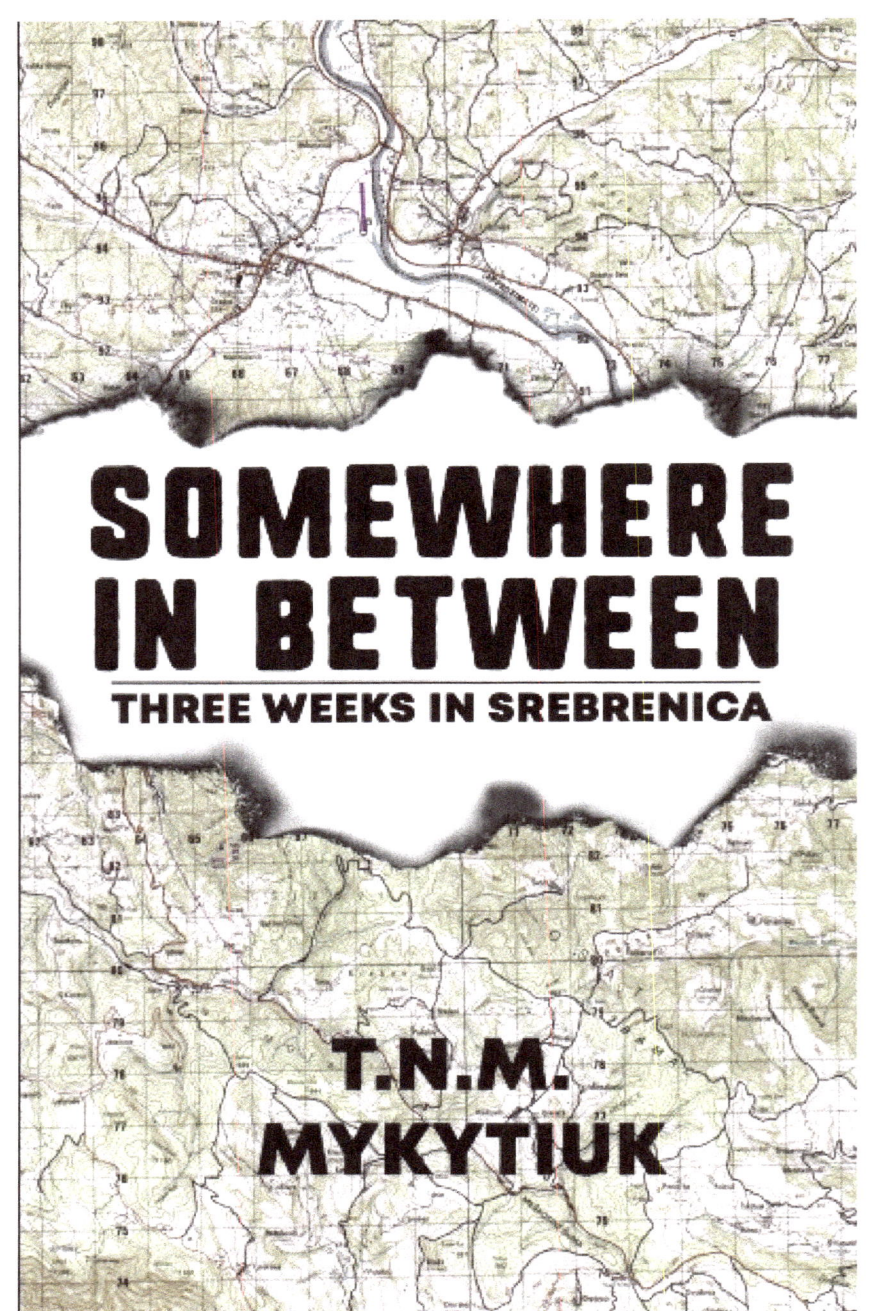

SOMEWHERE IN BETWEEN
THREE WEEKS IN SREBRENICA

T.N.M. MYKYTIUK

SOMEWHERE IN BETWEEN

In 1992, Bosnia imploded into civil war.

Under the flag of the United Nations, Canada sent its soldiers into the midst of violence and bloodshed to bring peace to the region. One of those soldiers was Lieutenant Tom Mykytiuk.

Drawing on his personal journal, he offers a first-hand account of the ethnic-fuelled violence in Bosnia and life in the besieged town of Srebrenica. "Somewhere In Between" is a gritty look at the conflict in Yugoslavia through the eyes of a young officer whose search for adventure ends in a grim understanding of the nature of war.

ABOUT THE AUTHOR

Tom Mykytiuk is a veteran of the Canadian Army. His service has taken him to many parts of the globe not advertised in tourist brochures. He includes John Le Carre, Steven King, and Nikos Kazantikus among his literary influences. Tom enjoys writing about his favorite people-soldiers and ex-soldiers- and his personal experiences often find their way into his novels. He admits to dabbling in short stories, and some non-fiction, but prefers writing thrillers with a historical theme. He lives in Smoky Lake, Alberta, Canada.

ABOUT THE AUTHOR

A serving Army officer, John Vintar has more than thirty years of Reserve and Regular Force service in the Canadian Armed Forces, with NATO or UN deployments to Bosnia, Sudan, South Sudan, and Mali. He was awarded two Command Commendations during these overseas missions – the first in 2006 for his actions in evacuating United Nations and civilian personnel during a firefight between rival factions in Sudan, and his second was awarded for his role in extracting United Nations peacekeepers forcibly detained by Opposition forces in South Sudan in 2015.

In addition to field experience with United Nations missions, he has been an instructor on the UN Military Expert on Mission course at the Peace Support Training Centre in Kingston, Canada. He has also lectured on the topic of contemporary peacekeeping in South Sudan at the University of Calgary, Mount Royal University, and the Royal Military College of Canada.

John has a life-long appreciation for history, folklore, literature, and storytelling. Educated in Canada and the United Kingdom, his master's degree research explored elements of the oral traditions of Anglo-Saxon and Icelandic literature, genres which contain both strong literary and warrior elements. He developed an abiding interest in East African history, anthropology, and literature while preparing for his South Sudan deployment.